SEXUAL CITIZENS

SEXUAL CITIZENS

The Legal and Cultural Regulation
of Sex and Belonging

Brenda Cossman

Stanford University Press
Stanford, California
2007

Stanford University Press
Stanford, California

Printed in the United States of America on acid-free, archival-quality paper

Library of Congress Cataloging-in-Publication Data
Cossman, Brenda, 1960-
  Sexual citizens : the legal and cultural regulation of sex and belonging / Brenda Cossman.
    p. cm.
  Includes bibliographical references and index.
  ISBN 978-0-8047-4996-1 (cloth : alk. paper)
  1. Social integration. 2. Sex--Social aspects. 3. Citizenship--Social aspects. 4. Sex
and law. 5. Sexual minorities. 6. Social control. 7. Self-control--Social aspects. I.
Title.
HM683.C67 2007
306.76--dc22
                                        2007003023

Typeset by Bruce Lundquist in 10/14 Minion

For Laura and Leah

Contents

Acknowledgments

I AM INDEBTED TO COLLEAGUES AND FRIENDS, near and far, for conversations both provocative and heartening: Nathaniel Berman, Davina Cooper, Dan Danielson, Katherine Franke, David Kennedy, Duncan Kennedy, Ummni Khan, Karen Knopp, Robert Leckey, Martha Minow, Annelise Riles, Kerry Rittich, Carol Rogerson, Bruce Ryder, David Schneiderman, and Lucy Williams have each enriched my thinking, and hopefully, my work. I am deeply grateful to former Dean Ron Daniels, who has been a source of unwavering institutional and intellectual support. I owe a special thanks to Daiva Stasiulus who first encouraged me to connect my work on the legal regulation of sexuality with the concept of citizenship and belonging. I am indebted to Laura Nemchin for almost everything I know about popular culture. And I feel very privileged for the critical engagement of Carl Stychin and Janet Halley. They each pushed me to cross many of the borders of my own imagination, and their engagement made this a better book. The borders that remain are my responsibility alone.

I was fortunate to be able to present parts of this work at various conferences and seminars, including the Subversive Legacies Conference at Texas School of Law, the Socio-Legal Regional Conference at SUNY Buffalo, the Law and Literature Series and the Faculty Seminar Series at the University of Toronto, the Dignity and Shame Symposium at Harvard Law School, the Gender and Sexuality Conference at Columbia Law School (a shorter version of Chapter Two appeared in the *Columbia Journal of Gender and Law* 2006), and the Association for the Study of Law, Culture, and the Humanities Conference at Syracuse University. I am grateful for the wonderful research assistance provided by Sean Rehaag, Amy Salyzyn, and particularly BJ Wray. Thanks also to Allyn Whitmore for her assistance with the manuscript.

A special thanks to Amanda Moran, my editor at Stanford, and her colleague Jared Smith, for their patience, support, and sage advice. Thanks also to Jennifer Gordon for her meticulous copyediting.

And finally, my thanks to Laura and Leah, to whom this book is dedicated—for sustaining, enduring, and everything else.

SEXUAL CITIZENS

Introduction

Sexing, Privatizing, and Self-Disciplining Citizenship

"Five gay men, out to make over the world—one straight guy at a time."
  Queer Eye for the Straight Guy

IN *QUEER EYE FOR THE STRAIGHT GUY*, Bravo's hit television show, a team of five gay men undertake an emergency makeover of one heterosexual man. Each week, the Fab Five—self-described as "an elite team of gay men dedicated to extolling the simple virtues of style, taste, and class"—descend upon their subject's home, diagnose his multiple fashion and style infractions, and whisk him off for a day of shopping and self-help (*Queer Eye*). Their mission is to "transform a style-deficient and culture-deprived straight man from drab to fab." Each member of the gay team has a specific self-improvement role. Carson takes him shopping for a new wardrobe. Ted shows him where to shop for food and wine and how to prepare it. Thom is the interior designer—he takes him to an upscale home furnishings store and then undertakes a miraculous makeover of his apartment in several hours. Kyan does the grooming—a hair cut, a visit to the spa, and then an education in multiple hair, face, and shaving products for home upkeep. Finally, Jai provides a rapid education in culture—how to dance, what play to see, how to handle himself at a cocktail party. By the end of the day, the straight guy has a whole new look—new clothes, new furniture, new hair products. The whole point of the shopping extravaganza is to make him more attractive—to his wife, girlfriend, or prospective girlfriend. Despite their relentless teasing of his many fashion crimes, the tone is upbeat and compassionate—the Fab Five want him to succeed; they want to make him a "better" person.

The Fab Five are icons of a new sexual citizenship. They are unapologetically gay, but they are on the front lines of defending masculinity, heterosexuality, and the domestic sphere. They are experts in the arts of self-conduct. And they shop. Their citizenship is sexualized beyond heterosexuality, commodified through a celebration of market consumption, and domesticated through a new emphasis on the intimate sphere not only as a site for caring for others but for care of the self. They are citizens who are sexed but not too much; citizens who not only consume but better yet, teach others to do so; citizens devoted to the conduct of self and other improvement. They represent the multiple transformations in the practices of citizenship that this book sets out to explore—that is, the ways in which citizenship is being sexed, privatized, and self-disciplined.

The gay men of *Queer Eye* present an interesting challenge to much of the sexual citizenship literature that has argued that citizenship is heterosexual (Bell & Binnie 2000; Richardson 1998) and that gay men and lesbians are sexual strangers within the body politic (Phelan 2001). Quite to the contrary, the Fab Five, like many other gay subjects, are becoming model citizens. But, this new sexual citizenship is about more than the inclusion and assimilation of gay subjects. It is about a makeover in the very terms of citizenship—a makeover that does not merely reverse the traditional heteronormativity of sexual citizenship but reconstitutes the practices of good citizenship beyond the gay/ straight dichotomy. Like the Fab Five, the new sexual citizenship is remodelling heterosexuality as well. From *Sex and the City* to *Oprah*, from the revival of Oscar Wilde to the recuperation of Larry Flynt in the *People vs. Larry Flynt*, a new modality of sexual citizenship is evident in which practices of belonging for gay and heterosexual subjects alike are being increasingly sexed but not too much, privatized through a celebration of market consumption, and transformed into projects of self-governance.

In this book, I explore the contours of this new sexual citizenship. Citizenship, I argue, is about a process of becoming. It is about the process of becoming recognized subjects, about the practices of inclusion and membership. But, this process of becoming requires its own interrogation, the question being: Becoming what exactly? What kinds of citizens are being produced? What are the norms of good and bad citizenship? The process of becoming citizens is one that operates its own technologies of inclusion and exclusion and constitutes subjectivities through these technologies. I argue that the new modality of sexual citizenship is one that is privatized, domesticated, and self-disciplined. But, I also argue that these new practices of citizenship are ambivalent, producing new and contested fissures in subjectivities and their governance. Since citizenship is also always about exclusion, I argue that these new practices are producing newly bad or failed sexual citizens, implicating a process not only of becoming but also of unbecoming citizens. From welfare mothers and irresponsible fathers to adulterers and pornographers, the new modality of sexual citizenship is always on border patrol, guarding the boundaries of good citizenship by producing and excluding the bad.

The Citizenship Debates

The recent interest in sexual citizenship is part of a broader proliferation in citizenship studies. As Will Kymlicka and Wayne Norman have observed, there has been a veritable "explosion of interest in the concept of citizenship among political theorists" (Kymlicka & Norman 1994, 352). This interest in citizenship has continued to burgeon across a multiplicity of disciplines, from history (Cott 2000; Kerber 1998; Schudson 1998; Smith 1997) to literary and cultural studies (Berlant 1997) to law. Yet, the concept of citizenship itself is deeply contested within this literature. For some, it is the formal legal status of membership in a nation state, demarcating citizens from aliens. But often, it is used more broadly to denote different dimensions of belonging, recognition, and participation within a nation state. Much of the current thinking of citizenship has been influenced by the work of T. H. Marshall, who defined citizenship in terms of three sets of rights: civil or legal rights, political rights, and social rights (Marshall 1950).[1] Working within this understanding of citizenship, many scholars have sought to expand the Marshallian conception, focusing for example on what Marshall overlooked, such as economic or cultural citizenship (Pakulski 1997; Turner 1994). Others have explored the exclusion of different groups from the full and equal enjoyment of rights, focusing for example on the gendered, racialized, and/or sexualized nature of citizenship and tracing the respective exclusion of women, minorities, and/or homosexual subjects (see, e.g., Lister 1997 and Voet 1998 on gendered citizenship; Plummer 2001; Richardson 2000; and Weeks 1999 on sexual citizenship). Others have focused on the transformation in Marshallian citizenship, with, for example, an increasing emphasis on consumer citizenship (Evans 1993; Ignatieff 1987) and a retrenchment from social citizenship (Held 1991; Rose 2000).

A second approach to citizenship focuses on political engagement. In this more civic republican tradition, citizenship is associated with active engagement in political life. It is critical of the liberal conception of citizenship as passive and formal, emphasizing instead political obligation and the value of engagement in the political sphere (Arendt 1958). Political activity is not simply a means to an end, but an end in itself; participation in the political life of the community is seen to be empowering in its own right for the individual citizen as well as contributing to the collective good. Some scholars have sought to reveal the exclusions of this civic republican vision of citizenship (Fraser 1997; Lister 1997). Other scholars, working within an understanding of citizenship as obligation and participation, have emphasized the "crisis of citizenship" and called for its revitalization (Scobey 2001).

Neo-conservatives like Lawrence Mead argue that welfare policies, affirmative action, and the decline of the family have led to a crisis of American citizenship. Citizens have lost their sense of obligation and moral virtue, focusing only on their rights or entitlements. A return to a more robust civic life thus requires a recentering of obligation through moral discipline. More progressive scholars, like Etienne Balibar and Jürgen Habermas, similarly denounce the erosion of citizenship but point to different culprits such as globalization, mass migration, and transnational capital. They, too, argue for its moment of possible redemption. As David Scobey has argued, tracing this metanarrative of rupture or crisis, the specter of citizenship is simultaneously present in laments of its demise and promises of its return (Scobey 2001).

Despite the considerable differences within this scholarship, much of it shares a normative commitment to an ideal of citizenship. As Linda Bosniak writes, most of the scholars in these debates "treat citizenship as embodying the highest normative value. The term rings unmistakably with the promise of personal fulfillment, community wellbeing, and democratic fulfillment" (Bosniak 1999–2000, 451). For many, then, citizenship remains a democratic ideal, an aspiration of civic participation and belonging, a norm for measuring equality and justice. Those who are excluded—fully or partially—should strive for inclusion. Democratic subjects should strive for a more robust notion of inclusion—social over consumer, or obligation over entitlement, or active over passive, depending on one's political perspective.

Others have taken a more critical stance on citizenship. A number of scholars, influenced by Michel Foucault's work on governmentality, have framed citizenship as a discourse of self-governance. Melanie White and

Alan Hunt, for example, approach citizenship as a technology of government, in which "modern practices of governing take place through the regulated and accountable choices of citizens" (White & Hunt 2000, 96). Barbara Cruikshank similarly argues that citizenship is a strategy of governance, whereby "individual subjects are transformed into citizens by . . . technologies of citizenships: discourses, programs and other tactics aimed at making individuals politically active and capable of self government" (Cruikshank 1999, 1). These technologies of citizenships are "modes of constituting and regulating citizens: that is, strategies for governing the very subjects whose problems they seek to redress" (Cruikshank 1999, 2). The will to empower is thus not simply approached as a democratic ideal, but as a practice that needs to be interrogated for the way it constitutes its subjects. Within this more critical literature, citizenship is not simply a normative ideal but rather a technology of governance. It takes a considerably less sanguine perspective on the role of citizenship discourse in both constituting and governing subjects.

There is, then, no consensus within the citizenship debates on the nature of citizenship. But, at its most general, it invokes the idea of membership. Bryan Turner defines citizenship as a "set of practices which constitute individuals as competent members of a community" (Turner 1994, 159). Rather than emphasizing the juridical or political dimensions of citizenship, it focuses on citizenship "as a bundle of practices that are social, legal, political and cultural." For Turner, it includes cultural citizenship, which he defines as "those social practices which enable a competent citizen to participate fully in the national culture" (Turner 1994, 159).

Borrowing from Turner's definition, I see citizenship at its most general as invoking a set of rights and practices denoting membership and belonging in a nation state. I frame citizenship as including not only legal and political practices but also cultural practices and representations. Borrowing from the more critical citizenship scholarship, I also see citizenship as invoking the ways that different subjects are constituted as members of a polity, the ways they are, or are not, granted rights, responsibilities, and representations within that polity, as well as acknowledgment and inclusion through a multiplicity of legal, political, cultural, and social discourses. It is about the way subjects are constituted as citizens and the way citizenship itself is constituted. It is about the discourses and practices of inclusion and exclusion, of belonging and otherness, and the many shades in between.

The citizenship literature has many subgenres that trace different dimensions of the exclusions, transformations, crises, and challenges of citizenship. In the section that follows, I highlight three of these subgenres that are most relevant for my purposes: sexual citizenship, privatization, and self-governance.

Sexing Citizenship

Sexual citizenship is also a contested concept. Some of the sexual citizenship literature, expanding on the Marshallian tradition, focuses on sexual citizenship as a set of rights to sexual expression and identity. Other scholars focus more broadly on the idea of belonging (Weeks 1999), on the transformation and privatization of political or democratic engagement (Berlant 1997), or on a new politics of intimate or everyday life (Plummer 2001). It is a concept that cuts across the multiple divisions of the citizenship literature more generally, with differing visions of citizenship as rights, political engagement, normative ideal, and/or disciplinary practice.

Two themes run through much of the literature. One is that citizenship has always been sexed, but in very particular ways. Citizenship, with its emphasis on either rights or political participation in the public sphere, has presupposed a highly privatized, familialized, and heterosexual sexuality. Citizenship in the public sphere was predicated on appropriate sexual practices in the private sphere.

A second theme that runs through this sexual citizenship literature is that something has changed within the once private sphere of intimate life, metamorphasizing into more expressly public and political concerns. Jeffrey Weeks argues, for example, that a new primacy has been given to sexual subjectivity, related to the democratization of relationships (see also Giddens), the production of new subjectivities, and the proliferation of new stories of the self, sexuality, and gender (Weeks 1999). Those who were once excluded—women, gay men and lesbians, amongst others—have demanded inclusion and begun to revise and expand the meaning of citizenship by claiming their rights and/or their political participation. In so doing, they have contributed to the politicization of the once private sphere, claiming that issues once relegated to this sphere are themselves the proper subject of political contestation.

Much of the sexual citizenship literature is located within gay and lesbian studies and queer theory and explores the ways in which citizenship has been constituted through the discourses of heteronormativity (Bell & Binnie 2000; Richardson 1998; Weeks 1999). Citizenship—as social membership in a nation state, as a set of rights and responsibilities associated with that membership, and as a set of practices defining membership in the community—has long been associated with heterosexuality: The sexual citizen was a heterosexual citizen (Richardson 1998). Lesbians and gay men were historically excluded from this citizenship, denied in varying degrees over time, civil, political, social, and cultural membership (Phelan 2001). From the criminalization of gay sexuality through sodomy laws to the legal condoning of discrimination, lesbians and gay men have been denied civil citizenship.

The nonrecognition of same-sex relationships and the refusal to allocate the rights and responsibilities of the welfare state to these couples denied lesbians and gay men social citizenship. The virtual exclusion of lesbians and gay men from the cultural representation in popular culture constituted a denial of cultural citizenship (Richardson 1998). Heterosexuality comprised a thick border of citizenship. Based on this history of exclusion, Shane Phelan concludes that "gay men, lesbians, bisexuals and transgendered people in the United States are strangers" (2001, 5). Phelan uses the term "stranger" to get at the way in which sexual minorities are neither enemies nor friends—they may be "neighbors, but 'they are not like us'" (Phelan 2001, 29, quoting Beck 1996, 382). This exclusion, this strangeness, this denial of full political citizenship, Phelan argues, is "at the core of contemporary American understandings and organization of common life" (Phelan 2001, 5).

The sexual citizenship literature explores the ways in which these practices of exclusion have been challenged in recent years by gay and lesbian subjects.[2] Gay men and lesbians have sought inclusion within the discourses and institutions of civil and social citizenship. Sodomy laws, employment discrimination, and the refusal to recognize same-sex relationships have each been challenged in recent years, with varying degrees of success. Gay and lesbian subjects have also sought a more fulsome cultural citizenship, challenging their invisibility in a broad range of cultural representations. Some scholars have embraced the gay and lesbian claim to citizenship, emphasizing the transformative potential to its insistence on entitlement and inclusion (see, e.g., Kaplan 1997; Phelan 2001).

Other scholars adopt a more critical stance to this claim to citizenship. Some focus on the disciplinary and normalizing nature of inclusion (Berlant

1997; Warner 1999). Steven Seidman, for example, argues that the struggle for sexual citizenship is a politics of civic inclusion and gay purification:

> Individuals aspiring to the status of citizen must claim to possess the psychological, moral and social traits that render them good and warrant their integration . . . gays have claimed not only to be normal, but to exhibit valued civil qualities such as discipline, rationality, respect for the law and family values, and national pride. (Seidman 1997, 323)

Normalization is a strategy for inclusion in the prevailing social norms and institutions of family, gender, work, and nation. It is a strategy that neutralizes the significance of sexual difference and sexual identity, "rendering sexual difference a minor, superficial aspect of a self who in every other way reproduces the ideal of a national citizen" (Seidman 1997, 324). These scholars argue that normalization deradicalizes claims for social transformation by incorporating sexual minorities into dominant political and social norms and institutions. As David Bell and Jon Binnie have argued, appeals to citizenship require the "circumscription of 'acceptable' modes of being a sexual citizen" (Bell & Binnie 1995, 3). In the current political climate, this compromise of acceptability "tends to demand a modality of sexual citizenship that is privatized, deradicalized, de-eroticized and *confined* in all senses of the word: kept in place, policed, limited" (Bell & Binnie 1995, 3).

Other critics have emphasized the normalizing costs of inclusion in the context of the privatization of citizenship. David Evans, for example, has argued that gay men have been included within consumer citizenship. Gay sexuality is commodified and identity is marketized (Evans 1993; Freitas 1998). This consumer citizenship has intensified with the rise of the neo-liberal state and its multiple strategies of privatization, in which citizens are reconstituted in and through the discourse of consumerism. Lauren Berlant has similarly argued that citizenship in the United States has been reprivatized under neo-conservative politics. The sphere of privacy, intimacy, and family has become the site of civic virtue (Berlant 1997). It is a vision of citizenship obsessed with sex—with normalizing private, procreative, heterosexual sex, and with demonizing all others. Yet others have emphasized that approaches to sexual citizenship that focus on the private, intimate sphere reprivatize sexual citizenship—by reinforcing the idea that sex and sexuality are naturally located with the private, not public spheres (Richardson 2000). The family and market are reinscribed as the natural sites of sexual citizenship.

Some critical scholars have emphasized the ambivalent nature of the claim to sexual citizenship. Carl Stychin, for example, has argued that citizenship is never wholly disciplined, but may simultaneously retain "an unruly edge" (Stychin 2001, 290). There are aspects of the struggle for sexual citizenship and its rights and responsibilities that are destabilizing. Similarly, Seidman has argued that the politics of sexual citizenship has led to "a weakening of a repressive heteronormative logic" (Seidman 2001, 323). There are also spin-off effects of these struggles, such as the awakening of a subaltern queer movement that explicitly resists the politics of assimilation and normalization (Plummer 2001; Seidman 2001, 326). Jeffrey Weeks has argued that the challenge of sexual citizenship involves both a moment of transgression and a moment of citizenship.[3] Stychin suggests that the interesting question is no longer whether citizenship is disciplinary or empowering "for undoubtedly the language of citizenship and rights can do both simultaneously" (Stychin 2003, 14). Rather, in his view, the interesting question lies in how citizenship has been and could be deployed.

Like Stychin, I begin from the premise that sexual citizenship is an ambivalent practice, simultaneously subversive and disciplinary. Membership may have its privileges, but it also has its costs. I also agree that the interesting questions have shifted; it is no longer productive to debate the normalizing versus transgressive dimensions of a prospective sexual citizenship. Rather, we need to turn our critical attention to the processes of becoming; that is, to what is happening as this citizenship becomes part of the present. Sexual citizenship has begun to transform: heterosexuality no longer operates as a preemptive bar to all forms of citizenship. Gay and lesbian subjects have begun to cross the borders of citizenship, unevenly acquiring some of its rights and responsibilities and performing some of its practices. They are in the process of becoming citizens, a complex and uneven process of crossing borders, reconstituting the terms and subjects of citizenship as well as the borders themselves.

But, sexual citizenship is about more than the process of gay and lesbian subjects becoming citizens. It is equally about the process of straight subjects becoming and unbecoming citizens. The literature's focus on the heteronormativity of sexual citizenship has limited its analysis of these multiple dimensions. Largely reflecting its location with gay and lesbian/queer studies, this focus on the homo/hetero axis of citizenship neglects the multiple ways in which the hetero side of the equation is subject to extensive regulation. As Anna Marie Smith has observed, "the equation of the official norms with heterosexuality tends to construct heterosexuality in a homogenous manner" (Smith 2001, 305). The concept of heteronormativity is not, for example, up to the task of analyzing the construction of the welfare mother or the adulterer as failed citizens. Rather, Smith argues that "we need to grasp the simultaneous operation of the multiple axes of power, constellations of exclusions and privileges, and diverse juxtapositions of rights and obligations that define the sexual subject's citizenship" (Smith 2001, 305).

Sexual citizenship must be more explicitly about the multiple processes of becoming and unbecoming citizens for heterosexual subjects as well. Some scholars, such as Ken Plummer in his work on intimate citizenship, have pointed in this direction. I seek to push the concept of sexual citizenship further in this direction, exploring some of the ways in which heterosexuality as well as homosexuality is contested and reconstituted. Sexual citizenship needs to broaden its lens to capture the multiple border crossings of gay and straight subjects alike, and the ways in which these border crossings are reconstituting the borders, the citizens, and the meaning of belonging.

Privatizing Citizenship

A number of scholars have focused on the transformation of citizenship with the decline of the Keynesian welfare state (KWS) and the rise of a neo-liberal state. The KWS, even in its more liberal versions, was informed by the Marshallian idea of social citizenship. The state was seen to be responsible for providing a minimum level of economic security to its citizens to ensure their political participation. With the progressive dismantling of the KWS in the United States, Canada, and the United Kingdom in the last two decades, this idea of social citizenship has similarly given way to a new privatized citizenship, which privileges self-reliance, self-governance, and free markets (Brodie 1997; Held 1991; Rose 1999, 2000). Governments are no longer responsible for ensuring even the most basic economic well-being of their citizens. Individuals must assume that responsibility and ensure their individual self-reliance through the market. At most, governments maintain some responsibility for helping citizens to help themselves, although this too is increasingly being shifted to the voluntary or charitable realm. Limited social responsibility has given way to individual self-reliance; social insurance has given way to individual risk management. Once-public goods and services are being commodified, that is, reconstituted as private, and thus are more appropriately distributed through the market (Brodie 1997, 236). Indeed, citizenship itself is increasingly being commodified, as the new mode of privatized citizenship recodes citizens as consumers, whose political participation is measured by their access to the market (Cooper 1993; Evans 1993).

Some scholars have also traced a new role for the family in this transformation of citizenship. Janine Brodie argues that this new privatized citizenship involves a process of familialization, whereby once-public goods and services are transferred back to the realm of the family. While the family has always been an important site for unpaid caregiving of dependents, the demise of social citizenship involves an even greater demand on families to meet the needs of its members, from child care to health care to welfare. Families are increasingly expected to take care of their own, "and it is up to the state to make sure that they do" (Abbot & Wallace 1992; Brodie 1997, 236).

The nature of this familialized citizenship is itself contested. While social conservatives seek to rearticulate the heteronormative family, with its gendered hierarchies and dependencies, fiscal conservatives are more concerned with reducing demands on the state by transferring responsibility to market, family, or voluntary sectors (Cossman 2002a, 2005). The latter place less emphasis on the normative structure of the family and more on the support functions of the family: A family is what a family does, and what a family does is support its members (Cossman & Fudge 2002). Yet both of these visions demand more rather than less of the family.

Much of the literature on the privatization of citizenship comes from the United Kingdom, Canada, and Europe where the KWS was far more developed and where there was a more robust vision of social citizenship in place. The United States, it is often said, never developed the same KWS, nor the same idea of social citizenship (Fraser 1997; Gordon 1994). There is, therefore, a question about whether it even makes sense to speak of its demise. While it is incontrovertible that the United States never developed a KWS to the degree seen in other Western nations, there was a limited welfare state in place from the time of the New Deal and a limited recognition of social citizenship (McCluskey 2003). From the passage of the Social Security Act in 1935 as part of the New Deal to the Great Society of the 1960s, the United States developed a limited welfare state, based on a mix of public and private provisions for the well-being of its citizens (Katz 2001).[4] While often associated exclusively with social assistance, such as Aid to Dependent Children (AFDC), food stamps, and Old Age Assistance, it also included a broad range of social insurance in both the public and private spheres, including Social Security, Unemployment Insurance, and Medicare, as well as a range of employee benefits, from health care to retirement benefits. Over the course of the twentieth century, there was an increasing bifurcation of these two dimensions of the welfare state. Social assistance, directed toward the undeserving poor, was increasingly stigmatized, while social insurance, directed toward the deserving poor, became a more legitimate entitlement. Yet, both were an important part of the state's provision for the well-being of its citizens.

Beginning in the 1970s, there has been a progressive discrediting of Keynesian economics and a dismantling of the programs it sustained (Katz 2001). From the ascendance of conservatism to international economic restructuring, Keynesian ideas of state intervention in markets were displaced in favor of a neo-liberal vision of limited governments and more robust markets. Part of the critique was a concerted attack on social assistance and the culture of dependency that it allegedly created. The very idea of social citizenship, that is, of citizenship entitlement to economic welfare and security, was rejected in favor of more explicitly marketized citizenship. While as Judith Shklar has argued, work has always been central in the construction of American citizenship (Shklar 1991), in recent years this role has intensified. As Michael Katz argues, "as a result, only those Americans with real jobs are real citizens"; work has become "the new criterion of full citizenship" (Katz 2001, 348).

Despite the absence of the ideas of "social citizenship" from the political lexicon in the United States, the history of the American welfare state is one marked by the rise and fall of a limited welfare state and with it, a limited vision of social citizenship. As I explore further in Chapter 3, it is a history marked in recent years by an increasing privatization and familialization of dependence, as even the limited extent of public support is retracted, and all citizens are expected to provide for themselves and their families.

Self-Disciplining Citizenship

A third and related theme in the citizenship literature involves the idea of citizenship as self-governance. Relying on Foucault's work on governmentality, some scholars have argued that the neo-liberal transformation of citizenship involves a new form of governance, relying more on the self-governance of its citizens (Dean 1999; Hunt 1999; Rose 1999, 2000). Foucault's later work on governmentality began to explore governance as the conduct of self-conduct and technologies of the self (Foucault 1988, 1991). These technologies of self consist of "those intentional and voluntary actions by which men not only set themselves rules of conduct, but also seek to transform themselves, to change themselves in their singular being, and to make their life into an oeuvre that carries certain aesthetic values and meets certain stylistic criteria" (Foucault 1985, 10). Individuals are called upon to cultivate their self; to make themselves a project of self-mastery and self-transformation. In contrast to his earlier work, which focused more exclusively on subjectification through techniques of domination, his work on governmentality explored the relationship between those techniques and the techniques of the self in the subjectification of individuals (Burchell 1996, 20).

Scholars such as Nicholas Rose and Alan Hunt have explored the particular ways in which contemporary regimes of subjectification rely on this kind of self-discipline and the government of oneself (Hunt 1999; Rose 1996, 2000). According to Rose, there has been a rise in a form of governance in which "individuals are incited to live as if making a *project* of themselves" (Rose 1996, 157). He connects a heightened emphasis on self-governance with the decline of the welfare state and the emergence of the neo-liberal state; as governments retract from the provision of social goods and services, individuals are called upon to become responsible for themselves and their families. He argues that "it has become possible to govern without governing *society*—to govern through the 'responsibilized' and 'educated' anxieties and aspirations of individuals and their families" (Rose 1999, 88). It is a politics of responsibilization, of becoming responsible risk managers for oneself and one's family; it is a politics that calls on individuals to make a project of oneself and to take responsibility for one's own and one's family's well-being and personal happiness.

Alan Hunt has similarly argued that this modality of governance "seeks to stimulate and activate the controlled choices of individual citizens" (Hunt 1999, 217). It is a mode of governance that is increasingly based on expertise, often "vested in the hands of experts" but also often reintroduced to allow non-experts to train themselves to become experts (Hunt 1999). Hunt argues that "self-help" has become one of the most important techniques for this self-regulation: "The self-government of subjectivity is effected through the stimulation of sustained and intense self-scrutiny" (Hunt 1999, 218). White and Hunt have connected this self-governance with the new discourses of citizenship. They argue that a vision of citizenship informed by the care of the self "marks a break with state-centered conceptions of citizenship" (White and Hunt 2000, 96). Contemporary citizenship is, in their view, constituted in and through the practices of regulated freedom. Individual citizens are required to make choices throughout this public sphere:

> Citizenship consists in a variety of practices of self-formation that are located within the tensions and choices inherent in a regulated freedom: Such freedom links practices of governance through the "shaping and utilizing the freedom of autonomous actors." (White & Hunt 2000, 111, citing Rose 1993, 295)

It is a citizenship that requires a practice of "self-inspection and self-regulation through choice."

Some scholars focus on the role of culture and consumption in this new self-disciplinary citizenship. Rose argues that a broad range of cultural practices are now constitutive of this new citizenship identity. "Advertising, marketing, the proliferation of goods, the multiple stylizations of the act of purchasing, cinemas, videos, pop music, lifestyle magazines, television soap operas, advice programs, and talk shows" all play an important role in the generating and regulating techniques of self-conduct (Rose 2000, 1339). Through a fusion of culture, consumption, and self-identity, individuals are called upon to shape their identities in and through market choices in "taste, music, goods, styles, and habits" (Rose 2000, 1402). The project of the self requires that individual citizens take responsibility for their identity and their well-being in and through their multiple cultural consumption choices.

According to these more critical approaches, citizenship emerges as a form of governance, constituted through practices of responsibilization, individual choice, and self-discipline. Citizenship is disarticulated from the state. It is, then, a broader notion of membership in a community, constituted through multiple sites of contact among individuals in the public sphere. Citizenship is not simply a normative aspiration, but a technology of governance that constitutes a highly self-disciplined citizen. Yet, it is also a citizen produced through the practices of autonomy and choice; citizens must choose among a range of available practices, discourses, and aesthetics: A citizen who is disciplined, but not wholly so.

Sexing, Privatizing, and Self-Disciplining Citizenship

In *Sexual Citizens*, I attempt to bring together the insights of these divergent literatures of citizenship to explore the multiple ways in which citizenship is being sexed, privatized, and self-disciplined. The chapters reveal some of the ways in which good citizens and bad citizens, becoming and unbecoming citizens, are being produced through the discourses of sex, markets, family, and self-governance. Sexual subjects once cast as outlaws or strangers, such as lesbians and gay men, are being brought into the folds of, and reconstituted in the discourse of, this new privatized and self-disciplined citizen. The reconstitution of outlaws as legitimate subjects in law has occurred within this dominant modality of citizenship in which the sexing of citizenship and the disruption of heteronormativity is accompanied by the privatization of sex. Other sexual subjects, such as the welfare mother and the deadbeat father, are being reconstituted as bad citizens through precisely this same marketized and familialized citizenship. Their sexuality is marked as deviant and dangerous, at the same time as their infractions are cast in terms of their failure to regulate through market and family. These sexual subjects are constituted as failing to live within this new modality of citizenship; they have failed to privatize and self-discipline. And the failure invites the state directly back into their lives, in all its coercive glory. Sexual subjects are also being brought into the folds of the new self-governing citizenship. Those sexual subjects who fail to self-discipline, just like those who fail to privatize, risk being marked as unbecoming, if not outright outlaws.

The privatization, familialization, and self-disciplining of citizenship are often inseparable processes. In the new modality of sexual citizenship, subjects are required to self-discipline according to the logic of the market. The good citizen emerges as the enterprising, self-regulating subject who manages his or her own risk. Individuals must conduct their lives, and that of their families, "as a kind of enterprise, seeking to enhance and capitalize . . . through calculated acts and investments" (Rose 1999, 164). It is a process that extends to the family, where individuals are expected to maximize the physical and emotional well-being of their children, their spouses, and themselves (Rose 1996, 163). It is a process that similarly extends to the practices of sexuality, where individuals are expected to promote their well-being by managing and minimizing risks. Bad citizens, on the other hand, are those who fail to self-regulate in these domains of family, market, and sex.

Sexual Citizens explores these and other intersections in the sexing, privatizing, and self-disciplining of citizenship, with a focus on the role of law in these processes. The literature on sexual citizenship has largely been located outside of law, and as a result, its analysis of law has been thin. With a few notable exceptions (Cooper 1993; Smith 2001; Stychin 2001), there has been little analysis of the role of legal discourse in constructing and disciplining sexual citizens. Historically, law has played an important role in constructing a narrow sexed and gendered citizen. As a result, law has been a crucial site of struggle and contestation in challenging the heteronormative and gendered constructs of citizenship. Criminal law, family law, social welfare law, and constitutional law, among others, are all deeply implicated in constituting and disciplining sexual citizens. The role of law is viewed here not exclusively in terms of its repressive and regulatory dimension but also in terms of its disciplinary and constitutive dimensions (Stychin 2003, 3). Law constitutes and regulates, punishes and self-disciplines.

The role of law in privatization has begun to attract some scholarly attention (Cossman & Fudge 2002; Freeman 2003; Minow 2002), although rather less has been directed to the implications for citizenship in particular. Often, the literature on privatization is associated with deregulation and the decentering of the state. Yet, as many have argued, it is a process better characterized as "re-regulation" (Cossman & Fudge 2002). The new modes of regulation, including the transfer of once public goods and services to the realms of market, family, and charitable sector require considerable state intervention. Law has an important role to play in operationalizing this privatization, as well as enforcing the new modalities of citizenship. There may be a range of changes in the preferred regulatory instruments and types of law—for example, from state ownership and supervision to an increasing delegation to private and quasi-private actors, from administrative regulation to contract, from social welfare law to criminal and family law. Yet, there continues to be a strong state and legal presence in this mode of governance (Cossman & Fudge 2002).

The role of law in the self-disciplining of citizenship has received even less attention. In part, the self-governance literature directs attention away from explicit forms of legal regulation in its vision of a less state-centered form of governance. The literature opens up a broad range of non-state practices to scrutiny for their role in the governance. This broader analysis, however, need not break completely with an analysis of state and legal regulation. Rather, it remains important to consider the role of law in these newer forms of governance. The rise of the neo-liberal state and its increasing reliance on self-governance is shifting the form and content of legal regulation. In some contexts, law regulates through the promotion of market relations, reconstituting individual subjects into market actors and citizen consumers. Law's role is both constitutive and regulatory; it seeks to regulate the subjects that it constitutes through marketized incentives. In other contexts, law regulates through the promotion of responsibilization within the family: It seeks to make individuals responsible for themselves and their family members. While the objective of both of these forms of regulation is the promotion of a privatized, self-disciplining individual, both are accomplished through a broad range of regulatory interventions in the market and family.

Further, an increasing reliance on self-governance has not led to an abandonment of the more coercive and authoritarian deployments of law. These more authoritarian forms of law are deployed against those who fail to self-discipline. As Rose has observed: "Those who refuse to become responsible and govern themselves ethically have also refused the offer to become members of our moral community. Hence, for them, harsh measures are entirely appropriate. Three strikes and you are out" (Rose 2000, 1047). Barry Hindness argues that authoritarian rule is an integral part of liberal government and that even with an increasing emphasis on self-governance "coercive and oppressive practices of government continue to play an important part . . . in the criminal justice system, the policing of . . . immigrant communities and the urban poor" (Hindness 2001). For some subjects, "the capacity for autonomous conduct can be developed only through compulsion, through the imposition of more or less extended periods of discipline" (Hindness 2001). It is therefore important to consider the uneven nature of legal regulation—self-disciplinary for some and correctively or punitively authoritarian for others.

Breaking with an exclusively state-centered vision of citizenship does, however, require attention to the ways in which these multiple forms of legal regulation intersect with other non-legal, non-state forms of governance. My interest is on the intersections between law and popular culture. While influenced by it, my approach diverges somewhat from the law and popular culture movement, which "treats works of popular culture about law and lawyers (such as films, novels or television shows) as legal texts, as important in their own way as statutes or judicial precedent" (Asimov 2001, 87). While I agree that much can be gleaned about law from studying popular culture as legal text, in *Sexual Citizens* I explore the intersections of law and popular culture for what it reveals about the sexing, privatizing, and self-disciplining of citizenship. Law and popular culture are both discourses that produce social meaning and constitute subjects. Influenced by the literature on cultural citizenship, I am interested in the ways practices of belonging are increasingly located in the cultural sphere. But, my analysis is moored to a legal studies approach. I deploy a cultural studies approach to law—an approach that Austin Sarat and Jonathan Simon describe as " . . . invite[ing] us to acknowledge that legal meaning is found and invented in a variety of locations and practices that comprise culture, and that these locations and practices are themselves encapsulated, though always incompletely, in legal forms, regulations and symbols" (Sarat & Simon 2001, 21). Like Sarat and Simon, I am interested in the "'cultural role' of legal practices, [in] their ability to 'create social meaning and thus shape social worlds'" (Sarat & Simon 2001, 159).

Sexual Citizens locates the legal regulation of sexual citizenship within a broader cultural context and explores the social meaning produced by its multiple practices. I am interested in the ways in which practices of belonging and, particularly, the sexing, privatizing, and self-disciplining of these practices are products of the porous borders between law and popular culture. I consider different ways in which images, norms, and narratives of popular culture seep into legal discourse and, conversely, the ways legal discourse casts its shadow over popular culture. I highlight the uneven and dialogic nature of the relationship between law and popular culture; the images, narratives, and social meanings in each sphere, sometimes complementary, sometimes conflicting, are produced dialogically, in explicit and implicit conversations with each other.

The first chapter considers ways in which sexual citizenship is produced through the regulation of consensual sexual practices. By examining the legal regulation of sexual privacy and sexual speech, the chapter explores the transformations and contestations of contemporary sexual citizenship. Subjects once constituted as outlaws, from sodomites and pornographers to sex toy users and hip-hop artists, continue to challenge their outlaw status, claiming inclusion within a new modality of explicitly sexualized citizenship. Some have successfully become citizens; others are in the process of becoming, and yet others continue to be cast as outlaws, unworthy of belonging. These are legal and cultural stories of a very explicit sexualization of citizenship; from the Oscar Wilde revival and the affirmation of sodomy in *Lawrence* to *Sex and the City*'s playful affirmation of the sex lives of single women and the contested right of women to sell sex toys in *Williams*, from Larry Flynt's claim to political citizenship to hip-hop artist Sarah Jones's indecency fight with the FCC—these are subjects who seek belonging without disavowing sex. Instead, their claim is that they deserve membership on its terrain.

The second chapter considers the role of sex in marriage in the practices of citizenship. It argues that marriage is being produced as a project of self-governance in which good citizens will make good choices and manage the risks to their relationship. Couples are called upon to make their sex life a project and minimize the risk of infidelity and relationship breakdown, practices unbecoming of a good citizen. It argues that this project of sexual self-governance is increasingly produced in the cultural sphere. Whereas law was once called upon to patrol the rigid sexual borders of marriage, now it is television talk shows, self-help books and magazines, and a range of films and television dramas, from *Dr. Phil* and *Oprah* to *Closer* and *Desperate Housewives* that articulate and promote the ethic of self-governance.

The third chapter turns further to the process of unbecoming citizens. It explores the contested stories of welfare reform and sexual citizenship, first, through the production of welfare queens and deadbeat dads in mainstream political discourse and then, in the effort to contest these images of failed citizenship in black popular culture. Both the welfare queen and the deadbeat dad were produced as unbecoming citizens through a shifting combination of market, sexual, and self-disciplinary failures, as well as an underlying repertoire of highly racialized stereotypes of African Americans. Their citizenship failures could then be deployed to legitimate a new and coercive regulatory regime. Despite the effort to tell explicitly counter hegemonic narratives, these icons of bad citizenship have cast their shadow over black popular culture. From the familial controversies around hip-hop artists Lauryn Hill and P. Diddy to films such as *Baby Boy* and *Disappearing Acts*, sexual citizenship for the African American subject can only be achieved through a repudiation of their failures in favor of highly privatized and self-disciplining practices of belonging.

The fourth chapter returns to where discussions of sexual citizenship often begin, namely, to the citizenship struggles of gay and lesbian subjects. The chapter uses the ambivalence of border crossing as an entry point into debates over same-sex marriage. It explores how the subjects, the borders, and the terms of citizenship are being transformed. Same-sex marriage becomes part of the present, and gay and lesbian subjects cross the borders into legitimate citizenship. The chapter looks at both legal and cultural stories of same-sex marriage: the constitutional challenges and the emerging divorces as well as the cultural representation of same-sex marriage and divorce in queer cultural productions such as *Queer as Folk* and *The L Word*. It explores the transformations in governance as same-sex marriage becomes part of the present, looking at the subjectification of gay men and lesbians through the new forms of self-governance. Finally, the chapter returns to *Queer Eye for the Straight Guy* to explore the implications of these transformations for the very categories of queer citizenship. As gay and lesbian subjects become citizens, the borders between gay and straight become rather less sharp.

1 Consensual Sex and the Practices of Citizenship

IN *SEX AND THE CITY*, HBO's acclaimed television show about the intimate, erotic, and neurotic pursuits of four single women in New York, Carrie Bradshaw and her posse are either having sex or talking about sex. While single women have been having sex on television for a long time, what distinguishes Carrie and company is the extent to which their sexualities are a crucial part of their citizenship in the republic of New York City. Carrie makes her living as a journalist who writes about sex. Samantha, a highly successful public relations agent, is unapologetically sexual in all aspects of her life—refusing the distinction between public and private. Miranda negotiates the tensions of the demands of an asexual profession—she is a lawyer—and her more intimate pursuits. And Charlotte is the traditionalist, the one who speaks about sex in hushed tones. Episode after episode explore once-racy topics, from the etiquette of oral sex and public sex to older women/younger men intergenerational relationships and lesbianism, all while Carrie reflects upon the deep inner truths of human intimacy.

The intimate public sphere explored in *Sex and the City* is part of the broader transformations of sexual citizenship, a process of becoming, which transgresses the borders of old and domesticates the citizens of new. These women are strong and independent and unapologetically sexual. But, they are also responsible market citizens, impeccably attired, with aspirations of relational and domestic happiness. They are part of the new sexual citizenry—a citizenry that, although highly sexualized, can be relied upon to self-discipline.

This normalization of the sexualized subject in popular culture signals a transformation in the terms of sexual citizenship. One-time sexual outlaws—like sexually active single women—are no longer so. Their sex lives are no longer hidden from public view, nor reason enough to cast them on the outside of citizenship. Indeed, their sex lives have become part of who they are. But this normalization of sex and recuperation of the sexual outlaw in popular culture is not without its detractors. The culture wars of the 1980s and 1990s witnessed social conservatives pushing back against the liberalization of sex in the public sphere. From the obscenity prosecutions of Robert Mapplethorpe's photography in the 1980s to the Clinton impeachment in the 1990s to the kafuffle over Janet Jackson's breast during Super Bowl halftime early in the 2000s, the status of sex and sexuality in the public sphere remains deeply contested.

While the status of the sexual subject may still be controversial within popular culture, it is even more so within law. Indecency, obscenity, and until recently sodomy are but a few examples of law continuing to regulate consensual sexual practices. Criminal law explicitly prohibits these practices and punishes those who engage in them—admittedly in an uneven and intermittent fashion. As some forms of consensual sex are marked as bad and thereby proscribed, the law not only draws lines between good sex and bad sex but also constitutes subjects as good and bad citizens: good citizens who learn to discipline themselves against the backdrop of the legal proscriptions and bad citizens who fail to self-discipline and who must then be punished by the law. The legal prohibitions of these sexual practices exemplify the ways in which the law operates both in juridical ways through repression and in more disciplinary ways through the construction of the subject and its appropriate modes of self-governance (Stychin 2003, 3).

This chapter considers some of the ways in which sexual citizenship is produced through the legal regulation of consensual sexual practices. First, it explores cases in which the idea of sexual privacy has been used to challenge legal prohibition on sodomy and the use of sex toys. Next, it looks at the regulation of sexual speech through indecency and obscenity laws, focusing on two legal controversies: the indecency charges against hip-hop artist Sarah Jones by the FCC and the federal government's obscenity prosecution of Extreme Associates, a company that produces extremely violent pornography. The chapter uses these cases to explore the contestations and transformations in contemporary sexual citizenship. Subjects continue to challenge their outlaw status, claiming inclusion within a new modality of explicitly sexualized citizenship. Some have successfully become citizens; others are in the process of becoming, and yet others continue to be cast as outlaws, unworthy of belonging.

The chapter highlights the role of the border in producing good and bad citizens. Much of the work done by law in this area is about border control—the judicial activity of patrolling the grid between good and bad sex, between legitimate sexual citizenship and illegitimate sexual outlaw. The idea of border patrol is hardly new to law; much has been written of the legal obsession with slippery slopes (Schauer 1985; Volokh 2003). The chapter highlights the extent to which the legal regulation of consensual sex is preoccupied with a similar border anxiety, heightened by a fear of sexual chaos. It also explores what happens when subjects cross borders. The process of crossing the border—from bad to good—is a process of incorporations and transformation, in which the sexual subject is reconstituted and reframed within the privatizing, domesticating, and self-disciplining discourses of contemporary citizenship. The chapter interrogates the ways in which subjects are normalized through the process of inclusion without, however, entirely negating the "unruly edges" (Stychin 2001, 290). It is not only the subjects who are changed through the process of inclusion but also citizenship itself, as explicitly sexualized subjects are incorporated into its folds. *Sex and the City* is a new modality of citizenship; Carrie and her gang of single women may be changed through their inclusion in it, but so too have their explicitly sexualized identities reshaped the contours of contemporary citizenship.

Sexual Privacy and the Borders of Citizenship

From its inception, the zone of protected sexuality, as judicially articulated by the constitutional right to privacy, was demarcated by what it was not: the good distinguished from and defined in relation to the bad. In *Poe v. Ullman*—the precursor to *Griswold v. Connecticut*—the majority of the Supreme Court dismissed a challenge to Connecticut's prohibition on the use of contraception on the ground of the lack of a constitutionally justiciable issue. Justice Harlan in dissent both recognized a right to privacy and asserted its limitations: "The right of privacy most manifestly is not an absolute. Thus, I would not suggest that adultery, homosexuality, fornication and incest are immune from criminal enquiry, however privately practiced" (*Poe*, 552). He further elaborated this limitation:

> Adultery, homosexuality and the like are sexual intimacies which the State forbids altogether, but the intimacy of husband and wife is necessarily an essential and accepted feature of the institution of marriage, an institution which the State not only must allow, but which always and in every age it has fostered and protected. It is one thing when the State exerts its power either to forbid extramarital sexuality altogether, or to say who may marry, but it is quite another when, having acknowledged a marriage and the intimacies inherent in it, it undertakes to regulate by means of the criminal law the details of that intimacy. (*Poe*, 553)

In these passages, the zone of privacy was highly circumscribed—marital sex good, nonmarital sex bad—with the articulation of good sex quivering in the shadow of the bad.

These passages were echoed by several of the justices in *Griswold v. Connecticut*, where the Supreme Court struck down Connecticut's prohibition on contraception use for married couples. Justice Douglas, writing for the Court, made it clear that the decision—and the right to privacy that it recognized—was all about marriage:

> We deal with a right of privacy older than the Bill of Rights—older than our political parties, older than our school system. Marriage is a coming together for better or for worse, hopefully enduring, and intimate to the degree of being sacred. It is an association that promotes a way of life, not causes; a harmony in living, not political faiths; a bilateral loyalty, not commercial or social projects. Yet it is an association for as noble a purpose as any involved in our prior decisions. (*Griswold*, 486)

Justices Goldberg, Warren, and Brennan in their concurring opinion, citing Harlan's words with approval, made it clear that the right to privacy was not about bad sex: "it should be said of the Court's holding today that it in no way interferes with a State's proper regulation of sexual promiscuity or misconduct" (*Griswold*, 499).

While this zone of privacy has evolved beyond marital sex—in *Eisenstadt v. Baird* the right to use contraception was extended to unmarried persons, and in *Roe v. Wade*, to a right to abortion in the first trimester, regardless of marital status—many of its extensions continue to be accompanied by an anxiety about patrolling the borders between legitimate and illegitimate sex. In this section, I examine two recent legal debates about the scope of the right to sexual privacy: sodomy and sex toys. In these debates, border control remains a central anxiety, with proponents of an expanded sexual citizenship building new borders and opponents defending the old against imminent collapse. This vigilance with border patrol is, on one hand, endemic to law in general and judicial review in particular, which by definition involves an exercise in demarcation. Yet, in the context of sexual citizenship, this border patrol is constitutive. Subjects who are allowed to cross borders are reconstituted in this process of becoming; they are partially remade in the disciplinary and domesticity terms of membership.

From Sodomite to Citizen

The late 1990s were marked by a Wildean moment (Plotz 1998). From the release of the film *Wilde* in 1998 and two Off Broadway plays (Moise Kaufman's *Gross Indecency* and David Hare's *The Judas Kiss*), to a statue in central London and a proliferation of books, Oscar Wilde was everywhere. As one film critic observed, "In the last few years, there has been a veritable Wilde explosion. It's not so much a revival of his work—that never really died—as a resurrection of the man himself" (Lloyd 1998). This Wilde revival coincided with two significant centenaries: 1995 marked the hundredth anniversary of his infamous trial and conviction for sodomy, and 2000 was the hundredth anniversary of his death. But the revival was more than simply an anniversary; it was animated by the rise of the gay citizen. Throughout the 1990s, the gay and lesbian sexual subject was on the move toward cultural citizenship— from Tony Kushner's Pulitzer Prize-winning play *Angels in America* and the Academy Award-winning film *Philadelphia*, to situation comedies like *Mad About You* and *Friends* featuring gay men and lesbians as minor characters, to shows like *Will and Grace* and *Ellen* with gay and lesbian characters in starring roles, to the coming out of celebrities like Ellen DeGeneres, Melissa Etheridge, and k. d. lang.

The resurrection of Wilde was very much part of the entry of the gay subject into sexual citizenship. The film *Wilde*, although marking the fourth film about the life of Oscar Wilde, was all about Wilde's sexuality; the multidimensional facets of his life, including his domestic marital life, faded into the background as the camera lens focused on his homosexual exploits and his relationship with Lord Alfred Douglas ("Boise"). As more than one film critic observed, *Wilde* seemed to remake Oscar Wilde in the discourse of respect-ability. The Wilde of the 1890s—sodomite, social outcast, mocker of society's social mores—was recast as a hero of the 1990s—sexual citizen, victim of in-justice, critic of outdated values and sexual hypocrisy. He was transformed from sodomite to sexual citizen, and in the process much of his unruly edge was left behind. As Carol Lloyd observed, "the domestication of Oscar epito-mizes the dangers of our current make-nice culture. Embracing perversity can also draw the delicious, vital poison from it" (1998). David Plotz similarly noted, "there is very little wildness in today's Wilde" (1998). The subversive-ness of Wilde with his endless transgression of Victorian social mores had given way to a new respectability (*Plotz* 1998).

Yet, the domestication of Wilde—no doubt part of the journey from sod-omite to sexual citizen—should not be overstated. Much of the popular cul-ture representation of the gay and lesbian subject in the 1990s was a highly desexualized one. The characters appeared on stage and on screen, but they did not have sex. The depiction of Oscar Wilde in *Wilde* was a rather more sexualized one. Oscar Wilde was shown having sex with men. While the focus was on the tortured relationship between Oscar and Boise, even their sexual relationship was not entirely domesticated: Both Oscar and Boise are shown having sex with other men. Unlike the other cultural representations of the moment, it was perhaps more difficult to avoid the sexual—Wilde was after all on trial for engaging in sodomy. Yet, unlike earlier depictions, the return to Wilde in the 1998 film version is all about the recuperation of sodomy as a defining gay male act. Oscar Wilde could not be as transgressive in the 1990s as he was in the 1890s. Yet his transformation from sodomite to sexual citizen was not accomplished through an erasure of the act of sodomy but, rather, in and through it.

Much the same can be said of the challenges to the sodomy laws and to the recent arrival of the gay sexual subject into the legal discourses of citi-zenship. The sodomite as sexual outcast survived surprisingly intact in legal discourse through much of the twentieth century. Although the gay libera-tion moment in the late 1960s and early 1970s began to challenge the crimi-nalization of gay sex, gaining momentum in cultural and social discourses, the infamous Supreme Court case of *Bowers v. Hardwick* upheld Georgia's sodomy laws as recently as 1986. The majority opinion written by Justice White held that the Constitution did not confer a right to privacy that ex-tended to homosexual sodomy. He distinguished the sexual privacy cases from *Eisenstadt* to *Carey* as dealing primarily with issues of family, marriage, and procreation and concluded that "No connection between family, marriage, or procreation on the one hand and homosexual activity on the other has been demonstrated" (*Bowers* 1986). In a single paragraph review of the history of the legal regulation of sodomy, the Court stated that "Proscriptions against that conduct have ancient roots," prohibited at common law, by the thirteen original states when they ratified the Bill of Rights, by all but five of the thirty-seven states when the Fourteenth Amendment was ratified, and until 1961, by all fifty states. With this brief history, the majority concluded: "Against this background, to claim that a right to engage in such conduct is 'deeply rooted in this Nation's history and tradition' or 'implicit in the concept of ordered liberty' is, at best, facetious" (*Bowers* 1986).

Justice White rejected the argument that the Court should follow the precedent of *Stanley v. Georgia*, in which the Supreme Court held that the First Amendment prevents criminal prosecution for possessing and using obscenity within the privacy of one's own home. In his view, "otherwise illegal conduct is not always immunized whenever it occurs in the home," noting, for example, that possession of drugs was not protected by *Stanley*. White further held: "And if respondent's submission is limited to the voluntary sexual conduct between consenting adults, it would be difficult, except by fiat, to limit the claimed right to homosexual conduct while leaving exposed to prosecution adultery, incest, and other sexual crimes even though they are committed in the home. We are unwilling to start down that road" (*Bowers* 1986).

Much has been written about the decision in *Bowers*, critiquing and condemning its reasoning (see, for example, Halley 1993; Thomas 1992). My point is that *Bowers* was characterized by many of the hallmarks of border patrol of sexual citizenship. The emerging right to sexual privacy was highly circumscribed—good sex and good citizenship being limited to the familial sphere, and the outlaw being cast as an outsider to this sphere. Good citizens were familial, marital, heterosexual. Sodomites were not. The Court expressly stated its border anxieties: that recognizing a right to engage in consensual gay sex would make it difficult if not impossible to continue to police other forms of consensual sex like adultery and incest—both clear violations of the highly circumscribed sphere of good familial sex. In addition to the obvious homophobic discourse informing the decision that has been well rehearsed in the literature, *Bowers* is a classic instantiation of the anxieties of patrolling a moving border: It must be contained and controlled, lest the center does not hold, and sexual chaos results.

In the two decades that followed, *Bowers* was very much out of sync with the cultural discourse around gay sex. Although social conservatives continued to denounce the immorality of homosexuality, popular culture embraced the gay and lesbian subject throughout the 1990s. While the image of the gay and lesbian subject was for the most part a desexualized one—these were not folks having public, promiscuous sex; in fact, they did not seem to be having any sex—it was a far cry from the image of outlaw. And it was an image in the public sphere that began to set the stage for the legal transformation.

In 2003, the Supreme Court reversed its ruling in *Bowers*. In *Lawrence v. Texas*, Justice Kennedy, writing for the majority, struck down a Texas sodomy law (*Lawrence*). The law stated that "a person commits an offense if he engages in deviate sexual intercourse with another individual of the same sex" and defined "deviate sexual intercourse" as "any contact between any part of the genitals of one person and the mouth or anus of another person" or "the penetration of the genitals or the anus of another person with an object" (*Lawrence*, 563 quoting Texas Penal Code). The definition of the proscribed sexual acts was thus expressly directed against same-sex sex; heterosexuals were free to engage in all the oral and anal sex they desired without fear of criminal prosecution.

Kennedy framed the right at issue as a liberty right, as a right to make certain private choices about intimate matters, that is, about matters "touching upon the most private human conduct, sexual behavior, and in the most private of places, the home" (*Lawrence*, 567). In his view, the decision to enter into a homosexual sexual relationship in the privacy of one's own home was precisely such a matter: "It suffices for us to acknowledge that adults may choose to enter upon this relationship in the confines of their homes and their own private lives and still retain their dignity as free persons. When sexuality finds overt expression in intimate conduct with another person, the conduct can be but one element in a personal bond that is more enduring. The liberty protected by the Constitution allows homosexual persons the right to make this choice" (*Lawrence*, 567).

But, that liberty right was at the same time carefully circumscribed. Throughout the opinion, Kennedy emphasized the private, the domestic, the home as the location of the liberty interest. Katherine Franke argues that the Court in *Lawrence* recognized a highly domesticated liberty right—"the liberty interest at stake is one that is tethered to the domestic private" (Franke 2004, 1403). She argues that "gay men are portrayed as domesticated creatures, settling down into marital-like relationships in which they can both cultivate and nurture desires for exclusivity, fidelity and longevity in place of other more explicitly erotic desires" (1408). As a result of this focus on the domestic, Franke worries that *Lawrence* will be of little assistance in advancing alternative "nonnormative notions of kinship, intimacy and sexuality" (*Lawrence*, 1414). Franke specifically ties her analysis to the idea of sexual citizenship, arguing that "[t]he world post-*Lawrence* remains invested in forms of social membership and, indeed, citizenship that are structurally identified with domesticated heterosexual marriage and intimacy" (1416). In her view, the sexual citizenship that emerges from *Lawrence* is a domesticated one, a "domestinormative sexual citizenship" (1416).

This domestication of the liberty right exemplifies the kind of border patrol of sexual citizenship evident in the sexual privacy cases. As the right is extended to nonheterosexuals—a radical transformation in its own right—it must simultaneously be contained; its radical edges must be controlled. Supplementing this focus on the domestic, there is in *Lawrence* an emphasis on what the right is not. Kennedy writes: "The present case does not involve minors. It does not involve persons who might be injured or coerced or who are situated in relationships where consent might not easily be refused. It does not involve public conduct or prostitution" (*Lawrence*, 578). In other words, the sexual conduct in question does not involve children, harmful sex, nonconsensual sex, public sex, or commercial sex. The gay sex that is being protected is carefully circumscribed: It is not all gay sex, nor is it all sex.

The sexual citizenship of *Lawrence* is articulated against the backdrop of what it is not; it is always against an identifiable border. Kennedy then returns to the trope of the domestic, which is deployed to constitute and patrol the border: "The case does involve two adults who, with full and mutual consent from each other, engaged in sexual practices common to a homosexual lifestyle. The petitioners are entitled to respect for their private lives. The State cannot demean their existence or control their destiny by making their private sexual conduct a crime" (*Lawrence*, 578). Kennedy is thus able to shift the homosexual from bad to good citizen by carefully ensuring that the borders between good and bad citizenship themselves are sustained. The normative content of good sexual citizenship remains—consensual, private, noncommercial—while gay men are reconstituted in its image. And the normative content of bad sexual citizenship similarly remains intact, with anything involving children, harm, coercion, public, and/or commercial as its harbingers.

There is one other thing in Kennedy's "what it is not" list: "It does not involve whether the government must give formal recognition to any relationship that homosexual persons seek to enter" (*Lawrence*, 578). The sexual citizenship of *Lawrence* is carefully articulated as not involving same-sex marriage or even same-sex relationship recognition. The gay subject is removed from outlaw status, but the process of legitimation is not one that grants the full rights of citizenship. This may simply be border patrolling compelled by political expediency: The Court wanted to make crystal clear that it was not deciding anything about gay marriage or civil unions or formal relationship recognition at a moment when these issues were politically explosive. Yet, it is an interesting limitation on the domestication of the gay subject. Although Franke quite rightly worries "that Lawrence and the gay rights organizing that has taken place around it have created a path dependency that privileges privatized and domesticated rights and legal liabilities, while rendering less viable projects that advance nonnormative notions of kinship, intimacy and sexuality" (1414), the decision itself attempts, perhaps unsuccessfully, to preempt this domesticated subjectivity by patrolling the borders of marriage.

It is precisely the anxiety over the majority's failed border patrolling that is amplified in Justice Scalia's dissent. Scalia vehemently opposes the majority conclusion that moral approbation is no longer a legitimate state interest sufficient to pass constitutional review. In his view, removing morality would lead inexorably to a collapsing of the borders between legitimate and illegitimate sex, and of government regulation thereof: "State laws against bigamy, same-sex marriage, adult incest, prostitution, masturbation, adultery, fornication, bestiality and obscenity are . . . sustainable only in light of *Bowers* validation of laws based on moral choices. Every single one of these laws is called into question by today's decision; the Court makes no effort to cabin the scope of its decision to exclude them from its holding" (*Lawrence*, 590). In Justice Scalia's eyes, this is nothing less than "a massive disruption of current social order" (591). On the majority assertion that the present case does not involve same-sex relationship recognition, Scalia retorts "Do not believe it" (604); in his view, the majority has dismantled the very "structure of constitutional law that has permitted a distinction to be made between heterosexual and homosexual unions" (604).

For Scalia, the outrage of the majority opinion is thus not only the overruling of *Bowers* and the recognition of the right of homosexuals to engage in sodomy, but also the utter failure of border patrol: Sodomy today, bestiality and same-sex marriage tomorrow. It is, on the one hand, a typical legal trope—the slippery slope is frequently invoked in judicial reasoning to justify a limitation on recognizing new rights or cognizable injuries (Lode 1999; Schauer 2003; Volokh 1985). But, it takes on a heightened salience in the context of the legal regulation of consensual sex where there are deeply embedded social anxieties about the excesses of sexual desire and the ever-present possibility of descent into sexual chaos. Indeed, the issue of border patrol is actually one on which Kennedy and Scalia tacitly agree: It must be ensured. Kennedy is of the view that the inclusion of gay men and lesbians can be done within secure borders, whereas Scalia believes that such inclusion actually calls into question the national security of sexual citizenship. Kennedy normalizes through inclusion, while Scalia demonizes through exclusion. But both maintain the importance of the border.

But, the domestication of the newly arrived sexual citizen is not without its "unruly edges" (Stychin 2001, 290). Much like the film *Wilde*, the transformation of the gay subject from sodomite to sexual citizen occurs not through an erasure of the sexual practices of sodomy, but in and through them. John Geddes Lawrence and Tryon Garner were, in the words of the Supreme Court, found by the police "engaging in a sexual act" (*Lawrence*, 563). The Court also referred to the sex as described by the complainants within the language of the statute as "deviate sexual intercourse, namely, anal sex, with a member of the same sex" (*Lawrence*, quoting the complainants, 563).[1] While the term "sodomy'" is used in the description of the history of its legal regulation, the actual sex that Lawrence and Garner had is otherwise described by the majority only in terms of "adult sexual intimacy" (564) or "sexual practices common to a homosexual lifestyle" (578). Despite this avoidance of the language of sodomy—or even anal sex—the fact that this is the "sexual practice common to a homosexual lifestyle" is unavoidable.

The case is all about the right to engage in sodomy and, in turn, the transformation of sodomite as outcast to gay subject engaged in sodomy as sexual citizen. Just like in *Wilde*, this transformation must occur on a highly sexualized terrain: Lawrence and Garner must be entitled to sexual citizenship in the face of their sexual performance. And while Lawrence and Garner may have actually had sex in the privacy of one of their homes, the performance of sodomy became rather more public, occurring on a legal stage with considerable public spotlight. Notwithstanding the efforts at domesticating the newly arrived sexual citizen, this performance of sodomy pushes at the edges of the previously respectable and desexualized citizen. There is no escaping the sexual desire and sexualized bodies of the new sexual citizen. Lawrence and Garner's newly acquired sexual citizenship is not one that disavows sex but, rather, is forced to embrace sex within its folds.

No Right to Vibrate? Sexual Privacy After Lawrence

In the first season of *Sex and the City*, Miranda introduces Charlotte to a vibrator—the candy-colored Rabbit (*Sex and the City* 1998). Despite her initial reserve, Charlotte takes to it like a fish to water—so much so that Carrie and Samantha have to stage an intervention; Charlotte is repeatedly canceling her social engagements in order to stay home with her new friend. The day after the show aired, sex shops across North America reportedly sold out of the model (George 2004). What Manolo Blahniks were to shoes, the Rabbit now was to vibrators, with the show again epitomizing the new sexual citizenship as a merging of sex and shopping. Although this was neither the first nor the last depiction of vibrators on the series—Miranda keeps one in her bedside table, Samantha spends an unsuccessful day at home with several vibrators in an attempt to get her orgasm back—it nevertheless represented a new high-water mark, as vibrators came out of the closet and into the public sphere.

While some might imagine that this new vibrating sexual citizen is limited to the city, there are tremors being felt well beyond the urban republics. Saucy Lady is a small Alabama-based company that conducts in-house Tupperware™-style parties for women at which sex toys are sold. Owner B. J. Bailey has been organizing these parties since 1993. Vibrators, dildos, lingerie, massage oils, lubricants, anal beads, and instruction manuals are among the products displayed and sold at these parties. Like larger scale direct-marketers specializing in sex products, such as Passion Parties™ based in Brisbane, California, and Ann Summers in the United Kingdom, Saucy Lady brings sex toys to women through local distributors—or party planners—who host house parties. The idea behind the parties is to take these sex products to the women who may otherwise be too timid to go to the sex products. By bringing them into the domestic sphere, these retailers demystify and normalize them for use by otherwise proper housewifely citizens. Passion Parties, described in a *New York Times Magazine* article as "one of the country's tamest, most pro-family peddlers of sexual paraphernalia," does good business in the southern Bible Belt: In 2003, Mississippi, Arkansas, and Tennessee ranked third, fourth, and ninth, respectively, in sales (Senior 2004). The company's home page describes itself as the "premier sensual party planner in the United States," "designed to promote intimacy and communication between couples." As further described in the *New York Times*:

> The Passion Parties training video, sent to all new representatives, begins with an endorsement from a board-certified sex therapist and licensed marriage, family and child counselor, and before the demonstration segment begins, one of the company's executive directors, a woman dressed in a bright indigo suit, declares: "Now, ladies, if you did come tonight looking for any vulgarity or pornography, you're going to be very disappointed. I don't have it. But if you came here for a fun evening, plus some tips to keep the excitement in your relationship, plus the parts to work with, you are definitely in the right place." (Senior 2004)

Despite their increasing popularity, the legality of these sex toys is at issue in some of the southern Bible Belt. Several states, including Texas, Alabama, Georgia, and Mississippi—have laws that criminally prohibit the sale of sex toys. In November 2003, Joanne Webb, a Texas-based Passion Party representative, was arrested for selling two vibrators to undercover agents, in violation of a state law prohibiting the sale of any device used to stimulate the genitals. While the charges were eventually dropped, a constitutional challenge to the state law was launched. Several years earlier, B. J. Bailey—the owner of Saucy Lady—along with Sherry Williams, who owns Pleasures, an upscale sex boutique in Alabama, challenged a similar law in Alabama. The Alabama Anti-Obscenity Enforcement Act, passed in 1998, prohibits the commercial distribution of "any device designed or marketed as useful primarily for the stimulation of human genital organs for anything of pecuniary value" and was based on the Texas law (Ala. Code 2003). The ACLU, on behalf of Williams, Bailey, and several other plaintiffs described as users of the sexual devices, challenged the law as violating the constitutional right to privacy and personal autonomy under the Fourteenth Amendment. The district court held that there was no recognized fundamental right to use sex toys, but in reviewing the statute under the rational basis review, concluded that the statute lacked any rational basis and enjoined its enforcement (*Williams* 1999). On appeal, the Court of Appeals for the Eleventh Circuit reversed the district court's conclusion, holding instead that the promotion and preservation of public morality was a rational basis for the legislation and remanded the case to the district court for further consideration of the as-applied fundamental rights challenge (*Williams* 2001).

On remand, the district court once again struck down the statute, holding that the statute burdened a constitutionally protected right to use sexual devices within private, adult, consensual relationships (*Williams* 2002). The decision included a detailed discussion of the history of sexual privacy in the United States, from the seventeenth century to the present, tracing the trend towards liberalization and the withdrawal of state regulation throughout the twentieth century. According to the court, this trend toward legislative and social liberalization supports the finding of a fundamental right to sexual privacy. This right was, in turn, burdened by the prohibitions on the sexual devices. The state of Alabama argued that it had a compelling state interest for this burden: specifically, to protect children from obscenity, to prevent assault on the sensibilities of the unwilling adult, to suppress the proliferation of adult-only stores, and more generally, to uphold the belief that "[t]he commerce of sexual stimulation and auto-eroticism, for its own sake, unrelated to marriage, procreation or familial relationships is an evil, an obscenity . . . detrimental to the health and morality of the state" (*Williams* 2002, 1301, citing the brief of the attorney general of Alabama). In the court's view, the statute was not sufficiently tailored to meet a compelling state interest. For example, the fact that the statute could apply to the Tupperware-style parties organized in private homes advertised solely by word of mouth meant that the statute was not narrowly tailored to prevent public exposure to children and unwilling adults. Nor was the statute sufficiently tailored to meet the objective of preventing "the commerce of sexual stimulation . . . unrelated to marriage, procreation or familial relations" (Williams 2002, 1301).

According to the court, the law "in fact, has the effect of accomplishing the reverse for the user plaintiffs. Each of the user plaintiffs has stated that use of sexual devices during marital and dating relationships has enabled them to, among other things, improve the quality of their marital communications, better their sexual relationships, encourage intimacy in their marital relationships, eradicate fears of infidelity between spouses, and to combat embarrassing or painful medical conditions" (*Williams* 2002, 1305). The court continued:

> ... "a great many" of vendor plaintiff B. J. Bailey's customers have "reported to Ms. Bailey that the products they purchased helped them to become orgasmic and greatly improved their marital and sexual relations." ... The parties further have stipulated to the opinions of two experts in the study of human sexuality that "sexual aids help in the revitalization of potentially failing marital relations," and that the use of sexual devices is recommended in "therapy for couples who are having sexual problems in their marriage...." Also compelling is the fact that the State of Alabama's own University Health System Internet site advocates applying a "powerful vibrator on the glands of the penis" to enable men who have suffered spinal cord injuries to ejaculate, for the specific purpose of "impregnat[ing] their wives and hav[ing] normal, healthy children." (Williams 2002, 1305, footnotes omitted)

The court thus goes to some lengths to emphasize the role of these sexual devices within marriage—improving marital relationships, preventing infidelity, even promoting procreation. It does so to make its point that the law is too broad, since it captures these legitimate marital uses. But in so doing, the reasoning effectively recuperates the legitimacy of sex toys by normalizing them within the domestic sphere. Rather like the Saucy Lady parties themselves, the legal discourse is redrawing the lines of good sex and legitimate sexual citizenship to include sex toys by recasting these toys as legitimate marital aids. The parties, and the legal discourse, are literally giving these toys a Good Housekeeping Seal of Approval.

This district court decision was appealed to the Eleventh Circuit, which despite the intervening development of the Supreme Court's decision in *Lawrence*, upheld the constitutionality of Alabama's statutory prohibition of the sale of sex toys (*Williams* 2004). The court held that there was no fundamental, substantive due process right of consenting adults to engage in private, intimate sexual conduct, as would trigger a strict scrutiny review of any infringement of that right. In the court's view, *Lawrence* simply did not establish a right to sexual privacy: "To do so would be to impose a fundamental-rights interpretation on a decision that rested on rational-basis grounds, that never engaged in *Glucksberg* analysis, and that never invoked strict scrutiny. Moreover, it would be answering questions that the Lawrence Court appears to have left for another day" (*Williams* 2004, 1238). Nor, the court held, should any new fundamental right be recognized. Applying the *Glucksberg* analysis for the recognition of new fundamental rights,[2] the appeals court held that the district court had failed to carefully describe the alleged right:

> In searching for, and ultimately finding, this right to sexual privacy, the district court did little to define its scope and bounds. As formulated by the district court, the right potentially encompasses a great universe of sexual activities, including many that historically have been, and continue to be, prohibited. At oral arguments, the ACLU contended that "no responsible counsel" would challenge prohibitions such as those against pederasty and adult incest under a "right to sexual privacy" theory. However, mere faith in the responsibility of the bar scarcely provides a legally cognizable, or constitutionally significant, limiting principle in applying the right in future cases. (*Williams* 2004, 1240)

The court observed that the only limitation provided by the district court was that the right would only apply to consenting adults. However, this "consenting adult formula" was not an appropriate constitutional standard. "If we were to accept the invitation to recognize a right to sexual intimacy, this right would theoretically encompass such activities as prostitution, obscenity, and adult incest—even if we were to limit the right to consenting adults" (*Williams* 2004, 1240). This passage was followed by a quotation from the Supreme Court's ruling in *Paris Adult Theatre I*: "The state statute books are replete with constitutionally unchallenged laws against prostitution, suicide, voluntary self-mutilation, brutalizing 'bare fist' prize fights, and duels, although these crimes may only directly involve 'consenting adults'" (*Williams* 2004, 1240). The court was thus explicitly concerned with patrolling the borders of sexual privacy, articulating the trope of potential sexual chaos: Sex toys would open the doors to prostitution and adult incest.

The court further articulated its anxiety over border control in addressing and rejecting the argument of the ACLU that the right to privacy and sexual privacy were at issue in this case. In its view, "[t]he statute invades the privacy of Alabama residents in their bedrooms no more than does any statute restricting the availability of commercial products for use in private quarters as sexual enhancements" (*Williams* 2004, 1241). In a footnote, the court further elaborated on this point: "The mere fact that a product is used within the privacy of the bedroom, or that it enhances intimate conduct, does not in itself bring the use of that article within the right to privacy. If it were otherwise, individuals whose sexual gratification requires other types of material or instrumentalities—perhaps hallucinogenic substances, depictions of child pornography or bestiality, or the services of a willing prostitute—likewise would have a colorable argument that prohibitions on such activities and materials interfere with their privacy in the bedchamber." Once again, the court is concerned with its ability to patrol the borders of good sex. If the privacy of the bedroom becomes the dividing line between good and bad sex and therefore between legitimate and illegitimate regulation, the use of child pornography and/or prostitution will necessarily fall on the side of good and, therefore, unregulated sex. This time, allowing sex toys would lead inexorably to the court's inability to prevent a free market of child pornography and prostitution.

The court concluded its discussion of the first part of the *Glucksberg* test by framing the alleged right as the right to use sexual devices and then turned to a consideration of the second part of the *Glucksberg* test: namely, whether the right can be said to be deeply rooted in the nation's history or implicit in the concept of liberty. In rejecting this right, the court criticized the district court for focusing on the history of sex in American culture rather than sexual devices, for overemphasizing the importance of contemporary practices, and for equating nonintervention in the access to sexual devices with historical protection. The majority referred several times to, and disagreed with, the district court's discovery of a constitutional "right to use sexual devices like . . . vibrators, dildos, anal beads, and artificial vaginas." Casting the right in these terms, as opposed to a more general right to sexual privacy (*Williams* 2004, 1244, 1247, 1250), is a way of belittling the interest at stake. A constitutional right to vibrators and dildos is intended to caricature the claim, by demeaning the seriousness of constitutional protection. It framed the right narrowly and thereby was able to dismiss the district court's discussion of the history of the legal regulation of sex and sexuality in America since it was simply not relevant to the right to use vibrators and dildos.

The court similarly rejected the district court's discussion of the "contemporary trend of legislative and societal liberalization of attitudes toward consensual, adult sexual activity" (*Williams* 2002, 1294, cited in *Williams* 2004, 1243) and the "specter of twentieth century sexual liberalism" (*Williams* 2002, 1291, cited in *Williams* 2004, 1243), on the basis that this contemporary practice is simply not relevant for the *Glucksberg* analysis. Indeed, in the majority's view, this focus on contemporary practice "ultimately proves too much. The fact that there is an emerging consensus scarcely provides justification for the courts, who often serve as an antimajoritarian seawall, to be swept up with the tide of popular culture" (*Williams* 2004, 1244). Popular culture—rather than influencing or shaping legal tradition—is held out as the very thing that law must resist. No *Sex and the City* for this court.

Williams is an example of law's reluctance to cede its policing power to the power of self-discipline. Not unlike Justice Scalia's dissent in *Lawrence*, the obsession with border patrol and containing the inevitable sexual chaos that would result from a failure to adequately protect these borders preempts the possibility of recognizing self-disciplining subjects. An irony lies in the fact that these new sexual subjects are an intensely self-disciplining lot. The women with sex toys—sellers and consumers alike—are constituted in and through the discourses of domesticity and self-discipline. The parties are private affairs: They are conducted in one of the women's homes, and the invitations are by word of mouth. Men are excluded, since a male presence would contaminate the pristine female domesticity. There is an implicit code of conduct at these parties: Women can talk about sex, they can laugh, and they can let their hair down. But, as the promotional materials caution, "if you did come tonight looking for any vulgarity or pornography, you're going to be very disappointed." Martha McCaughey and Christina French, in their participant-observation research of women's sex toy parties, similarly observe that despite the sexual explicitness of these parties, the "atmosphere attempts to retain some sense of refinement by avoiding putatively dirty words for body parties. . . . Saleswomen use nice-nellyisms such as 'button' for clitoris, 'lily' for vulva and/or vagina and 'unit' for penis" (McCaughey & French 2001, 81).

The parties and their emphasis on women's sexual pleasure are also often contained with the discourses of romance and self-help.[3] Passion Parties uses the tag line "Where every day is Valentine's Day" and has a flagship product line entitled Romanta Therapy. These products are expressly marketed as relationship enhancing. Indeed, the products are often described by the distributors as relationship saving. Joanne Webb, the Passion Party representative charged under the Texas obscenity statute, described her work as helping keep couples together: "I thought . . . if I could educate women on how to get the most out of their sensuality, how to give the most in their relationship through their sensuality, maybe, just maybe some of these divorce rates would go down" (*ABC News* 2004). Kim Airs, who runs two retail sex toy stores specifically directed to women, similarly says: "I cannot tell you how may times I hear, 'This saved my marriage, this has saved my relationship'"

(Alexander 2004). The distributors see themselves not only as saleswomen but as sex educators and therapists, helping women to help themselves toward more fulfilling sexual relationships. This role was not lost on the district court in *Williams*, which considered the marital-enhancing use of these products in striking down the law.

McCaughey and French have suggested that these sex toy parties be seen through the lens of Anthony Giddens's life politics, that is, as self-actualization projects (Giddens 1991; McCaughey & French 2001, 91, 97). They argue that these sex toy parties are part of a self-help narrative in which women can enhance their sexual pleasure and their relationships by "expect[ing] less from men and learn[ing] to satisfy themselves" (McCaughey & French 2001, 93).

I would argue that these sex parties are part of an increasing emphasis on self-help and self-actualization, but they are also about women taking greater responsibility for the couple's sex life. It is part of a related project of responsibilization in which individuals are being called upon to make their lives a project and to take responsibility for this project (Rose 1996). It is part of a new modality of self-governance that includes an emphasis on taking responsibility for one's intimate, romantic, and sexual life (Rose 1996). As I discuss in greater detail in Chapter 2 on the role of sex in marriage, sexual citizens are being asked to take responsibility for their sex lives as part of a broader responsibility for the health of their marriages. Women's sex toy parties are located within this project of self-governance. As some of the distributors suggest, women are being taught to make sex a priority, to make their sex lives a project, and in so doing, to save their relationships.

The sex toy parties can then be framed within a discourse of the self-disciplining of sexual citizenship. Rather than challenging the heteronormativity of sexual citizenship, women are assuming a central role in the project of intimate self-governance, with a view to sustaining the marital relationship. It is admittedly a modality of citizenship with a new emphasis on women's sexual pleasure—one that disrupts the foreclosure on women's sexual agency. It makes women's sexual pleasure speakable, but not entirely for its own hedonistic sake. Rather, this pleasure is contained with the marital, the heterosexual, the domestic, where it is put to work to produce a better relationship.

It is also important to recognize that Passion Parties is big business. In 2003, it sold $20 million of goods, and projected sales for 2004 were $35 million. Sales have been growing at a rate of 50 percent annually between 2001 and 2004 (Alexander 2004). And Passion Parties is not alone: Its major competitors,

Slumber Parties and Pure Romance, each have more than 3,000 consultants across the United States. The economic success of these sex toy parties has been incorporated into the marketing of the parties. For example, Passion Party promotes becoming a Passion Party associate as an avenue for women's financial independence and economic empowerment. The sex toy Tupperware parties are partially framed and legitimated within the discourse of market citizenship. The distributors—the party planners—are good citizens by virtue of the norms of market self-reliance. The consumers are similarly being constituted as good citizens by virtue of the norms of market consumption. As McCaughey and French have argued, the consumption of sex toys—like the consumption of a range of novel lifestyle goods, becomes part of the project of self-actualization (McCaughey & French 2001, citing Giddens, 91). Self-help, sexual enhancement, and market consumption are integrated into a new synthetic citizen.

Women's sexual pleasure is incorporated into sexual citizenship, but in a way that ensures its containment. The discourses of domesticity, marketization, and self-discipline ensure that any recognition of women's sexual pleasure does not lead inexorably to sexual chaos. Rather, just as Carrie and Samantha stepped in to discipline Charlotte in the face of her inability to control her desire for her vibrator, the discourses within which women's access to these sex toys is being constituted ensures that sexual excess will be controlled by the women themselves. Women themselves will provide all the lessons in self-governance. But, in *Williams*, the Eleventh Circuit was unable or unwilling to recognize the ways in which these sexual practices and the citizens they constitute will discipline themselves. The court, in its zeal to protect the borders of traditional sexual citizenship, refuses to recognize the new modalities of normalization, which would make the kind of regulation imposed by the court redundant. Charlotte, like the women who attend Saucy Lady parties or Passion Parties, does not need the Eleventh Circuit to ensure that she does not descend into sexual chaos: She has her friends who can hold up a mirror and make sure that she does it herself.

It is important not to underplay the extent to which the sexual citizen is being reconstituted on the terrain of the sexual. Notwithstanding the domestication of sex toy party participants, this performance pushes at the edges of the previously respectable and desexualized citizen. This is a sexual citizenship that is explicitly sexual; it is a desiring, pulsating, pleasure-driven, orgasmic body. This is a new modality of sexual citizenship. It is also an explicitly gendered sexual citizenship. *Williams*, and the broader Passion Parties phenomenon, are all about women—otherwise respectable, often married women who are buying and selling sex toys. There is no escaping the sexual desire and sexual pleasure of women—married or otherwise.

But, it is a modality of citizenship that has its detractors, from Justice Scalia and the Eleventh Circuit, to the townspeople of Burleson, Texas, who simply could not tolerate the sexualized citizenship of Joanne Webb. Webb, the Passion Parties distributor in Burleson, Texas, was charged under the Texas statute for selling an obscene object. She ran into trouble because she failed to conduct herself according to the local norms.[4] Her infraction? She was a little too sexy. She wore her skirts a little too short and her shirts a little too low cut. But she was no Bible Belt Carrie Bradshaw. Joanne Webb was married for over twenty years to a veteran, a former major in the U.S. Army. She and her husband were Southern Baptists. Her short skirts, indeed, her whole overly sexualized appearance, was described as exclusively for her husband's pleasure: "more than anything else, my husband likes them. It's one of the basic things he asks me to do." Like a good Southern Baptist wife, she was following the authority of her husband. But, for the citizens of Burleson, Texas, her husband was telling her to be a little too sexy. In fact, they both were too sexy. He was flirtatious and had a collection of 1940s advertising trinkets featuring voluptuous women. She not only wore her skirts too short, but she had breast enhancement, sexy blond hair, and drove a red convertible. In other respects, Joanne Webb was a model citizen—she was a member of the Chamber of Commerce, she was involved in her church, she was married and dedicated to her husband—all markers of good citizenship. But her overtly sexualized appearance outweighed these factors. The local community attempted to sanction her; they even tried to impose a dress code for members of the Chamber of Commerce. The pastor of their church demanded that her husband make her dress differently. He refused, and they left the church. All of this led to swirling rumors of sexual excess: They were having affairs, they were causing divorces, they were swingers.

When Joanne became a representative for Passion Parties, the rumors erupted into a full-scale sexual panic. They must be having orgies. An anonymous complaint lodged with the local police led to a police investigation. Two undercover police officers posing as a married couple asked to see Joanne's catalogues. She encouraged the woman to get some friends together for a party, but the couple insisted on buying two vibrators right away. The 30-minute operation was captured on video. Several weeks later, Joanne was under arrest. She hired a lawyer, BeAnn Sisemore, who made Joanne's case a personal crusade. They got the national media involved, with stories in the *New York Times*, and on CNN, NPR, and some of the networks, all belittling the town of Burleson. [5] Joanne's trial was supposed to take place in the summer of 2004, but the charges were subsequently dropped.

The controversy around Joanne Webb might be dismissed as the machinations of small-town, red-state politics, in much the same way as the national media portrayed the story and the town of Burleson. But, the fault lines of this controversy have broader ramifications. Joanne Webb was constituted as a subject who failed to self-discipline, despite repeated warnings by the community. She and her husband chose to flout the local norms of appropriate sexual citizenship. In so doing, they aroused a series of border anxieties of sexual chaos: They must be committing adultery, they must be having orgies. Their sexual excess could not be contained, nor could it be reined in through self-discipline, despite repeated efforts. When all else failed and when the sexualized behavior reached unprecedented proportions—when Joanne started having sex toy parties that were perceived as a cover for orgies—the law had to be called in. Community efforts to cast her as a sexual outlaw were not enough to make her self-discipline. The punitive and constitutive power of the law was then deployed to mark her as an outlaw. This is a story very familiar to the legal regulation of consensual sexual practices; the law is called in when the borders appear to be at stake and when the subjects have failed to self-discipline.

Joanne Webb fought back, though at considerable personal cost. Her husband lost his business, and they declared personal bankruptcy. Yet, she refused to self-discipline. She continues to be a Passion Party distributor. She has filed a federal civil suit seeking to have the Texas law declared unconstitutional. Joanne Webb has refused to accept her status as a sexual outlaw. Rather, she continues to demand her citizenship status: as a sexual being, as an entrepreneur, as a mother and wife. She is emblematic of those subjects challenging the contours of traditional sexual citizenship from the perspective of a marketized and self-disciplined but explicitly sexual subject.

Joanne Webb also exemplifies the normalizing role played by those sexualized subjects who challenge the borders of sexual citizenship. Her contested citizenship creates space for others to live more sexualized lives. In this respect, Joanne Webb, like B. J. Bailey of Saucy Lady parties charged in the *Williams* case, has rather more in common with Samantha from *Sex and the City* than with Charlotte.

Throughout the series, Samantha is unapologetically sexual. Indeed, her character is framed through a discourse of sexual excess; she has sex with multiple partners, often with virtual strangers. She dresses provocatively. She interacts with men seductively—both professionally and socially, often mixing the two. Her life project seems to be the pursuit of sexual pleasure. Samantha's character does more than provide the show with sexual titillation; her sexual excess helps to normalize the sexuality of the other three characters. Carrie, Miranda, and particularly Charlotte seem tame in comparison. While they, too, are explicitly sexual citizens pursuing their sexual desires, Carrie, Miranda, and Charlotte are also pursuing their romantic desires. Sex and romance are more intricately interwoven for these three characters. Their sex—whether good, bad, or otherwise—simply never appears as outrageous as Samantha's sex. Further, while Samantha's explicit sex talk and her sexual exploits often shock her friends, it also creates space for the foursome to share their sexual desires and anxieties. Samantha is constituted in the discourse of sexual excess, and her role is to push the boundaries of legitimate sexual citizenship; indeed, at times her role is to exceed those boundaries. In so doing, her character creates more citizenship space and more normalized citizenship space for the others to inhabit. Much like the border dweller contesting the lines between good and bad citizenship discussed in the next section, Samantha—like Joanne Webb and B. J. Bailey—reconstitutes the domain of legitimate sexual citizenship, allowing others to become more explicitly sexual without losing their citizenship status. Others can be good precisely because they are just a little bit bad; good citizenship is once again constituted in the shadow of the bad.

Sexual Speech, Sexual Subjects

"If the First Amendment will protect a scumbag like me, then it'll protect all of you—'cause I'm the worst," declares *Hustler Magazine* publisher Larry Flynt in the midst of one of his many court cases represented in *The People vs. Larry Flynt.* The controversial film, released in 1996, tells Flynt's story—from poor boy selling moonshine to strip club manager to multimillionaire CEO of *Hustler*'s empire and political crusader against America's morality police. Flynt's idea was a fairly simple one: provide a graphic and crass alternative to *Playboy* and *Penthouse.* It was a matter of being in the right place at the right time—a photo series of Jackie Kennedy Onassis sunbathing nude put *Hustler* over the top, and it never looked back. But along come the antipornography crusaders and so began his seemingly endless legal battles defending himself against charges of obscenity. He pays a high price—arrest, imprisonment, and paralysis as a result of an attempt on his life. He is also sued by none other than Jerry Falwell, the self-appointed head of America's Moral Majority. The suit involves a parody advertisement for the alcoholic drink Campari in which Falwell reminisces about his first sexual experience—an incestual one with his mother. Falwell sued Flynt for libel, invasion of privacy, and intentional infliction of emotional distress. The trial court awarded Falwell damages for the intentional infliction of emotional distress. But, Flynt was ultimately vindicated by the U.S. Supreme Court.

In the film, a sexual outlaw is reconstituted as a political citizen. Larry Flynt—the unapologetic pursuer of sexual pleasure and scandal—becomes Larry Flynt—the defender of America's civil liberties and freedom of speech. Flynt is represented sympathetically: He loves his unconventional wife in unconventional ways, he overcomes drug addiction when the pain of his back injury is relieved through successive surgeries, and he adamantly defends the constitutional rights of Americans. He is, basically, a good guy, notwithstanding his self-description as a "scumbag." It is a story of becoming, of transformation, and of normalization. But this normalization of the sexual subject occurs not so much through a transformation in the sex itself—Flynt and *Hustler* are represented as the sexual extreme, as "the worst." Instead, the story of citizenship is told through Flynt's impassioned legal struggles and his unrelenting commitment to America's constitutional principles. It is a kind of modern-day sexualized version of *Mr. Smith Goes to Washington*: instead of a naïve protagonist, we have a crass one; instead of a fight against graft and corruption, we have sexual hypocrisy and censorship. Yet both men stake their futures and that of their country on their unshakable belief in democracy and its institutions. And they both win.

The People vs. Larry Flynt is a story of political idealism and constitutional vindication. But, Flynt's story is at the same time a story about sexual citizenship that traffics in the ongoing tension between sex and politics, between the sexual edginess of its protagonist and his political commitment. The story of pornographer as citizen is effective precisely because the sex is more than a little bit bad. It is titillating because it is illicit: The sex that *Hustler* celebrates is crass, raunchy, and promiscuous. And while Larry Flynt's legal struggles and the representation of these struggles in the film are intended to defend the right of Americans to engage in this sex, the film does this more by shift-ing the lines of legal liability than by redrawing the lines between clean and dirty sex. The message of the film is this: This is dirty sex, and it is our right to have it. Even in the mid 1990s, pornography was still an outlier.

Fast forward to 2004, and much of the landscape has shifted. It is no lon-ger clear that pornography is a genre of the sexual outlaw. Jenna Jones—one of the pornography industry's hottest stars—has written an autobiography that appeared on the *New York Times* best-seller list. The fashion industry has assimilated pornography's style. Fortune 500 companies distribute por-nography. Its audience has expanded, with women and couples as new target markets. While pornography has long been marketized—sexual images for sale—its mass marketization and aestheticization have begun to reconstitute the genre. Its outlaw status has made it hip, and in the process it has become rather less outlaw.

And Larry Flynt is no longer "the worst." He is, in the corporate world of the adult entertainment industry, the mainstream. He funds Democrats, runs for mayor, takes out full-page newspaper ads soliciting information about the adulterous relationships of members of Congress, and distances himself from the new sexual outliers. In the new sex wars discussed below, where the Ashcroft/Gonzales administration is cracking down on what it has identified as extreme pornography—particularly sex with violence—not only is Larry Flynt no longer the worst, but he has declined to provide financial assistance to the new worst. There has been a transformation in the relative outlier status of the pornographic genre, with much of it coming in from beyond citizenship.

It is a story of transformation—of the assimilation and domestication of much of the genre—that presents new and interesting challenges to legal regulation and its mandate of drawing the lines between good and bad sex. Drawing these lines has long been the very *raison d'être* of obscenity. As Joan DeJean has argued, obscenity has a long history of operating as "a boundary maker, signaling the frontier between the indecent and the decent, the filthy and the clean" (DeJean 2002, 6). From the introduction of obscenity laws in Victorian England to the Comstock laws of the early twentieth century to the culture wars of the 1980s and 1990s, sexually explicit representations have been seen as posing a threat to the family, to the social order, and to the nation. The law has evolved over time, allowing a broader range of representations to cross into the realm of legitimate speech. Yet, the urge to draw lines between legitimate and illegitimate speech and protecting society from the corrosive effect of sexual representations endures. The law continues to try to draw the line on speech, by declaring that some has gone too far and that it represents too great a threat to our children, our communities, and our nationhood. Each era seems to produce its own set of cultural contestations and anxieties over legitimate sexual representations.

Drawing lines in an era of cybersex presents new challenges—technological and discursive. At a time when the availability of sexual imagery has virtually exploded—when the Internet is flooded with adult websites always only a click away, and cable and digital television offer a veritable menu of sexually explicit videos—it has become more difficult to restrict access. The profusion of sexual imagery has also presented challenges to the law of obscenity and indecency, which has long relied on the concept of community standards, that is, on whether the sexual representation violates contemporary community standards. As explicit sexual imagery becomes ubiquitous on the Internet as well as on television, and spills over into popular culture through music videos, advertising, fashion, and best-selling novels, it becomes more difficult to argue that it violates community standards. The ubiquity of sexual imagery is producing a range of border anxieties and skirmishes. While social conservatives seek to prop up the borders between legitimate and illegitimate speech, commercial pornographers push back against any curtailment of the expanded borders of presentability. But, beneath these border scuffles that erupt in censorship controversies lie deeper questions of border patrol.

The ubiquity of sexual imagery, for example, also challenges the categories of pornography and obscenity themselves. Obscenity was, by definition, that which was not presentable; it acquired its meaning in and through transgression. Pornography similarly has acquired much of its erotic meaning through its prohibitors—legal or otherwise. Its titillation lay, at least in part, in its transgression of the norms of presentability and speakability. But, what happens to pornography as more and more sexual imagery crosses into the realm of the presentable? To what extent does pornography need borders to be pornography?

The shifting borders of legitimate sexual speech is thus about more than the shifting lines of the judicial power of law. Rather, as more recent scholarship on obscenity laws and censorship have begun to highlight, these shifting borders also implicate the productive power of these laws. Judith Butler, for example, has argued that censorship "is not merely restrictive and privative, that is, active in depriving subjects of the freedom to express themselves in certain ways, but also formative of subjects and the legitimate boundaries of speech" (Butler 1997b, 132). This productive and constitutive power of censorship "operates to make certain kinds of citizens possible and others impossible" (132).

The line between legitimate and illegitimate speech is then not simply about the law repressing the speech of individual subjects but, more profoundly, involves constituting the line between legitimate and illegitimate subjects. "To become a subject means to be subjected to a set of implicit and explicit norms that govern the kind of speech that will be legible as the speech of a subject" (Butler 1997b, 133). According to Butler, these norms are constitutive of the "domain of the sayable," of "speakable discourse." To move outside of this domain is then not simply to risk the sanction of the law but to risk one's very "status as a subject" (133). By contrast, to speak within the domain, "[t]o embody the norms that govern speakability in one's speech is to consummate one's status as a subject of speech" (133).

Butler's analysis has been criticized for collapsing marginal and normatively disfavored speech with that speech that is impossible to utter—the domain of the truly unspeakable. Despite the significant limitations in her analysis of implicit censorship, her passing observations on the paradoxical nature of explicit censorship may nonetheless be helpful in analyzing the marginal and normatively disfavored.

> Explicit forms of censorship exposed to a certain vulnerability precisely through being more readily legible. The regulation that states what it does not want stated thwarts its own desire, conducting a performative contradiction that throws into question that regulation's capacity to mean and do what it says, that is, its sovereign pretension. Such regulations introduce the censored speech into public discourse, thereby establishing it as a site of contestation, that is, as the scene of public utterance that it sought to preempt. (Butler 1997b, 130)

Explicit censorship—like indecency and obscenity legislation—constitutes the site of public contestation over legitimate and illegitimate speech (rather than between utterable and unutterable speech). In the analysis that follows, I borrow the idea of speakability but attempt to loosen it from its Butlerian moorings. More specifically, I deploy it to explore explicit censorship and the speech of "border speakers"—subjects who speak at the borders of legitimate, rather than utterable, speech. I use speakability to capture not only the contested lines between legitimate and illegitimate speech, but also to illustrate the constructive nature of this speech producing legitimate and illegitimate subjects, citizens, outlaws, or something in-between.

Border Seekers, Border Speakers

> A subject who speaks at the border of the speakable takes the risk of redrawing the distinction between what is and is not speakable, the risk of being cast out into the unspeakable.
>
> Judith Butler (1997b, 139)

Sarah Jones, a hip-hop poet, playwright, and performance artist, was censored and then uncensored by the FCC for her song, "Your Revolution." Lizzie Borden, a pornographic filmmaker specializing in depicting graphic sexual violence, is currently being prosecuted by the federal government for obscenity. Both of their cases raise deeply contested questions of the appropriate line between speakable and unspeakable sexual representations. Both of their cases also raise questions of the gendered nature of this speech: Can women say what men can say, or is the domain of speakability a gendered domain? Both cases require an analysis that moves sexual citizenship beyond heteronormativity since the alleged border violations are not along a hetero/homo axis. Both of their cases raise questions of explicit censorship, of the law's juridical power being deployed to punish those subjects who fail to discipline themselves. Both of their cases also raise questions of the constitutive power of law, of the ways in which explicit censorship operates to constitute some subjects as legitimate sexual citizens and relegate others to the unspeakable beyond.

But, while Sarah Jones and Lizzie Borden may both be border speakers, they could not be further apart. Some border speakers move the lines. They become sexual citizens, and in the process, change the domain of citizenship and themselves. Other border speakers fall over the line and are cast right back into the domain of the outlaw. Sarah Jones is a border seeker on the side of speakability. Lizzie Borden is not. Borden's speech is unspeakable, and by virtue of its utterance, she is risking her status as a subject and confirming her status as an outlaw. Sarah Jones is a border speaker who ended up on the side of speakability and legitimate sexual citizenship by shoring up the very borders that divide citizen from outlaw. In yet another instantiation of the paradoxes of the process of becoming sexual citizens, Sarah Jones transformed sexual citizenship while reinforcing its limits. Lizzie Borden, from the other side of the border, also reinforced its limits, yet she does so in a way that disrupts its foreclosure. Her speech may be unspeakable, but it has been spoken.

The Revolution of Sarah Jones

> Your revolution will not happen between these thighs
> Your revolution will not happen between these thighs
> Your revolution will not happen between these thighs
> Will not happen between these thighs
> Will not happen between these thighs
> The real revolution ain't about bootie size

After receiving a listener complaint for airing Sarah Jones's poem/rap song, "Your Revolution," the FCC issued a notice of apparent liability for forfeiture (NAL) to the radio station KBOO-FM in Portland Oregon. According to the FCC, "Your Revolution" "contains unmistakable patently offensive sexual references" (KBOO 1991, para. 8) and was indecent within the meaning of the federal Communications Act. The radio station was issued a fine of $7,000 for having willfully aired the indecent material. As a result of the NAL, other radio stations ceased airing the song. With the support of People for the American Way, Sarah Jones then sued the FCC in federal court. The suit was dismissed on procedural grounds, and Jones filed an appeal in the U.S. Court of Appeals for the Second District. February 23, 2003, the day before its brief was due, the FCC reversed its earlier ruling and concluded that "Your Revolution" was not indecent.

"Your Revolution" is a feminist critique of the misogyny of hip-hop music. Based on Gil Scott-Heron's "The Revolution Will Not Be Televised," it parodies the degradation of women by many hip-hop artists such as LL Cool J and Notorious B.I.G. by quoting and then denouncing their macho lyrics. The lyrics are, as a result, sexually explicit but also politically explicit.

> You will not be touching your lips to my triple dip of
> French vanilla, butter pecan, chocolate deluxe
> Or having Akinyele's dream, um hum
> A six foot blow job machine, um hum
> You wanna subjugate your Queen, uh-huh
> Think I'm gonna put it in my mouth just because you
> Made a few bucks

Jones is no outsider to hip-hop. In an interview with the *Washington Post*, Jones stated, "I'm not attacking hip-hop. . . . I'm attacking sexism in the larger culture. I'm a cultural critic and a member of the hip-hop generation" (O'Neal Parker 2002). She describes her work as creating an alternative conversation within hip-hop culture and emphasizes the need to appreciate the different voices within hip-hop music. Her song is written in its codes, while challenging the increasingly dominant representation of women as little more than sex objects. Perhaps more explicitly political than some—she was after all talking about the revolution—Jones is part of a generation of women in hip-hop, from rappers Yo-Yo and Missy Elliott to neo-soul artists Erykah Badu, Lauryn Hill, and Jill Scott, who each challenge the unidimensional image of hip-hop as hypermasculine and sexist. Nor were her lyrics any more sexually explicit than those of the rappers she was quoting.

But, her words—spoken by an African American woman whose citizenship is always at best precarious—produced a rupture. The failure of the listener (and in turn the FCC) to appreciate that Jones was citing the lyrics of others, never mind criticizing them, erased all possibility of parody, replacing it with a reductive literalism. The words were interpreted through the mainstream image of hip-hop—a ghetto culture of violence, drugs, misogyny, promiscuous sex, threatening the fabric of the American nature. What was heard, instead, was an African American speaking of graphic, explicit, misogynist sex. And so came the call for the censor.

According to FCC guidelines, indecent speech is defined as language that "describes or depicts sexual or excretory organs or activities" in a manner that is "patently offensive as measured by contemporary community standards for the broadcast medium" (Federal Communications Commission 2001, para. 7 & 8). The guidelines state that three factors are central in determining indecency: "(1) the explicitness or graphic nature of the description or depiction of sexual or excretory organs or activities; (2) whether the material dwells on or repeats at length descriptions of sexual or excretory organs or activities; (3) whether the material appears to pander or is used to titillate, or whether the material appears to have been presented for its shock value" (para. 10). The guidelines emphasize the importance of context in examining each of these factors, as well as noting that the factors are not exclusive and that "[n]o single factor generally provides the basis for an indecency finding" (para. 10).

In the NAL issued in the Sarah Jones case, the FCC found that "[t]he rap song 'Your Revolution' contains unmistakable patently offensive sexual references" (*KBOO* 2001, para. 8). The FCC rejected KBOO arguments that the song should be considered in its cultural context as "a feminist attack on male attempts to equate political 'revolution' with promiscuous sex'" and therefore not indecent. According to the FCC, "considering the entire song, the sexual references appear to be designed to pander and shock and are patently offensive." The mere fact that the song may have merit does not mean that it is not indecent. Similarly, the contemporary social commentary in "Your Revolution," although a factor to be considered, is not determinative (para. 8). The FCC concluded that KBOO willfully broadcast the material and imposed the basic forfeiture of $7,000.[6]

Sarah Jones filed a suit against the FCC in federal court. Jones claimed that the FCC labeling of "Your Revolution" as indecent caused her harm and violated her constitutional rights. She sought a declaration that "Your Revolution" is not indecent and an injunction barring the FCC from indecency enforcement against the song. In her petition, Jones sought to establish her credentials as an accomplished poet, playwright, and performance artist, highlighting the venues and critical acclaim of her most recent play, *Surface Transit*. The petition sought to explain the content of "Your Revolution," placing it within its hip-hop tradition and noting that the song both incorporates and critiques the denigrating lyrics from popular songs that are regularly broadcast on the radio and featured on music videos:

> "Your Revolution" exposes the highly offensive treatment of women in popular hip hop by referencing its vocabulary and thereby criticizing the message that these songs are sending. At the same time, "Your Revolution" celebrates hip hop by using the hip hop form and vocabulary that so often denigrates women to instead send a message of self-determination to women. (*Jones*, para. 21)

The petition emphasizes the many feminist messages of the song, including its warning "against the dangers of sexual promiscuity and unwanted pregnancy" (para. 24), its protest against "the subjugation of women to male sexual fantasy and women's compliance, where sex is considered quid pro quo for material comfort and status" (para. 25) , and its message of abstinence and "women reclaiming traditional values of sex as an expression of intimacy, love and commitment" (para. 26). It concludes that "Your Revolution" does not pander or titillate in its sexual references, but rather, "is a political and cultural critique that challenges young women and men to reject a social order that is foisted upon them by much of popular radio, television, and magazines and seek a true revolution, which promotes relationships based on equality rather than power" (para. 29).

Throughout the petition, the focus of the argument is that "Your Revolution" is not indecent. It argues that the FCC failed to consider the "full context" of the song and failed to apply the community standard, concluding that the FCC "censored speech that is not indecent and that is entitled to the highest First Amendment protection" (para. 45). It emphasized that it has been "extremely damaging to her reputation to have 'sexually indecent' attached to her name. The Commission ruling is particularly unjustified since 'Your Revolution' is a strong statement against indecency" (para. 46). Over and over again, the petition states "'Your Revolution' is not indecent" but is, rather, "a protest against indecency in popular culture" (para. 49).

The main argument of the petition does not challenge the FCC criteria for indecency. Rather its message is that "Your Revolution"—properly understood—is itself a condemnation of indecency in popular culture. The FCC and "Your Revolution," it is implicitly argued, are actually on the same side—the side of legitimate speech and sexual citizenship—defending decency against its encroachments. This was, of course, a most reasonable defense. Jones did not need to challenge the criteria for indecency in order to argue that she had been sanctioned inappropriately. She could rightly argue that the FCC had simply drawn the wrong line given its own criteria. She was wrongly singled out—as an artist, a dissenter, an African American woman. Yet, her argument is one that tacitly accepted the power of the FCC to draw these lines and reinforced the category of indecency for future use. Notwithstanding her defense of hip-hop music, her legal arguments could be seen to implicitly sanction future prosecutions of the very hip-hop artists that she critiques, since the implication of her arguments is that their work is in fact indecent.

Such is the paradox of being cast into the world of legal defenses—Jones needed to deploy the available legal categories, which in turn operate to reinforce the legitimacy of those categories. Yet, there is a question of the extent to which the category of indecency was used—its repetition, not unlike the rhythmic repetition of her songs, is intended to discursively construct the proposition as true. And the category is deployed complete with its internal dichotomies: Jones's work is a critique of the indecency of others; Jones's work is not indecent, but others are; Jones is good, others are bad.

The U.S. District Court rejected the petition on procedural grounds (*Sarah Jones v. FCC* 2002). The court held that there was an absence of final agency action in the matter, since Jones could have filed a request for further action with the FCC and, subsequently, with the circuit courts, where exclusive jurisdiction resides for the review of agency decisions. In discussing the narrow exception to this rule of exclusive jurisdiction, the court held that only broadcasters and not artists were entitled to this recourse.

Jones appealed, arguing that the district court erred in ruling that Jones needed to wait for further action from the FCC. She argued that if the FCC were allowed to censor her speech and force her to wait for years before making a final determination that she could then appeal, then the FCC indecency enforcement regime constituted a form of prior restraint in violation of the First Amendment. While there was less emphasis on the question of indecency in this appeal, a new term appeared in the appeal—"indecency blacklisting"—that was used throughout to describe the FCC action in issuing the NAL against "Your Revolution."

The appeal to blacklisting is an effort to frame the censorship in explicitly political terms, by discursively linking the FCC actions with those of other notorious censorship moments in U.S. history. It is intended to cast the FCC action as illegitimate, by deploying the normativity of blacklisting. The appeal petition as a whole, despite its heavily technical language of judicial review and constitutional law, is one that shifts the emphasis from indecency to citizenship. Jones is now presented as a citizen who has been denied her First Amendment rights and her right to procedural fairness. She is an artist and political actor, whose political speech was censored arbitrarily through a regime of prior restraint. Again, this is an entirely reasonable and persuasive argument, given the nature of the district court ruling denying her any recourse. It is nonetheless interesting to see how the legal argument deploys—and attempts to constitute—notions of citizenship. The sexual dimensions of the speech are downplayed, while its political dimensions are highlighted.

The appeal was never heard. Several days before the FCC's response was due to be filed, the enforcement bureau rescinded the NAL against KBOO-FM (*KBOO* 2003). The decision states that although it is "undisputed that KBOO-FM aired material that describes sexual activity . . . we now conclude that the material is not patently offensive and therefore not indecent" (para. 8). The following is the sum total of the explanation provided for the change in opinion:

> While this is a very close case, we now conclude that the broadcast was not indecent because, on balance and in context, the sexual descriptions in the song

are not sufficiently graphic to warrant sanction. For example, the most graphic phrase ("six foot blow job machine") was not repeated. Moreover, we take cognizance of the fact presented in this record that Ms. Jones has been asked to perform this song at high school assemblies. While not controlling, we find that this is evidence to be considered when assessing whether material is patently offensive. In sum, we find that The KBOO Foundation has demonstrated that the lyrics of "Your Revolution" measured by contemporary community standards, are not patently offensive and therefore not indecent. (para. 9)

The district court ruling was vacated as moot, and the case was dismissed. "Your Revolution" was removed from the indecency blacklist, and Sarah Jones's battle with the FCC was over.

Jones successfully challenged a dubious decision on the part of the FCC enforcement bureau. Her case highlighted the arbitrary nature of censorship, particularly the ways in which the discretionary and often unaccountable power of the censor is used against artists and political dissidents. Her case could be—and was—framed as a classic case of the juridical power of censorship law and the sovereign individuals who battle it. But, it was also a case about the productive power of censorship that constitutes the very terms of speakability and makes certain forms of sexual citizenship possible and others not. Sarah Jones was produced as a subject within "the domain of the sayable"; she embodied the norms of speakability consummating her status as a subject, and as a citizen. Jones's defense deployed all of the codes of speakability: political speech, blacklisting, prior restraint. The structure of indecency remained firmly intact. Indeed, the consummation of her status of a speaking subject was performed to a considerable degree through the denunciation of indecency itself, rather than its regulation. As Butler argues, "[a] structure only remains a structure through being reinstated as one. Thus, the subject who speaks within the sphere of the speakable implicitly reinvokes the foreclosure on which it depends and thus, depends on it again" (Butler 1997b, 139). Sarah Jones's legal challenge to her FCC censorship reinstated the structures of speakability, denying her status as a border speaker, arguing only that she had been misclassified. Her successful defense thereby reinvoked the very foreclosure that puts other border seekers on the other side.

Further, while claiming her place within hip-hop culture, Jones's defense echoed some of the troubling images of it in the mainstream imagination. While making the obvious points of parody—deployment of the hip-hop form and inappropriate censorship—part of the success of Jones's defense lay in her critique of the hypermasculinity and sexualized violence of the male rappers. Once she was able to convey that her song was parody and critique, it could be reinterpreted through the lens of the dominant discourse and its condemnation of the sexual violence of hip-hop. She was successful at least in part because she was able to play to the anxieties of the dominant culture.

Try as she might to position herself within hip-hop culture, the Jones controversy becomes all too similar to the many controversies in which the dominant culture selectively deploys African American women against African American men (see, for example, Crenshaw 1982). Jones ultimately falls on the right side of the border, because she has the right message about the other more insidious border speakers. Not only does the structure of indecency remain intact, but so too does the mainstream image of male hip-hop artists as falling on the wrong side of it.

The Jones controversy thus tells an enormously complex story about citizenship, racialization, and the speakability of sex. Her citizenship is precariously balanced on the border of speakability; she is reconstituted as a good citizen through the very discourses that produce the erasure of women like her and the outlaw status of the men that she critiques. Establishing her citizenship was no small feat—indeed, "Your Revolution" marks a disruption in the terms of sexual citizenship for African American women. Her process of becoming is simultaneously a process of transformation, normalization, and exclusion; her membership is accomplished through the repeated foreclosure of other possibilities. Yet, this foreclosure is never complete; the mere utterance of that which should not be spoken creates its own future possibilities, sustaining the unruly edges of sexual and racialized citizenship.

The Extremes of Lizzie Borden

Extreme Associates, owned and operated by Robert Zicari and Janet Romano, is a company that produces extremely violent pornography. It has created a niche market, sometimes called slasher porn, distinguishing itself from the mainstream pornography industry by virtue of the often shocking and violent nature of its videos. Janet Romano—who goes by the name Lizzie Borden—produces many of the films. She describes herself as a gender warrior of sorts, doing things that women do not do, in fact, doing things that many men do not do. She intends to shock.

Zicari and Borden were featured in a PBS *Frontline* documentary entitled "American Porn" in 2002. During their exploration of the pornography industry, the *Frontline* producers visited the set where Borden was filming her latest work *Forced Entry*. The producers were so disturbed by what they saw—rape and violence—that they filmed themselves walking off the set. The *Frontline* documentary also included an interview with Zicari, in which he defended the material that his company produced and set out his readiness to do battle with government censors and their conservative agenda: "I'm not out there saying I want to be the test case. But I will be the test case. I would welcome that. I would welcome the publicity. I would welcome everything, to make a point in, I guess, our society" (*Frontline* 2002).

In April 2003, reportedly as a result of the *Frontline* documentary, the federal government seized five of Extreme Associates videos, including "Forced Entry," and shortly thereafter laid charges against Zicari and Romano. They were indicted on ten counts relating to the production and distribution by mail and Internet of obscene materials. The charges were the first major federal prosecution for obscenity in ten years, and many have suggested that it signals an effort by the Ashcroft administration to crack down on the pornography industry by targeting its most extreme elements. Despite the location of the company's operations in California, the arrests and indictments occurred in the western district of Pennsylvania, a state where it is believed convictions for obscenity come more easily. (Videos were allegedly sent there, and video clips allegedly downloaded there).

Mary Beth Buchanan, the federal prosecutor in the case, said in an interview with *60 Minutes*: "We have just had a proliferation of this type of material that has been getting increasingly worse and worse. And that's why it's important to enforce the law, and to show the producers that there are limits. There are limits to what they can sell and distribute throughout the country" ("Porn in the USA" 2003).

The case against Extreme Associates is a test case of the limits of pornography. The federal government chose the most extreme and violent within the genre and laid charges in what is perceived to be the most conservative of jurisdictions. It is determined to establish that, despite the proliferation of pornography, there are still limits between the speakable and unspeakable.

There is little doubt that Extreme Associates represents the extreme of the genre. Indeed, their videos traffic in their unspeakability. *Forced Entry* depicts a graphic beating, rape, and murder of women by a serial killer. The Extreme Associates website describes it as "the most controversial movie" in their "video arsenal": "A Stunningly Disturbing Look at a Serial Killer, Satanic Rituals, and the Depths of Human Depravity." The other films listed in the indictment are equally extreme, involving representations of sexual violence and a host of bodily fluids including spit, excrement, and vomit.

Both Zicari and Borden admit—and celebrate—the fact that their films are shocking and disgusting. In an interview with *Salon Magazine,* for example, Borden says "It's disgusting but I like to watch it because it's shocking" (Brown 2002). Both Zicari and Borden compare their films with slasher movies and the new wave of reality television, such as *Fear Factor,* which people watch in order to be shocked. Again, Borden says, "Those reality shows, where people eat bugs and shit: That's disgusting! How can you watch it? But I watch it. It's the same with what we do: People are shocked by it, but they watch it" (Brown 2002).

The U.S. Supreme Court defined obscenity in the 1973 case of *Miller v. California.* The Court established a three-part test: "(a) whether 'the average person, applying contemporary community standards' would find that the work, taken as a whole, appeals to the prurient interest; (b) whether the work depicts or describes, in a patently offensive way, sexual conduct specifically defined by the applicable state law; and (c) whether the work, taken as a whole, lacks serious literary, artistic, political, or scientific value" (*Miller* 1973). The Court in *Miller* specifically stated that the community standards were local rather than national standards.

Applying the legal category of obscenity to the Extreme Associate films, it is difficult to argue that the material does not appeal to the prurient interest. The films are located within the pornographic genre; their objective is to sexually arouse their viewers. It is also hard to argue that the material does not depict sexual conduct: They include graphic depictions of vaginal intercourse, oral sex, and anal sex. It is similarly difficult to argue that the depiction is not patently offensive, given that both Zicari and Borden acknowledge that their very intention in creating this niche material is to shock and offend. They could try to argue that the material does not offend the local community standard. Yet, the decision of the federal attorney general to seek the indictment in the western district of Pennsylvania seemed specifically intended to neutralize any possibility of this argument. It is considered to be a very conservative community, which by all accounts, would be patently offended by depictions far less extreme than those in the Extreme Associate films.

Unlike the Sarah Jones case, there is rather less room to maneuver within the legal category. Borden and Zicari are challenging the limits of speakability. Their graphic and violent sexual representations effect their shock by virtue of their transgression of these limits. Given the structure of obscenity law and the Court's repeated affirmations of its constitutionality, it seemed likely that they would be convicted on obscenity charges and thereby reaffirmed as sexual outlaws, as subjects who must be disciplined. But, they were not, at least not initially. The defendants moved to dismiss the indictments on the ground that the federal obscenity statutes violated the constitutional guarantees of liberty and privacy protected by the due process clause. Relying on *Lawrence v. Texas*, as well as *Stanley v. Georgia* (1969), they argued that there is a broad fundamental right to sexual privacy that includes a right to possess and view sexually explicit material in the privacy of one's own home. This right, they argued, was not diminished by the fact that the material was devoid of literary or artistic merit. They argued that because the federal obscenity laws imposed a complete ban on the distribution of materials that individuals have the right to possess, the law is unconstitutional.

The Court agreed (*U.S. v. Extreme Associates* 2005a). District Judge Lancaster held that the law violated an individual's fundamental right to possess and read what he chooses in the privacy of his own home. Given that a fundamental right was violated, the law was therefore subject to strict scrutiny level of review, according to which the government must establish a compelling state interest. But, the two interests argued by the government—protecting unwitting adults from exposure to obscenity and protecting minors from exposure to obscenity—were rejected by the Court. Even assuming that these were legitimate government interests, the Court held that the federal statute was not sufficiently narrowly tailored to meet these interests and could not justify a total ban on obscene material.

The deployment of *Lawrence* in the decision is noteworthy. The Court agreed with the government that *Lawrence* did not create a broad and new fundamental right to engage in private sexual conduct. Instead the Court relied on *Stanley v. Georgia*, which established a fundamental right to private possession of obscene material. However, the Court did rely on *Lawrence* for the proposition that the government could not rely on public morality as a legitimate state interest justifying the infringement of adult, consensual, private sexual conduct. It further relied on the dissenting opinion of Justice Scalia for the idea that the holding in *Lawrence* calls the nation's obscenity laws into question, since the government could not legislate a "moral code" of conduct. Lancaster wrote, "It is reasonable to assume that these three members of the Court came to this conclusion only after reflection and that the opinion was not merely a result of over-reactive hyperbole by those on the losing side of the argument" (590). He then cited the numerous constitutional scholars who have similarly observed that the majority's ruling on *Lawrence* calls these obscenity laws into question.

Paradoxically, the district court ruling relies on the border anxieties of the dissenting opinion in *Lawrence* to move the borders of obscenity law. For Justice Scalia, highlighting the implications of the majority ruling was intended as a call to arms to defend the borders. It was not only hyperbole; it was also a grave concern about the imminent collapse of the borders between legitimate and illegitimate sex. It was all about defending the borders of contemporary sexual citizenship. Yet, in the Extreme Associates case, these border anxieties are deployed to move the borders of contemporary sexual citizenship: Border dwellers like Zicari and Borden are brought within its constitutional folds. Their representations were protected—not through the First Amendment protection of speech but rather through the privacy rights of substantive due process. The rights of some citizens to possess these materials—regardless of just how offensive they may be—is extended to provide a kind of umbrella protection for those who produce the materials.

But, the legal battle over the lines of speakability continued. The federal government appealed the decision to the Court of Appeals for the Third Circuit. The Justice Department said that ruling, if upheld, "would undermine not only the federal obscenity laws, but all laws based on shared view of public morality, such as laws against prostitution, bestiality and bigamy" (U.S. Department of Justice 2005). The Third Circuit reversed the district court and reinstated the indictment (*U.S. v. Extreme Associates* 2005b). In its view, the lower court was bound to follow Supreme Court precedent upholding federal obscenity legislation. The district court should not have struck down the obscenity law based on "speculation" that *Lawrence* would undermine this precedent. Extreme Associates appealed, but the petition was dismissed by the Supreme Court.

This contestation over the legitimate borders of sexual citizenship gets even more complicated when one considers the response of the adult entertainment industry to the Extreme Associates case. Zicari and Borden's productions have been described as beyond the limits of acceptability even by those who defend their rights to produce it. Paul Fishbein, president of Adult Video News, the trade journal of the adult entertainment industry, described Extreme Associates' films as "horrible, unwatchable, disgusting, aberrant movies." However, he added that they should be protected by the First Amendment (Tapper 2005).

Some within the adult entertainment industry have gone further and attempted to distance themselves from Extreme Associates, in no small part due to the industry's attempts to self-discipline and thereby avoid the prosecutorial threat of the Ashcroft and now Gonzales justice department. One such self-disciplining initiative is the Cambria list: a set of guidelines for the adult entertainment industry setting out sexual acts that should be avoided. Named after adult entertainment industry lawyer Paul Cambria who drafted it (and who, not coincidentally, is among Larry Flynt's lawyers), the list sets out a series of sexual acts that have attracted the attention of obscenity prosecutors in the past. The list of prohibited sexual acts includes sadomasochistic (s/m) sex ("No shots with appearance of pain or degradation . . . no blindfolds, no wax dripping . . . no bondage-type toys or gear unless very light . . . no forced sex, rape themes etc."); no bodily fluids and explicit or "nasty" sexual shots such as "no two dicks in/near one mouth . . . no shot of stretching pussy, no fisting." It also includes a range of other taboo topics including "no male/male penetration, no transsexuals, no bi-sex" and "no black men/white women themes." [7] The list is an extraordinary example of the imperative to self-discipline in the shadow of the threat of criminal prosecution. Although controversial within the adult entertainment business, it is intended to provide guidelines for those who wish to avoid obscenity prosecutions. It is a graphic list of "bad sex," the kind of sex that will get its producers in trouble. The list signals a transformation in the terms of sexual citizenship: Sexually explicit sex is no longer a marker of bad sex; only a subset of sexually explicit sex now qualifies and identifies its makers as sexual outlaws.

There is little concrete evidence of the influence of the Cambria list. A quick perusal of Internet sex sites reveals a plethora of the alleged bad sex acts: from bodily fluids to transsexuality to interracial sex of all varieties. Indeed, each one appears as a specialty niche, readily available to the consumer. However, there are suggestions within the industry that the mainstream players within the adult entertainment industry, like Vivid Video, VCA Pictures, and *Hustler,* are carefully monitoring the content of their films according to the Cambria guidelines. This internal divide within the pornography industry is an interesting indication of the extent to which the Cambria list is intended to capture—but is simultaneously constituting—the prevailing sense of good and bad in sexual representations. Good citizens within the industry are self-disciplining, agreeing to produce representations within a realm of legitimate sexually explicit sex. Bad citizens are not. The mainstream adult entertainment industry may not agree with the definition of good and bad sex, but it is agreeing to discipline itself along its lines, thereby reinforcing the dichotomy.

Further, according to Paul Cambria, law enforcement authorities are themselves using the list in their prosecutions (Calvert & Richards 2004). The self-disciplining list—intended to reflect the morality of the obscenity prosecutors—is thus being used by the obscenity prosecutors themselves as a marker of good and bad industry citizens. And according to the Cambria list, Borden and Zicari are unapologetically bad citizens. They traffic in the very images proscribed by the list. They are border speakers, flouting the distinction between good and bad sex, and thereby reproducing themselves as bad citizens, not only in the eyes of social conservatives but also those within the mainstream adult entertainment industry.

Even Larry Flynt, who once prided himself in being "the worst," now casts Borden and Zicari in these terms. In his words, "Most of the obscenity cases being brought today involve pretty rough stuff that's demeaning and humiliating to women—pedophilia, rape, necrophilia. They're aberrations and they're out of the norm. I like to think that we stick to plain old vanilla sex . . . it seems to keep us out of trouble" (Flynt 2004). A debate between Flynt and Zicari has been seen in the pages of the *Adult Video News*. Zicari solicited financial assistance for his legal defense from others in the adult entertainment industry, including Larry Flynt, who declined. While Flynt stated that Zicari deserves First Amendment protection since "all forms of expression are legally protected by the First Amendment," he does not believe that he is under any obligation to provide him funding. Moreover, he is highly critical of Zicari for bringing on the prosecution (Farrar 2004). "I had a request from them for money for their defense fund. I spoke with (other producers) who just echoed my feelings, we've got a guy who's bringing a lot of heat on the adult industry" (Farrar 2004). Flynt did not shy away from the financial dimensions of his position. "What we're talking about here is an industry that everybody is doing very well in," Flynt said. "Everyone is following certain guidelines. Not just what they produce but where they ship them to, where they're being sold from. And as a result, this industry has grown from a $600 million industry in the early 1970s to an $11 billion industry today. But it's because, you know, we have businessmen running it, not people that wanted to see how kinky or weird they could get" (Farrar 2004). Flynt added that very few adult entertainment industry directors are "bent on doing, you know, things that are real demeaning toward women. . . . You don't want a jury of at least half women sitting there seeing this. It's cutting your own throat. This has nothing to do with the First Amendment; it takes an idiot to create a product that he knows he can't defend in court that's going to send him to prison" (Farrar 2004).

Zicari responded with an open letter to Larry Flynt, stating that Flynt was hypocritical for suggesting that Extreme Associates has gone too far. In Zicari's view, he was only doing what Flynt had done years before, namely, pushing the envelope of pornography:

> What I am under indictment for tests the limits of the current administration position of obscenity, much the same as you did Larry, before I was born. In 1974, showing a close-up of a woman's open vagina was undeniably extreme. You brought to the masses crude and extreme pictures of naked women. It was a magazine with a controversial and some said dangerous edge and I proudly say, what you achieved was revolutionary and still remains a defining moment for freedom of speech and expression. It changed the world of print pornography forever. (Zicari 2004)

Zicari argues that his videos are simply the contemporary version. Flynt again responded, rejecting Zicari's attempt to draw parallels between their work. "I have never been in favor of forced sex, whether real or imagined. I have always promoted consensual sex and portrayed consensual sex," Flynt wrote. "Bad taste should not be confused with physical abuse. This is where I part company with Mr. Black [Zicari]" (Brown 2004).

We come full circle then, back to Flynt's conversion to citizenship, which is now far more complete. While the Larry Flynt in *The People vs. Larry Flynt* was still a sexual outlaw of sorts, defining himself on the outer edges of speakability, he has since circled the wagons of speakability around himself—and others like him. It is Flynt himself who is now producing and policing the lines between good and bad sex, between what can be said and what remains unspeakable, precisely because his own citizenship depends on it. The legitimacy—and profitability—of the adult entertainment industry depends on these new lines, and all of its members, from AT&T to *Playboy* to *Hustler*, are prepared to discipline themselves accordingly. Flynt has now subjected himself to "a set of implicit and explicit norms" that constitute the realm of the speakable and constitute subjects as cognizable, if not entirely legitimate, subjects

(Butler 1997b). The new sexual citizen—the sexual entrepreneur—acquires its status as a subject through self-discipline, and an implicit recognition that a legitimate subject requires a shadow of illegitimacy cast elsewhere. There is a convergence of the multiple dimensions of contemporary sexual citizenship—sexualization, marketization, aesthetization, and moral regulation.

The commodification of sex was once enough to cast it into the domain of the bad. And there is no doubt that its commodification is still highly suspect. For example, the very regulation of prostitution continues to be premised on the idea that the commodification of sex is, in and of itself, a social or moral harm. Yet, the commodification of sex, particularly of sexually explicit imagery, has become so widespread across a multiplicity of genres, from the expressly pornographic to advertising to music videos, that it has become more difficult to suggest that the marketization of sex is *per se* a transgression, an act of border crossing between legitimate and illegitimate sex. The "adult entertainment industry"—the phrase itself a legitimating rhetorical device—has become such a successful financial enterprise that it has begun to dissolve the lines between legitimate and illegitimate economic citizenship.

No longer relegated to the disreputable, the economic players in the industry are increasingly located near the epicenter of American capital. More Mouseketeer than black-marketeer, the new industry leaders are successful entrepreneurs and CEOs who speak in the language of product, audiences, profit, and shareholders. Their citizenship is constituted in the neo-liberal discourse of the market—provided that they remain on the right side of the new line. The marketization of sex—once the marker of illegitimacy—has provided a measure of legitimacy, as long as these new market citizens abide by the new norms of unspeakability. As long as they do not venture into the realm of the Cambria list—of s/m sex, nonconsensuality, bodily fluids, transsexuality—as long as they self-discipline, the transformation of pornographer to adult entertainment industry entrepreneur is complete. Larry Flynt does; Robert Zicari does not.

This difference is itself no mere failing on the part of Zicari. He is not simply a sexual anarchist or nihilist, transgressing for the sake of transgression. Zicari is an entrepreneur—in fact, he is a small business entrepreneur, attempting to carve out a space for his company in an industry increasingly dominated by large corporations. He is a small player, creating a niche market based on taboo and transgression. His market is constituted in and through the very lines between good and bad sex that the mainstream adult entertainment industry has produced. It is his way to produce for a small target audience that will return a profit. Yet, for Zicari, the market language of product, audiences, and profit are not enough to constitute him as a legitimate economic citizen, since his business is premised on violating the stated and unstated codes of the legitimate adult entertainment industry citizen; his is a market in unspeakability. He needs the border if he is to transgress it.

The mere utterance of this unspeakability challenges the borders between legitimate and illegitimate sexual citizenship. The fact that Zicari and Borden have spoken their unspeakable words operates to rupture the foreclosure on speakability. The trial court finding, despite being overruled, suggests the extent to which the legitimacy, or at least the criminality of their representations, has become contested. The story of Extreme Associates exemplifies Butler's argument about the vulnerability of explicit censorship, since the very regulation of this speech introduces it "into public discourse, thereby establishing it as a site of contestation, that is, as the scene of public utterance that it sought to preempt" (Butler 1997b, 130). While Borden and Zicari may continue to be constituted as outlaws, they will simultaneously have transformed the limits of unspeakability. The images of graphic sexual violence and bodily secretions have been introduced in the public sphere and have been rendered a site of contestation.

The Contested Citizenship of Border Dwellers

There is a degree of incommensurability to the indecency charges against Sarah Jones and the obscenity charges against Extreme Associates. Indecency regulation under the FCC and obscenity regulation under both federal and state law are judged by entirely different standards. Indecency for the purposes of the broadcast medium has a much lower threshold than criminal obscenity law, and the penalties are of an entirely different nature: fines and removal from the airwaves versus fines and imprisonment. There is also incommensurability to the speech in question: political poetry versus violent pornography; condemnation of the degradation of women versus its celebration.

Yet, a comparison of the speech of Sarah Jones and Extreme Associates highlights some uncomfortable equivalencies. Sarah Jones and Lizzie Borden both became border speakers by virtue of their sexualization of speech. If Jones had engaged in a critique of mainstream rap without reproducing their sexualized and misogynist speech, she would not have run afoul of the lines of indecency. If Borden had produced a film about assault, rape, and murder without its sexualization, she would not have transgressed the lines of obscenity nor of speakability. It is, in other words, the sex that produces the transgression.

The NAL against Jones and the obscenity charges against Borden and Zicari are both the product of a crackdown on sexual speech. The censorship of Sarah Jones is an admittedly misfired missive in the FCC enforcement against broadcast indecency. Since the Jones controversy, the FCC has intensified its surveillance of broadcasting, in what many commentators are calling a new episode of the culture wars. While pressure had been building, the controversy that erupted as a result of the exposure of Janet Jackson's breast at the 2004 Super Bowl halftime show marked a turning point in the crackdown. Half a million complaints were lodged with the FCC, and in an act of almost immediate self-discipline, ABC added a 5-second delay to the Academy Awards, and CBS did the same for the Grammy Awards. CBS was eventually fined $550,000 for the infraction. In October 2004, Fox was fined $1.18 million for an episode of *Married by America* that depicted a blurred bachelor party calling it "sexually suggestive." The self-censorship continued, as a month later sixty-six ABC stations refuse to air uncensored *Saving Private Ryan* for fear of being fined by the FCC over expletives. NBC obscured shots of an 80-year-old woman's breast during *ER*. While some broadcasters initially sought a clarification of the indecency rules from the FCC, others rejected the idea.

Congress is considering increasing the fines for indecency for broadcasters and subjecting cable television to the same regulation. A bill to extend indecency rules to cable failed by one vote to pass the Senate Commerce Committee in 2004, chaired at the time by Senator John McCain. His successor, Senator Ted Stevens, has similarly stated that cable television programs should be subject to the same indecency rules as broadcasters using public airwaves. "We wonder why our children are sexually active at a young age," Stevens said in a speech to the National Association of Broadcasters. "The public airwaves are increasingly promoting sex. . . . Cable is often worse" (Hofmeister 2005).[8] Despite their own battle against FCC censorship, it is a position that the broadcasters support. Broadcasters argue that cable operators have an unfair market advantage, since they are not subject to the same indecency guidelines and therefore are able to depict more sexual and violent content. The cable operators are overwhelming opposed to the move (with one notable exception—Walt Disney Co., which owns ABC). However, some cable providers are beginning to talk about self-regulation, such as a voluntary rating code, and some have begun to rein in the content of their more explicit shows.

Similarly, the obscenity charges against Borden and Zicari are the first in a new wave of federal obscenity prosecutions against adult pornography. As Buchanan stated in an interview on ABC *Nightline*, "The current prosecution of Extreme Associates should put the pornography industry on notice that the U.S. Department of Justice is vigorously enforcing the federal obscenity laws" (*Nightline* 2003). According the Department of Justice, since 2001 the department has significantly increased the prosecution of adult obscenity, with forty convictions and nineteen indictments pending as of spring 2005 (U.S. Department of Justice 2005, 2). By contrast, between 1993 and 2000 under the Clinton administration, there were only four obscenity cases (U.S. Department of Justice 2005, 2). "The renewal of obscenity prosecutions during this Administration is a direct result of the emphasis placed on the importance of obscenity law enforcement by the President and the Attorney General" (U.S. Department of Justice 2005, 2). Not all of these charges are directed at the likes of Extreme Associates but rather have included more mainstream adult entertainment videos—described by the Department of Justice as "hard core adultery pornography . . . depicting ultimate sexual conduct between adults with penetration clearly visible" (U.S. Department of Justice 2005, 4).

The intensification of the campaigns against indecency and obscenity are part of an effort by social conservatives to reestablish the lines between legitimate and illegitimate speech. These crackdowns on sexual speech are unlikely to reverse the proliferation of sexual speech into everyday life (only in their extreme do censorship regimes have such an effect). But, they are intended to signal the imperative of limits and self-discipline. In an era of the intense sexualization of everyday citizenship, social conservatives are determined to signal that there are limits and that those who fail to impose limits on themselves will have it done for them. While many social conservatives would like to see a more complete erasure of the pursuit of sexual pleasure from the public sphere (and many libertarians argue that these crackdowns are merely the tip of the impending iceberg), one of the discursive effects of these prosecutions might be a disciplining of the already highly sexualized citizen.

The adult entertainment industry has responded to the threat of pending indictments with the Cambria list. The broadcast industry is responding to the FCC crackdown and the congressional threat of significantly increased fines by more carefully monitoring its content. Even the cable industry is beginning to discipline itself in an effort to avoid being brought under the same indecency standards as the broadcast industry. Representations of the sexualized citizen will not disappear, but they might become more circumspect. This disciplined sexual subject is one that must establish its legitimacy within the borders of legitimate citizenship that are being redrawn. The legal proceedings against both Jones and Extreme Associates were the harbingers of this re-disciplining of the sexual subject.

The juxtaposition of Sarah Jones and Extreme Associates, despite the incommensurability of their cultural productions, also tells a story about the limitations of the privatized discourse of market citizenship for some border citizens. Neither Zicari nor Jones could deploy this privatized discourse to reconstitute themselves as legitimate citizens but for entirely different reasons. Both Jones and Extreme Associates are entrepreneurs of sorts. Both are seeking to distribute their cultural productions; they are both seeking market commodification of their products. Yet neither was cast in the redemptive language of the market citizen. Zicari is a self-described small business entrepreneur, attempting to create a niche market in an adult entertainment industry virtually dominated by large corporations. But, his product is sexual transgression. The rhetorical weight of the small businessman battling corporate dominance could not displace that of sexual deviant.

Nor did the discourse of market citizen work for Sarah Jones, but the process of exclusion was quite different. Performance artist, poet, songwriter— Jones too is an entrepreneur, attempting to make a living, a profit, from her cultural productions. But, even upon redemption, she was not constituted in the neo-liberal discourse of market citizen and economic citizenship. The shadow of noncitizenship that still haunts the subject status of African Americans, in conjunction with the specifically racialized fears of hip-hop culture and the sexualization of African American women, made Sarah Jones highly susceptible to regulatory discipline. Caught up in the cultural representations of black women and hip-hop culture, her words were suspect and her citizenship precarious. But, once it was established that she was an artist, a cultural critic engaged in political critique of the very hip-hop culture that produced her as a border speaker, Sarah Jones was transformed into a full-fledged political citizen whose speech was deserving of the highest form of protection, unsullied by the pursuit of profit. Jones is produced as a good citizen against the backdrop of the questionable citizenship of many of her rapper colleagues. But neither she nor they are cast in the language of the market. It is this exclusion from the cultural logic of citizenship—African Americans simply are not cast as potential market citizens—that operates to constitute Jones as a border speaker without the obvious possibility of market redemption. Jones is not Larry Flynt—successful entrepreneur—because that is not what African Americans are. And so the market offered little to no protection. Rather, Jones had to wrap herself in the flag—in the rhetoric of high political citizenship and its privileging of political speech—because it is that discourse alone that may, and in her case did, offer redemption. Jones's case suggests some of the ways in which the offerings of neo-liberal citizenship, as well as self-discipline, operate through highly racialized discourses.

Their juxtaposition also reveals something about the ways in which some border speakers can cross the lines into legitimate citizenship and reconstitute themselves in the language of sexual citizens, while others cannot. Those who cross do so by respecting the existence of the border. Jones crosses by repeating the mantra of the lines between decency and indecency. Flynt crosses but reinforces the idea of a realm of unspeakability beyond the border. Borden and Zicari are not ultimately allowed to cross—in large part because they refuse the legitimacy of a border. Their legal arguments constituted a wholehearted rejection of the line-drawing exercise of obscenity.

Border speakers may push the borders or cross the borders, but they cannot dissolve them, for it is the borders that produce them as legitimate citizens, or not. The self-disciplining citizen needs an unruly subject against which to emerge, an obscenity against which it can be produced as normal. But it is not only citizens that need borders; transgressors need them just as much. Borden and Zicari may have lost their legal battle, but they have ended up on the "right" side of the border if they are to traffic in the unspeakability that produces the appeal of the pornographic. They are resisting the banalification of pornography, reestablishing the very borders that are required if they are to be transgressed. While exclusion has its costs, for Borden and Zicari, it may also have its privileges. But borders are porous, seepage occurs, and even outlaws remain in the public sphere. Borden and Zicari refuse to be shamed. Their mere presence will continue to produce border anxieties and skirmishes, and the future borders of speakability—including a border that could undermine their own unspeakability—remains unknowable.

2 Marriage, Sex, and Adultery as Practices of Self-Governance

I N *RELATIONSHIP RESCUE*: *A Seven Step Strategy to Reconnecting with Your Partner*, Dr. Phil McGraw—America's pop psychologist talk show host extraordinaire—comes to the rescue of couples on the verge of divorce with some hard-hitting advice (McGraw 2000). In this *New York Times* best-seller and its companion workbook *Relationship Rescue Retreat*, as well as on television and on his website, Dr. Phil insists that "It all starts with you."

> You have to be willing to admit that when it comes to conducting a relationship, whatever you are thinking and feeling and doing is not working. You have to be willing to move your position on some very deep beliefs and long-held emotions and behavioral patterns. You must be willing to utterly change the way you think, feel, and act in relationship to yourself and your partner. (www.drphil.com)

His second piece of advice: "Put Your Relationship on Project Status":

> To rescue your relationship, you have to put it on Project Status. This means that you must consciously decide to actively, purposefully work on improving your situation each and every day. It's not that you just "want to" or "intend to" work on it. You need to do it, every single day. Discipline yourself to do the work. (www.drphil.com)

As with so much of his talk show and advice books, Dr. Phil takes a tough love approach, telling his guests the difficult truth about what they need to do to improve their relationship. Over and over, his message is that individuals have the power to change. They simply must take responsibility for their lives, their decisions, their actions and commit themselves to the hard work of change. While Dr. Phil dishes out advice on a wide range of issues from losing weight to managing debt to parenting disorderly teenagers, marriage is a recurrent theme. Dr. Phil tells his flock that they must make their marriage a project. Marriage is hard work, and the only way to make it work is to work on it.

This public performance of marriage is yet another instance of the way in which "the political public sphere has become an intimate public sphere," wherein citizenship has increasingly become "produced by personal acts and values, especially acts originating in or directed toward the family sphere" (Berlant 1997, 4). It is part of a proliferation and intensification of marriage politics: questions about how we should, do, or do not live our marital lives abound. Same-sex marriage, adultery, premarital sex, marriage promotion, and divorce have all become sites of intense political contestation.

But, this politicization of the intimate sphere goes beyond the conservative/liberal fault lines of ideological debate. In this chapter, I argue that contemporary marriage politics reflect a new practice of self-governance produced by transformations in intimacy. The individualization of intimacy is producing practices of responsibilization, wherein individuals are being called upon to manage the risk of the increasing fragility of their relationships.

This responsibilization of marriage is occurring on multiple sites: sex, emotion, parenting, financial. Individuals must learn to be better lovers, nurturers, parents, consumers, and financial managers. This chapter focuses on sex. It begins by tracing a transformation in the way in which the sexuality within marriage has been regulated, from a regime based on law and social sanction to a regime increasingly based on self-governance. It then looks at consummation and adultery: two areas where the law has long taken an interest in sex in marriage and produced a very particular kind of sexual citizen. As these laws have waned in significance, however, the importance of sex in marriage has not. It now relies more on sexual self-governance. It is individual sexual subjects who are responsible for becoming or unbecoming citizens. Citizenship success, failure, and/or redemption lie in their own hands.

Some sexual citizenship literature has focused on marriage as a right of citizenship, noting the denial of this right to gay men and lesbians as an example of the heterosexuality of citizenship (Phelan 2001; Richardson 1998). I argue, however, that marriage is much more than a right in the sexual citizenship basket; it is one of citizenship's central and constitutive practices. As

Nancy Cott has argued, marriage has long been deeply implicated in American public policy and the construction of the nation, establishing "terms for the inclusion and exclusion of new citizens" (Cott 2000, 2). "By incriminating some marriages and encouraging others, marital regulations have drawn lines among the citizenry and defined what kinds of sexual relations and which families will be legitimate" (Cott 2000, 3). Cott demonstrates how marriage laws throughout American history have "sculpt[ed] the body politic" (Cott 2000, 5). In this chapter, I look at how the laws and practices of marriage continue to sculpt sexual citizenship. Marriage is not simply a status line demarcating who is in and who is out. It is also an ongoing practice—a verb, something one does—and as such, must be done in a particular way. The practices of marriage constitute the terms of the heteronormativity of marriage, not simply for the gay men and lesbians that it traditionally excluded but also for the expected norms and behaviors of the heterosexual subjects that it includes. The chapter focuses on the sexual practices of marriage and the ways in which its norms both constitute and judge the subjects of marriage as good or bad, becoming or unbecoming citizens.

Self-Governance and the Transformation of Intimacy

Sociologists of the family have identified, analyzed, and debated the terms of a transformation of intimacy. Marriage has changed from a life-long status to an increasingly individualized and voluntary relationship designed to promote the happiness of the parties (Beck-Gernsheim 1999; Giddens 1992). Rather than a stable and life-long commitment, marriage is now characterized by the pursuit of individual fulfillment. Marriage can be entered and exited by choice. It is a transformation in the terms of intimacy whereby individuals now seek an emotionally rich and companionate relationship.

This transformation has, in turn, produced the divorce revolution. When relationships no longer fulfill their intimacy objectives, they can be dissolved. Sociologists have offered differing analyses of this transformation. Some nostalgically bemoan the loss of stability and commitment with the detraditionalization of intimacy and argue for a return to these values (Fevre 2000). Others celebrate the possibilities of democracy and equality that accompany this transformation (Giddens 1992). However, most agree that a change has occurred in the discourse of intimacy.

These intimacy theorists suggest that as family life and intimacy come to be associated with more risk and fragility, more care needs to be placed on encouraging responsibility within these relationships. In his promotion of the politics of the Third Way in Britain, Anthony Giddens has argued that individuals must learn to embrace their individualized citizenship and become "responsible risk takers" (Giddens 1998, 100). Other more conservative voices have argued that the individualization of intimacy has undermined the values of love, caring, and responsibility (Fevre 2000; Lasch 1977).

While seeking to reverse the effects of detraditionalization, these conservatives also argue for a return to individual responsibility (Mead 1997). Despite their significant differences, liberal and conservative theorists alike seek to minimize the negative consequences—in particular the fragility of relationships and the increase in rates of divorce—by encouraging individuals to become more responsible.

This increasing emphasis on responsibility is part of a more general shift in governance. Michel Foucault's later work on governmentality began to explore governance as the conduct of conduct and technologies of the self (Foucault 1988, 1991). Foucault described the technologies of the self as a form of governance "which permit the individual to effect by their own means or with the help of others a number of operations on their own bodies and souls, thoughts, conduct and way of being, so as to transform themselves in order to attain a certain happiness, purity, wisdom, perfection or immorality" (Foucault 1988, 18). Individuals not only set themselves "rules of conduct, but also seek to transform themselves, to change themselves in their singular being, and to make their life an oeuvre" (Foucault 1985, 10). As discussed in the Introduction, many scholars have explored how contemporary regimes of subjectification increasingly rely on the self-discipline and the government of oneself. Nicholas Rose describes the analysis as one that directs attention to "the ways in which individuals experience, understand, judge, and conduct themselves" (Rose 1996, 29, citing Foucault 1986, 1988):

> Technologies of the self take the form of the elaboration of certain techniques for the conduct of one's relation with oneself, for example, requiring one to relate to oneself epistemologically (know yourself), despotically (master yourself), or in other ways (care for yourself). (Rose 1996, 29)

It is an approach to governance that presupposes the freedom of the governed to make choices. It seeks to shape the conduct of others by acknowledging and using this capacity of the subject (Rose 1999, 3–4). Alan Hunt similarly focuses on the role of self-help in this modality of governance; through sustained self-scrutiny and self-control, the individual is "obliged to live life harnessed to projects of its own identity, its normality, its weight, its mental and physical health" (Hunt 1999, 218). As Rose argues, "individuals are incited to live as if making a *project* of themselves: they are to work on their emotional world, their domestic and conjugal arrangements, their relations with employment and their techniques of sexual pleasure, to develop a 'style' of living that will maximize the worth of their existence to themselves" (Rose 1996, 157). For Rose, the family plays a particularly important role in this project of self-governance as one of the multiple sites where individuals are called upon to make "a project of themselves." Individuals must make their families, their marriages, their children, their sex lives, their domestic happiness a personal project. They must actively assume responsibility for the pursuit of their well-being and that of their family.

This responsibilization of marriage is a response to the instability produced by the transformation of intimacy. If marriages are now fragile, then they require work. In Dr. Phil's words, they must be put "on project status." The proliferation of self-help books, marriage counseling, relationship workshops, and marriage mentoring has transformed marriage into a project and produced a new message: Marriage is hard work. In what I call the *Dr. Phil* effect, marriage has become both a project of self-transformation—you must first change yourself—and a collaborative project—working together to make it work. Indeed, the public performance of marriage malfunction and transformation of the *Dr. Phil* show is a performance in the contemporary expectations, roles, and responsibilities of marriage. Individuals must be prepared to do the hard work of saving their marriages: They must take responsibility for their actions and for their marriages. They must learn to become better, more responsible risk managers in the project of maintaining fragile relationships.

This transformation of marriage is producing a new meaning to the "I do" vows of marriage. "I do" was a public performance of consent and commitment to the covenant of marriage. At one time, it was a commitment to a life-long status. It was performative and constitutive of the conjugal body (Austin 1962; Brook 2000), a performance that could not be easily undone. In the transformation of intimacy, it became a performance of individual choice and a voluntary statement of commitment that could just as easily be revoked with a subsequent "I don't."

With the shift toward marriage as a project of self-governance, "I do" has again begun to shift its meaning. It is no longer a passive consent to the status or contract of marriage. Rather, it has become a doing; it is the doing of marriage. It is what individuals must do within their marriage. It is a commitment to the practice of self-governance, to making one's marriage a project that is to be worked on everyday. Whereas marriage was once passive—it was something you were—it has become active. Indeed, marriage has become a kind of verb. In the new politics of intimacy, it is something that you do, over and over.

Much of this transformation of marriage is occurring within the cultural realm. It is part of a more general and "increasing role [of] culture and consumption . . . in the generation, regulation and evaluation of techniques of self-conduct" (Rose 2000, 1339). From advertising to film and lifestyle magazines to talk shows, popular culture is playing a more significant role in governance (Rose 2000, 1399). Through a fusion of culture, consumption, and self-identity, individuals are increasingly involved in an "active and detailed shaping . . . of their daily lives in the name of their own pleasures, contentments, or fulfillments" (Rose 2000, 1402).

The sections that follow focus on several of these cultural sites and practices that are shaping the self-conduct of sexual citizenship. The chapter draws on examples from film, television, lifestyle magazines, and talk shows to illustrate the ways in which individuals are being called upon to become responsible and govern themselves ethically in relation to their spouses, particularly in relation to their sex lives. It argues that this emphasis on making one's marriage and sex life a project is a consequence of the transformations of intimacy. If marriage is now a question of individual choice and happiness, then individuals must make better choices and commit themselves to the hard work of making themselves happy. But, it is also "self-governance intensely imbricated in public practices."[1] While individuals are called upon to make these choices for themselves, to take responsibility for their own lives and happiness, it is hardly a practice of unrestrained freedom.[2] The ethics of the choices are prefigured, an army of experts is deployed to promote and scrutinize these choices, and good sexual citizenship stands or falls on the basis of them.[3]

Consummating Marriage, Consecrating Citizenship

Sex is central to the legal construction of marriage. Heterosexual sexual intercourse has long been considered by the courts to be an implied condition of marriage (see Borten 2002). As the New York Superior Court stated in a 1940

case, "Capability of consummation is an implied term in every marriage; potential copulandi is of its very essence" (*Steinberger v. Steinberger* 1940, 597). The
ability to consummate the marriage was sufficiently important that the inability to do so was a ground for annulment at common law. As statutes replaced
the common law, failure or inability to consummate marriage has remained
a ground of annulment in many states. Some statutes describe the ground in
terms of impotence, others in terms of physical incapacity or physical incapa-
bility of consummation by sexual intercourse. Some statutes require that the
incapacity be incurable. Others allow for annulment simply on the basis of
the failure to consummate. Many allow for annulment if there has been some
fraudulent representation in relation to consummation, such as a concealed intention not to consummate the marriage. Notwithstanding these differences,
the idea underlying this ground for annulment is that without sex, a marriage
is missing one of its most basic requirements and, therefore, may not be valid.

The courts have long insisted that the ground for annulment is about the
ability to have sex, not the ability to have children. "Impotence consists, not
of sterility but of the want of power for copulation" (*Turney v. Avery* 1921; see
generally Perlmutter 1974). In these cases, sex is distinct from reproduction:
The ability to have sexual intercourse is disarticulated from the ability to have
children. This disarticulation has led to cases in which an annulment has
been granted on the basis of incapacity notwithstanding the fact that the wife
became pregnant and/or had children. In *T. v. M.*, for example, a husband was
granted an annulment on the basis of his wife's incapacity, notwithstanding
the fact that she became pregnant through a "splash pregnancy" caused by the
husband's ejaculation against her vulva (*T. v. M.* 1968). It was sex, not the ability to reproduce, that operated as a defining feature of marriage.

And sex for the purposes of consummation has been defined in very specific terms. It is all about heterosexual sexual intercourse. Even more specifically, it is about the ability of the husband to penetrate the wife (Borten 2002,
1099). In *Stepanek v. Stepanek*, for example, the test for incapacity was whether
the couple could engage in "normal copulation" (1961). In *Stepanek*, "copulation" was defined as "the act of gratifying sexual desire by the union of the
sexual organs of two biological entities" (*Stepanek* 1961, 1942, citing *People v.
Anglier*). This union of sexual organs had to take a very particular form—
vaginal intercourse, with successful penetration.

At times, the courts have made this requirement quite explicit. For example, in *Donati v. Church* the court held that the wife was impotent where "The

introitus or opening of the vagina is infantile in type and too small to allow of copulation, although her husband was able to, and did frequently, insert the tip of his penis" (*Donati v. Church* 1951, 634).[4] In *Heller v. Heller*, a wife sought an annulment on the basis of her husband's impotence, and the husband opposed on the ground that he was not impotent but that the failure to consummate the marriage was due to the wife's "nervous resistance." The court stated:

> The defendant is not without virile qualities. It is conceded that he regularly made sexual response to his wife's body by an erection and an effort at intercourse, but that discharge took place before penetration was accomplished. The reason for the premature emission is ascribed by the wife to the husband's inability, and by the husband to the exercise of restraint occasioned by the wife's protestations. One of the medical witnesses produced by the petitioner testified that the probability of a cure attends such a condition as the petitioner imputes to the defendant. He also testified that the petitioner's vaginal opening was extremely resistant. (*Heller* 1934, 544)

The court concluded that if the wife's testimony was accepted, then the husband was impotent—defined as want of power for copulation. The court was not, however, convinced that the wife had established that the impotence was incurable and therefore dismissed her case. Nevertheless, the definition of impotence in these cases is very clear—it is the inability of the husband to vaginally penetrate the wife.

The courts have also emphasized that a marriage is not consummated by virtue of other forms of sex: Only "natural heterosexual intercourse" could satisfy the requirement. For example, in *Santos v. Santos*, the wife "refused to have normal sexual intercourse and wanted only unnatural sexual intercourse" (*Santos* 1952, 7). After three days of marriage, the wife left "to associate with a girl friend of questionable reputation for whose love she professed a preference." This "unnatural sexual intercourse," although never described in any detail, was presumably some form of oral and/or masturbatory sex and did not constitute a consummation of the relationship. Similarly, in *Kshaiboon v. Kshaiboon*, a husband was held to lack the physical and mental capacity to engage in "normal sexual intercourse." The court stated, without any additional description, that "his sexual activities after the marriage were only of the unnatural type" (*Kshaiboon* 1983, 220).

In earlier times, both courts and commentators were explicit about the objectives underlying this ground for annulment, namely, the importance of channeling sex into marriage (Carbone 1996; Graff 1999; Lindsay 1998). In the nineteenth century, the courts expressly sought to "prevent sexual promiscuity by legally ensuring the satisfaction of sexual desires within marriage" (Lindsay 1998). According to one treatise on the law of husband and wife, "the natural indulgence of natural desire" and the "prevention of adulterous intercourse" were amongst the most important objectives of marriage (Lindsay 1998, citing Bishop 1864, 276). Bishop, citing the 1845 case of *Deene v. Avery*, wrote that denying a petition for annulment on the ground of nonconsummation would place the innocent party in a state of "constant temptation" generating "the probable consequence of other . . . connections" (Lindsay, citing Bishop 1864, 299). Lindsay argued that in these actions of nonconsummation, the courts were primarily concerned with marriage as "a vitally important institution that functioned as a bulwark against promiscuity" (Lindsay 1998).

Consummation played an important constitutive role in marriage. The act of consummation transformed the marriage contract from civil contract to something larger, more sacrosanct, more public. As courts stated, "Although marriage is a civil contract, immediately upon its consummation public policy endows the marital relationship with enduring rights and responsibilities concerning which the State attaches primary importance and exercises ultimate control" (*Dolan v. Dolan* 1969, citing Whitehorse 1925). As Heather Brook argues, consummation—or "consummative sex"—operates performatively; it "finalize[s] the performative utterances of wedding" (Brook 2000). The act of consummative sex operates to produce the conjugal body; it is the final act producing the state recognition of the union and endowment of a range of relational rights and responsibilities. Sex within marriage was thus not only good sex; it was transformative. Consummation transformed the marriage, making it more than a private contract between the parties. It produced the conjugal body and the public status conferred upon this body.

Consummative sex was also transformative of sex. Consummation law was intended to ensure that a couple could have "natural" sex and in so doing oversaw the redemption of sex from dangerous and out of control to domesticated and socially desirable. It operated to sequester sex. It was a kind of public oversight—a moment where sex was spoken in the public sphere to ensure that the right kind of sex was produced in the private sphere. It highlighted the permeability of marital privacy—private in this case only if the couple had the right kind of sex. If they proved unable or unwilling to have "natural sex," the private world of marital sex would be made very public; indeed, it became the site of a performance of failure for all the world to see. As a performance of the norms of marital sex through its failure, it thereby reproduced the terms for marital self-discipline.

It was, in turn, the act of consummative sex that produced the legitimate sexual citizen; a citizen whose sexuality was then appropriately marked as private, heterosexual, married and who was entitled to a sexuality precisely because it was cordoned off into this private world. The legal regulation of consummative sex was not simply about policing borders but about producing those borders and the very subjects that inhabited them. It produced sexual subjects who entered their sexuality on their wedding night, whose sexuality could even be celebrated once it was domesticated. It transformed the subject—from nonsexual to sexual, from virgin to conjugal. Moreover, the law of consummation had the power to transform them back again. If the marriage was not consummated and an annulment was granted, the previously married subjects were recast in their virginal, pre-sexual form.

But, what of consummation today? Non-consummation has been retained in many states as a statutory ground for annulment. Individuals can choose to pursue an action for annulment on the basis of inability to consummate their marriage. It therefore remains a ground for a fairly serious form of marital relief: the legal obliteration of a marriage; a court can literally pronounce that there is not and never was a marriage. Sex, and a particular form of sex at that, continues to operate to finalize a marriage, to make it real. And its absence continues to operate as a potential exit option. This is not insignificant, given that marriage continues to be an important social institution, which grants access to a range of public and private rights and responsibilities. From actual legal citizenship through immigration and naturalization laws, to private support to Social Security, marriage is the basis for the recognition of relational rights and, with them, access to many dimensions of civil and social citizenship. Sex, then, or more specifically—natural heterosexual intercourse—continues to formally mediate access to a full panoply of rights and responsibilities and, in turn, to full social citizenship, in T. H. Marshall's sense.

Yet, despite the brief return of the celebrity annulment—with the likes of Dennis Rodman, Mick Jagger, and Britney Spears all having sought to annul their marriages in the last few years—proceedings for annulment have become rare. Divorce is the preferred exit option, and there are now relatively few reported annulment cases. As a result, annulment law remains in a kind of stasis—it is still good law—yet the case law has not evolved since the courts are rarely given an opportunity to interpret it.

Occasionally, the consummation requirement is mentioned in same-sex marriage challenges. For example, in *Dean v. District of Columbia*, a case involving two men who were denied a marriage license, the majority opinion mentioned in obiter that "consummation by the marital partners would be biologically impossible" (*Dean* 1991). Consummation, in this case, thus continues to be understood in traditional terms as heterosexual intercourse. No other form of sex can satisfy the requirement. Yet, such mentions of the underlying sexual requirements of a valid marriage are increasingly rare.

Much of the law of consummative sex seems like an anachronistic throwback to an era before the sexual revolution and its normalization of a multiplicity of forms of "non-natural" sex, including pre/extra/post marital sex. To the extent that marriage and the laws of consummation were once intended to channel sex into marriage, it is fair to say that they are not working. Of course, the fault can hardly be placed exclusively at the feet of the consummation laws. At one time, there was an extensive network of legal prohibitions on any and all forms of pre- or extramarital sex: criminal and civil laws against adultery, fornication, criminal conversation, and seduction among them. Most of these laws have since been repealed or lie dormant on the statute books. Overall, the law seems to take less interest in explicitly regulating and containing marital sex.

Yet, marriage is not understood as any less of a sexual institution: Sex has not become less important in constituting marriage as marriage. Nonmarital sex is no longer regulated in quite the same way; indeed nonmarital sex has to a large extent been normalized, for at least some sexual citizens. It is recognized by many as the path to marriage and marital sex. This normalization of sex before marriage, however, has done little to displace the centrality of sex within marriage. Sex remains partially constitutive of the institution.

For example, Giddens has argued that the transformation of intimacy and the emergence of the idea of confluent love—a contingent love based on intimacy—has actually brought sex "into the core of the conjugal relationship and makes the achievement of reciprocal sexual pleasure a key element in whether the relationship is sustained or dissolved" (Giddens 1992, 62). While this confluent love and its emphasis on sex is not necessarily marital nor monogamous, it has nonetheless left its mark on marriage.[5]

In recent years, marital sex has been the subject of a kind of renaissance.

Sex within marriage has been rediscovered as good sex and as important sex. While some conservative discourses seek to reestablish its normative superiority, through an emphasis on sexual abstinence before marriage, there is a more general resurgence of cultural interest in the sex that occurs within marriage. Many cultural discourses focus on the importance of sex to a marriage and the importance of making sex a project within marriage. Unlike the law's channeling function in the past, this new interest in marital sex is one that relies increasingly on self-governance. In this renaissance, married individuals must take responsibility for their sex lives; they must make their sex lives a project; they must commit themselves to making their sex lives the best it can be. And the price of failure is grave. Marriages without sex are marriages at risk of infidelity and divorce and therefore of citizenship failure. In this sexual renaissance, marital sex has become a citizenship project. Sex continues to be central in the construction of sexual citizenship, but it is increasingly accomplished through the practices of the self.

Consider, for example, the proliferation of marital self-help books, advice columns, and programs that emphasize the sexual dimension of marriage. According to Dr. Phil, sex is an important part of the emotional intimacy of a healthy marriage. In a discussion of his top ten relationship myths, Dr. Phil says "The belief that sex is not important is a dangerous and intimacy-eroding myth. Sex provides an important time-out from the pressures of our daily lives and allows us to experience a quality level of closeness, vulnerability and sharing with our partners" (drphil.com, Top Ten Relationship Myths). While sex is not the foundation of a healthy relationship, it is "a natural extension of a relationship in which giving and receiving mutual support and comfort are common. If you want a good sexual relationship, it needs to be embedded in a good overall relationship." An emotionally open, giving, and trusting relationship is the *sine qua non* of a good sexual relationship. If this healthy emotional relationship is in place, then "the sexual interaction is still crucial. The intimacy that comes from sexual interaction takes the relationship to a completely different level" (McGraw 2000).

Sexual intimacy is then all about emotional intimacy—about attaining an even higher level of emotional intimacy within a relationship. This vision of sex as emotional intimacy is also seen in Dr. Phil's advice that couples should have a broader understanding of what actually constitutes sex. "Don't restrict your thinking by considering sex to be something that only consists of the actual physical act. Touching, caressing, holding hands and any means by which you provide physical comfort to your partner can all be viewed as part of a fulfilling sex life" (drphil.com, Top Ten Relationship Myths). Couples are urged to see sex as part of any physically intimate interaction. The point is the sexual intimacy, not the sexual act. It is sexual intimacy that has become a defining element of marriage.

It is because of this fundamental importance of sexual intimacy within marriage that Dr. Phil urges couples to make their sex lives a project. In one of his advice columns about "putting passion back into your relationship," Dr. Phil writes:

> Put your sex life on project status. Make a conscious decision to recommit to each other and move sex higher on the priority list. Physical intimacy in a relationship deserves a lot of attention. You can start by making small changes. Put your kids to bed earlier, don't fall asleep on the couch and go to bed at the same time as your partner. (drphil.com, putting passion)

Sex in marriage is produced as a project. It is not a dimension of marriage that can be taken for granted but, rather, must be worked on. Putting "your sex life on project status" becomes part of the project of responsibly managing the risk of relationship failure; it is part of the hard work of responsible marital citizenship. Dr. Phil lists sex—or the lack thereof—as one of the three top threats to a marriage (along with in-laws and money). "Sexless marriages are an undeniable epidemic," says Dr. Phil. "And since sex and intimacy are a meaningful part of a relationship, loss of sexual desire can severely affect a marriage" (drphil.com, sexless marriage). Sexless marriages are thus framed as a problem, as a way not to practice marriage.

The explicit message is that without sex, a relationship is at risk of failure. The somewhat more implicit message is that without sex, a spouse may wander. While Dr. Phil does not blame affairs on sex alone but rather on a turning away from the relationship, the absence of sex is part of the lack of connection between the partners. Not unlike nineteenth-century consummation doctrine, the importance of sex in marriage is still associated with the fear of adultery. But, unlike in the earlier era, sex in marriage is not simply about containing sexual desire but about marriage as intimacy. Sex is now part of the emotional intimacy of marriage, and without it, the intimate core of the relationship is weakened and threatened.

The importance of sex within marriage is also a force behind a new consumer market. From sex toys and lingerie to pornography for couples, there has been a veritable explosion in the marital sex market. Like the Passion Parties discussed in Chapter 1, sexual enhancement aids such as massage oils, lingerie, and sex toys are increasingly marketed to married women. This sexual consumer market is cast in the new language of sexual intimacy. Passion Parties, for example, describes itself as "enhancing the sexual relationships of our clients with sensual products designed to promote intimacy and communication between couples." Their trademarked product line entitled Romanta Therapy includes a range of body oils, scrubs, enhancement gels, and edible body products. Eli Lilly has launched a $100 million advertising campaign for Cialis™, its erectile dysfunction drug, specifically targeting romance in marriage. In a move designed to distinguish it from competitors like Viagra™, the ads show nuzzling middle-age couples in romantic settings with soft jazz playing the background. The ad campaign was designed to include women in the target market, since women are the health care managers in many households. "The harder, jocky kind of advertising excludes the partner," explains Colleen Meehan, Cialis's creative director. "It's not just about the ability to have an erection. It's about getting back the emotional bond with your partner" (*Newsweek* 2004). These products are marketed as all about intimacy.

Marital sex enhancements are part of a more general discourse about the importance of sex within marriage and the power of individuals to make their sexual relationships work. Individuals must assume responsibility for managing their sexual relationships. It is part of the shift toward self-disciplining sexual citizenship and what Rose has identified as the fusion of culture, consumption, and self-identity, in which individuals are involved in the "active and detailed shaping . . . of their daily lives in the name of their own pleasures, contentments, or fulfillments" (Rose 2000, 1402). Individuals must pick and choose from a wide range of consumer products. The specific characteristics of their sex lives have become a matter of lifestyle choice, depending on their individual and relational needs and desires. Enhancement gel or edible lingerie, erotic massage videos or Cialis—whatever works for the couple in their pursuit of sexual intimacy. This new consumer market in sexual enhancements for married couples produces a fusion of privatized sexual citizenship: markets, marriage, and self-help. While there is nothing particularly novel about using romance or sex to sell products, there is a unique twist to this advertising discourse. Sexual intimacy is being framed as within one's own power, as a project of the self. Both sex in markets and sex in marriage are being produced in and through the discourse of self-help. Good citizens are produced as both consumers and good marriage partners who make their sexual intimacy part of their marriage project.

The New Cultural Politics of Adultery: From Crisis and Contagion to Responsibility and Redemption

Adultery is nothing new. Nor are social sanctions against it. But, there is something new in the contemporary cultural politics of adultery and its role in the production of sexual citizens. It is a politics that begins with an ever-expanding definition of infidelity. Once restricted to "natural heterosexual intercourse," infidelity now extends to a variety of sexual practices. Indeed, these days, infidelity can occur without sex. Computer sex, telephone sex, e-mail flirtations are all being included within the ambit of adulterous relationships, violating the marital relationship.

As the definition of infidelity expands, so too do its practitioners. In several recent exposés of the new infidelity, women have been shown to be increasingly equal opportunity cheaters. This expansion of infidelity and infidels has in turn produced a new crisis of adultery; a virtual epidemic of adultery has swept the nation. Crises in turn require intervention. The epidemic of infidelity has produced a new emphasis on both prevention and treatment. The first line of protection against adultery is a prevention strategy, based on identifying and then minimizing the risks. It is a politics of self-discipline, of individuals recognizing and taking responsibility for managing the risks to their relationship. If this fails, then the new politics of adultery shifts into treatment. Redemption is possible, if individuals are prepared to take responsibility for their actions and undertake the hard work of relationship repair. In the new politics of adultery, sex—particularly sex within marriage—is a project of self-governance. If the new intimacy has produced greater individual choice in intimate relationships, then the new politics of adultery is about disciplining individuals to make the right choice—to just say no to adultery, or if that fails, to undertake the hard work involved in saying sorry. And it is a politics of self-governance that is "intensely imbricated in public practices and expert disciplinary discourses" (Leckey).

This new politics of adultery no longer relies quite as heavily as it once did on legal regulation to promote marriage as a monogamous relationship. Adultery remains a criminal offense in a number of states, although it is rarely prosecuted.[6] Individuals who commit adultery are also still at risk of losing the privileges of marriage—adultery remains a ground for divorce in the majority of states. However, since the divorce revolution, divorcing parties are much more likely to rely on no-fault grounds for divorce, such as irreconcilable differences.[7]

Despite this change in the grounds most commonly relied upon for divorce, adultery remains a cause célèbre of marriage crisis and failure. But, it no longer needs to be proven or even asserted. A married person can simply choose to exit from a marriage on the basis on his or her spouse's infidelity. Paradoxically, the divorce revolution has maintained the potential legal consequences of adultery. It is in the shadow of a divorce regime of unilateral exit that adultery continues to be produced as a threat to marriage and that a self-disciplining ethicality has been produced to avoid this risk to the relationship. Today, the politics of adultery is no longer produced by direct criminal or legal sanction, but rather, in the shadow of no fault divorce law (Mnookin & Kornhauser 1979). Moreover, the sanctions against adultery have become more diffuse and self-disciplining. It is increasingly television talk shows, magazines, best-selling self-help books, television dramas, and Hollywood films that warn us to avoid this road to certain disaster. The meaning of adultery as a violation of marriage is now produced culturally more than legally.

While the adulterer has never been a particularly good citizen, in the new politics of adultery, the adulterer is becoming a new kind of unbecoming citizen. Adultery is now a citizenship failure on the part of a subject who has failed to take responsibility for the marriage, who has failed to minimize the risk of marriage failure by engaging in an irresponsible but seductive pleasure. It is a failure of self-discipline. It is a failure of the good citizen's marriage project. The appropriate response to this citizenship failure is for the adulterer to recommit him- or herself to the marriage project—to not only discipline their sexuality by redirecting it to their spouse, but to recommit themselves to the project of managing and minimizing the risks of the marriage project. While the adulterer is being constituted as an unbecoming citizen, as something not to be, he or she is no longer a sexual outlaw. Or at least, they need not be. Citizenship redemption for the adulterer now lies in the practices of the self and the project of marriage.

From Adultery to the New Infidelity

There is a new infidelity in town. In 2004, the cover of *Newsweek* magazine announced "The New Infidelity: The Secret Lives of Wives" (Ali & Miller

2004). The article was an exposé of the epidemic of cheating women: As many as 50 percent of women are said to have an extramarital affair during their marriage. An article in *USA Today* in 2003 also announced "the new infidelity," but this time it was about emotional affairs (Peterson 2003). According to its experts, infidelity need not be sexual. In *Salon*, the new infidelity marks the rise of Internet cheating (Goodwin 2003). Yet others spin the new infidelity as the workplace romance (Moll 2005). According to an article in the *Washington Post*, the office is "the new home wrecker" (Shallenbarger 2003). Women and men working in close proximity have apparently produced a new epidemic of infidelity.

With the arrival of each of these new infidelities, the category itself expands. No longer restricted to heterosexual intercourse, infidelity includes more sexual encounters. Indeed, increasingly, it includes more nonsexual encounters. There has been a transformation in the underlying harm of adultery, increasingly understood in terms of a violation of emotional intimacy. This expansion of the category, along with heightened attention to all the women and men engaging in it, has produced a new crisis of infidelity—a new crisis that in turn sets the stage for the new politics of therapeutic intervention: self-discipline and responsibilization.

The New Harm of the New Infidelity   Historically, adultery, like consummation, was all about heterosexual sexual intercourse. The criminal and civil laws sanctioning adultery were focused not simply on prohibiting immoral sexuality. Rather, these laws were explicitly justified in terms of ensuring that the children of a marriage were actually the biological children of the father. It was this objective of preventing the introduction of false blood lines into a family that provided the justification for treating a married woman's adultery more seriously than a man's. For example, criminal adultery was long defined as sexual intercourse with a married woman. Sexual intercourse with an unmarried woman was fornication. In *State v. Lash*, for example, the Court explained this distinction and the definition of adultery explicitly in terms of the introduction of a false blood line into the husband's lineage and its implication for inheritance: "The heinousness of [adultery] consists in exposing an innocent husband to maintain another man's children, and having them succeed to his inheritance" (*State v. Lash* 1838, 387). Indeed, the Court specifically said that the harm to the husband, which is the gist of adultery, lies not in "the alienation of the wife's affections, and loss of comfort in her company" but rather, in "its tendency to adulterate the issue of an innocent *husband*, and to turn the inheritance away from his own blood, to that of a stranger" (State, 388).

In some states, women's adultery was also treated more harshly than men's for the purposes of divorce. Whereas a single act of adultery on the part of a woman was sufficient ground for her husband to divorce her, a husband had to be either "living in adultery" or committing habitual adultery for a woman to be entitled to a divorce (Clark 1968). This double standard was again explicitly justified on the basis of the potential adulteration of the husband's blood line. As a Texas appellate court explained in *Franzetti v. Franzetti* (1938), this distinction is based on "the tendency to adulterate the issue of the innocent husband and to turn the inheritance away from his own blood to that of a stranger" (*Franzetti*, 127). By contrast, if the woman was unmarried, "her incontinence produces none of this evil, because her illegitimate offspring can be heir to nobody" (*Franzetti*, citing 1 Am. Jur. 683, s. 3).

Over time, this double standard in the definition of adultery was removed, and adultery for the purposes of both criminal and divorce law came to be defined as the voluntary sexual intercourse between a married man or woman with a person other than the offender's wife or husband. While the requirement that a woman be married was thus removed, the requirement that sexual intercourse occur was retained. However, in recent years, this requirement has also begun to change, and the case law is now on whether adultery requires intercourse.

Some courts have broadened the definition to include other sexual encounters. For example, in *Bonura v. Bonura*, a Louisiana appellate court held that a wife had committed adultery even though she had not had sexual intercourse (*Bonura* 1987). The court cited an earlier case of *Menge v. Menge* in which the appellate court had concluded that oral sex was included within the definition of adultery (*Menge* 1986) and concluded that "adultery, as grounds for divorce . . . is not limited to actual sexual intercourse" (*Bonura*, 144). In *Bonura* the wife admitted that she had slept "in the same bed with another man, that she had touched the other man's sexual organ and that he had touched hers and that they laid on top of each other" (*Bonura*, 145). The court concluded that "these repeated acts of marital infidelity constitute adultery" (*Bonura*, 145).

Similarly, in the case of *S.B. v. S.J.B.*, a New Jersey court considered whether gay extramarital sex could constitute adultery (*S.B.* 1992). The husband alleged that the wife had had a lesbian relationship. The wife denied the relationship but also argued that even if it was true, a nonheterosexual relationship could not constitute adultery. The court held that all laws dealing with the termination of marriage "must be looked at through the eyes of the injured spouse" (S.B., 126).

> An extramarital relationship viewed from this perspective is just as devastating to the spouse irrespective of the specific sexual act performed by the promiscuous spouse or the sex of the new paramour. The homosexual violation of marital vows could be well construed as the ultimate in rejection. (S.B., 126)

In the court's view, the impact of a homosexual relationship on the injured spouse is extraordinary. It cites with approval a passage from a 1959 case:

> It is difficult to conceive of a more grievous indignity to which a person of normal psychological and sexual constitution could be exposed than the entry by his spouse upon an active and continuous course of homosexual love with another. Added to the insult of sexual disloyalty *per se* (which is present in ordinary adultery) is the natural revulsion arising from knowledge of the fact that the spouse's betrayal takes the form of a perversion." (H. v. H. 1959, 236)

The court concluded that "adultery exists when one spouse rejects the other by entering into a personal intimate sexual relationship with any other person, irrespective of the specific sexual acts performed, the marital status, or the gender of the third party. It is the rejection of the spouse coupled with out-of-marriage intimacy that constitutes adultery" (S.B., 127).

Somewhat paradoxically, the court in *S.B.* expanded the definition of adultery to recognize same-sex sex in a way that was anything but normalizing of that sex. The court was able to condemn same-sex sex as deviant at precisely the same time as it expanded the definition of adultery to recognize that its violation to marriage lay in the violation of sexual intimacy. It was not concerned with a particular sexual act, but with the emotional harm caused by entering into an intimate sexual relationship with another person; an emotional harm that was only exacerbated by the fact that it was with a person of the same sex.

The question of whether same-sex sex constitutes adultery remains a contested legal issue. In *Blanchflower*, the Supreme Court of New Hampshire held that the legal definition of adultery still requires heterosexual sexual intercourse (*Blanchflower* 2003). The Court cited the 1838 case, *State v. Wallace*, for the proposition that "adultery is committed whenever there is an intercourse from which spurious issue may arise" (*State v. Wallace* 1838). In contrast, the dissent in *Blanchflower* concluded that same-sex sex *does* constitute adultery: "It is hard to comprehend how the legislature could have intended to exonerate a sexually unfaithful or even promiscuous spouse who engaged in all manner of sexual intimacy, with members of the opposite sex, except for sexual intercourse, from a charge of adultery. Sexual infidelity should not be so narrowly proscribed" (*Blanchflower*, 232). In the dissent's view "Under our fault-based divorce law, a relationship is adulterous because it occurs outside of marriage and involves intimate sexual activity, not because it involves only one particular sexual act" (*Blanchflower*, 232).[8]

This expansion of the legal definition of adultery to include oral sex, genital touching, and same-sex sex reflects the broader transformation of intimacy, whereby marriage has increasingly become a relationship about emotional and sexual intimacy. Adultery is no longer framed in terms of a particular sexual act. While there continues to be some social anxiety about married women becoming pregnant as a result of an extramarital affair—there are *Oprah* and *Dr. Phil* shows highlighting this nasty consequence of adultery—it is no longer the central harm of adultery. Rather, adultery is now framed more in terms of the violation of the promise of emotional and sexual exclusivity.

This issue was brought into the public spotlight with the Clinton/Lewinsky sex scandal, when the question of what constitutes sex became the subject of a national political and cultural seizure. It was this changing understanding of infidelity that helped to produce the Clinton scandal of presidential adultery, and in turn the sex scandal garnered further support for the idea that any sexual encounter constitutes infidelity. Bill Clinton, rather unwisely, insisted that he "did not have sex with that woman." In the lurid facts that emerged in the national voyeuristic fest, culminating in the 445 pages of the Starr Report, the truth that was produced was that Clinton never had sexual intercourse with Monica Lewinsky, but rather, had a range of other sexual encounters, including oral sex, genital masturbation, and the insertion of sex toys, namely, the now infamous cigar sex.

At one time, it would have been legally accurate to say that Clinton and Lewinsky had not committed adultery. But, the discourse of "having sex" instead of "committing adultery" put Clinton's statement on an already slippery slope. The meaning of sex and of adultery was changing in America. In 1998, at the peak of the Clinton/Lewinsky sex scandal, *Harper's* magazine reported

that only one in eight American men, and one in nine American women believed that oral sex did not constitute adultery (*Harper's* April 1998, citing Fox
News/Opinion Dynamics poll). While there was a fractious political debate
about the appropriate meaning and consequences to attach to his sexual an-
tics, there was very little debate about the fact that Clinton had violated his
marital relationship; he had clearly cheated on Hillary, regardless of whether
there had been sexual intercourse.

As infidelity expert Shirley Glass, described by the *New York Times* as "the
fairy godmother of infidelity research," has authoritatively pronounced, "oral
sex *is* infidelity" (Glass 1998). Glass has found that oral sex is often viewed
as a particularly serious form of infidelity: "Some spouses are more upset if
the partner had oral sex than if they had intercourse; it just seems so much
more intimate" (Glass 1998). It is the breach of intimacy, rather than the sex
act itself, that constitutes the violation of the relationship. Glass explains the
nature of the harm in infidelity:

> The infidelity is that you took something that was supposed to be mine, which
> is sexual or emotional intimacy, and you gave it to somebody else. I thought
> that we had a special relationship, and now you have contaminated it; it doesn't
> feel special any more, because you shared something very precious to us with
> someone else. (Glass 1998)

This understanding of the harm of infidelity is leading to a more expansive definition, wherein virtually any violation of the emotional and sexual
exclusivity of marriage is increasingly cast as infidelity. In the proclamations
of the new infidelity, some have argued that infidelity does not even require
sex. In fact, Glass argues that affairs need not include sex (Glass 2003, 2). An
article in *USA Today* describes her position on this new infidelity: "Sometimes
the greatest betrayals happen without touching. Infidelity is any emotional or
sexual intimacy that violates trust" (Peterson 2003). Glass argues that "a new
crisis of infidelity is emerging in which people who never intended to be unfaithful are unwittingly crossing the line from platonic friends into romantic
friendship," without ever actually having sex (Peterson 2003, quoting Glass).

Glass appears to be on to something. As another infidelity commentator
has observed in the pages of *Salon*: "affairs do not begin with kisses; they
begin with lunch" (Goodwin 2003). A *Newsweek* poll found that 45 percent of
women and 30 percent of men were of the view that emotional betrayal was
actually more upsetting than sexual behavior. While often interconnected,

emotional infidelity has become as much a violation of the marriage as sexual infidelity. Sex has become an expression of the underlying emotional intimacy, rather than the *sine qua non* of marriage.

The idea of emotional infidelity is evident in emerging public debates about whether viewing Internet pornography and cybersex constitutes adultery. According to Glass, "Internet infidelity" epitomizes emotional infidelity, where betrayal occurs in the absence of any sexual contact (Glass 2003, 25–26). Dr. Phil seems to agree. In his view, watching Internet pornography is disrespectful of one's relationship, and may cause "a negative emotional harm" to a spouse ("Dr. Phil on Adultery" 2002). He was even more direct on his own advice page, "Is Internet Porn Cheating?" His answer: "It is not OK behavior. It is a perverse and ridiculous intrusion into your relationship. It is an insult, it is disloyal and it is cheating" ("Is Internet Porn Cheating?" drphil.com). While it does, in his view, constitute "cheating," the next passage suggests that there are various degrees of infidelity: "Viewing Internet pornography or engaging in cybersex is a short step to taking cheating to the next level." According to Dr. Phil, while cybersex constitutes a violation of the marital relationship in its own right, it is also dangerous because it opens the door to the next step of cheating, which presumably involves actual physical sex.

The New Infidels   In the film *Unfaithful* (2002), Connie Sumner (Diane Lane) is a beautiful, seemingly happily married suburban housewife and mother who, after a chance encounter on a windy day in New York City, decides to have an affair with an exotic rare book dealer named Paul Martel. Like the wind that blows Connie off her feet and into the arms of Martel in their first encounter, so too does the affair knock Connie off of her moral center. The affair becomes increasingly sexual and emotionally intense, as Connie succumbs to her obsessive desires. She simply can no longer control herself. The film is loosely adapted from Claude Chabrol's *La Femme Infidèle* by screenwriters Alvin Sargent and William Broyles Jr. Connie's husband Edward (Richard Gere) becomes suspicious, hires a private detective to follow her, and on discovering the truth, goes to Paul's apartment to confront him. The film then takes a violent turn: In a moment of uncontrollable jealousy, Edward smashes Paul on the head with a metal object, killing him almost instantly. Edward must then cover up his crime of passion, to the police and to Connie, who slowly and without words between them, realizes what her husband has done. Through a sobering silence, Connie now sees the very real threat to marriage and the couple comes together, in a combination of fear and marital solidarity, to stare down the threat of discovery.

Director Adrian Lyne is no stranger to infidelity. *Fatal Attraction*, his 1987 blockbuster, was also about infidelity gone bad. Dan (Michael Douglas) is the cheating husband who has very dangerous sex with Alex (Glenn Close), a single professional woman who rapidly transforms from attractive sexual predator to psychotic killer. The cheater is the husband, but the real threat to the family comes from the dangerous other woman, intent on destruction. As Linda Singer has argued, the problem that the film frames "is not Douglas's desire . . . but its object. His mistake was to have picked the wrong woman" (Singer 1993, 183). Fast forward to 2002, and the story of infidelity is a very different one. In *Unfaithful* it is the wife who cheats, the wife who chooses to act out her sexual desires. And now desire is the problem. Connie has not simply chosen the wrong man—in fact, Paul seems a rather nice fellow, not out to destroy her family in any malicious way. The problem is Connie's desire and her decision to act on it, which unleashes the destructive powers of jealousy and deceit. If the blame in *Fatal Attraction* was placed squarely on the backs of professional women, in *Unfaithful* it is shifted inside the marital relationship; now the threat lies within. And it is women now, as much as men—even happy, suburban, stay-at-home mothers—who must also shoulder the risk of and eventual blame for infidelity.

Unfaithful is part of an unfolding narrative of another new infidelity—the infidelity of women. The 2004 *Newsweek* exposé of women's extramarital affairs (Ali & Miller 2004) seemed to unleash a wave of interest in the topic. An *Oprah* show on "Secret Sex in the Suburbs" included a segment on women who cheat and an interview with Lorraine Ali, the *Newsweek* reporter who "helped blow the lid of off . . . the New Infidelity." CBS followed suit with a feature on *The Early Show* entitled "When Women Cheat" (2005). Then there are the books. January 2005 saw the publication of Stephanie Gertler and Adrienne Lopez's *To Love, Honor, and Betray: The Secret Life of Suburban Wives*, focusing on twenty-six married women who have had, are having, or are considering having affairs (Gertler & Lopez 2005). Hot on its heels was *Undressing Infidelity: Why More Wives Are Unfaithful* by Diane Shader Smith in February 2005, which tells the stories of twelve women "who choose to cheat" (Shader Smith 2005). Each of these cultural representations seeks to reveal the "truth" about women's infidelity—that women are having extramarital affairs in increasing numbers.

While the articles, books, and news stories all emphasize that statistics about infidelity are notoriously unreliable insofar as they rely on self-reporting, the experts all seem to agree that women's infidelity is on the rise and beginning to equal men's. According to the *Newsweek* article, "Couples therapists estimate that among their clientele, the number is close to 30 to 40 percent, compared with 50 percent of men, and the gap is almost certainly closing" (Ali & Miller 2004). *The Early Show* quoted infidelity expert Susan Shapiro Barash that 60 percent of married women have extramarital affairs ("When Women Cheat" 2005).

The discovery of married women's affairs as the new infidelity is paradoxical, since the very legal definition of adultery at one time required that the woman be married. Indeed, the most famous—albeit fictional—adulteress in American history was Hester Prynne of *The Scarlet Letter* fame. Hester was married. Admittedly, her husband was nowhere to be seen, having abandoned her in the colonies and then refusing to reveal his identity upon his return. But, the very commission of the offense of adultery required that the illicit sexual intercourse be with a married woman. The other famous fictional adulteresses—Madame Bovary and Anna Karenina—were also married women.

As the legal and social definition was slowly broadened to include sexual intercourse between a married person and someone who was not their spouse, the focus on the adultery of married women faded. The stereotype of an affair was more typically one of a married man and "the other woman." When married women did appear in popular culture as adulteresses, the portrait was often one of an overly desirous subject, the evil femme fatale. In *Double Indemnity* (1944), Billy Wilder's classic film noir, Barbara Stanwyck plays the ultimate adulterous femme fatale who seduces her insurance salesman into helping her kill her husband for the insurance money. She is both heartless and lustful, a deadly combination, for which she and her paramour must ultimately be punished. Adultery and murder again go hand in hand in the 1946 film noir *The Postman Always Rings Twice*. Lana Turner plays Cora, a sexually unsatisfied married woman whose affair leads her and her paramour to kill her husband. As the posters for the film said, "Their Love was a Flame that Destroyed." Both are duly punished: Cora is killed in a car accident, and Frank is executed for her murder. In *The Graduate* (1967), the infamous Mrs. Robinson, played by Anne Bancroft, is a desirous older married woman who seduces Ben (Dustin Hoffman), the son of her husband's business partner. She is bored, overly sexed, and ultimately vengeful when Ben falls in love with her daughter. Admittedly, she does not commit murder—a shift from the adulteresses of the 1940s—but she is a mean and heartless seductress who attempts to sabotage Ben's new relationship.

None of these filmic married adulteresses is presented as the every-woman, but as an exceptional femme fatale whose lust and/or greed lead her to her infidelity—and often, her demise. In the new infidelity, the married adulterous is now the woman next door: She is the suburban housewife or the working mother. The vignettes of the women who have had affairs are stories of an average woman; she may be young or old; she may have been married for only a few years or for several decades; she may live in the Midwest or Manhattan. Her husband might neglect her, or she might be happily married. As the promotional materials for *Undressing Infidelity* asks and answers: "Who are these cheating women? They are your neighbors, your friends, your coworkers. They go to your gym. They shop at your grocery store. They are the women you see every day who seem to have it all" (Shader Smith, 2005) The bottom line of the stories is that she is unexceptional.

While the stories include stay-at-home moms as adulterers, many of the news stories focus on the particular threat of the workplace. As *Newsweek* asks and answers: "Where do married women find their boyfriends? At work, mostly" (Ali & Miller 2004).

> Nearly 60 percent of American women work outside the home, up from about 40 percent in 1964. Quite simply, women intersect with more people during the day than they used to. They go to more meetings, take more business trips and, presumably, participate more in flirtatious water-cooler chatter. If infidelity is an odds game, then the odds are better now than they used to be that a woman will accidentally bump into someone during the workday who, at least momentarily, interests her more than her husband does. (Ali & Miller 2004)

According to Glass, "today's workplace is the most fertile breeding ground for affairs" (Glass 2003, 28). An article in the *Wall Street Journal* puts it even more starkly, accusing the workplace of being "the new home wrecker" (Shallenbarger 2003). It reviews a Swedish study that found that working with people of the opposite sex increases the chances of divorce. The message of these stories is the same: More married women in the labor market translates into more opportunity for and therefore risk of infidelity. The workplace is a dangerous place because the sexes intermingle—because it provides a space of intimacy and opportunity.

An Epidemic of Adultery   The net discursive effect of the broader definition of adultery and the larger group of infidels is that there is simply more infidelity than ever before. Many infidelity experts conclude that this infidelity is reaching virtually epidemic proportions. The new infidelity is often framed in the discourse of disease, epidemic, and contagion. Sometimes the language of disease and contagion is specifically invoked. For example, an article in the *Wall Street Journal* announced that "divorce is contagious" (Shallenbarger 2003):

> By showing that office divorces can break out in what a separate study in Ohio called "a measles pattern," the research highlights the need for working couples to take steps to vaccinate their marriages.

The language of immunization and vaccination is recurrent. For example, Peggy Vaughan says that preventing affairs begins by "being aware that no one is immune from having an affair" (Vaughan 2003, 9). She states "Preventing affairs is not like having a one-time inoculation—or even getting occasional booster shots. It's more like taking a pill every day for the rest of your life" (Vaughan 2003, dearpeggy.com). Shirley Glass similarly writes "A happy marriage is not a vaccine against infidelity" (Glass 2003).

Sometimes the reference to disease and contagion is more subtle, likening infidelity to a virus. For example, an article in *USA Today* speaks of the "new 'crisis of infidelity' breeding in the workplace" and of the workplace as "the truly fertile ground for dangerous emotional attachments" (Peterson 2003). Sometimes, the risk of infidelity is cast as a genetic one. Glass, for example, states that risk factors include, "Family patterns: Unfaithful parents tend to produce sons who betray their wives and daughters who either accept affairs as normal or are unfaithful themselves" (Glass, quoted in Peterson 2003).

This discourse of infidelity as disease mirrors Linda Singer's work on sexual politics in an age of epidemic. Singer argues that the sex panic created by AIDS has pervaded American social, political, and cultural life and in turn produced a discourse of contagion and epidemic (Singer 1993; see also Sontag 1989). The discourse is used to describe "an ever increasing number of cancers, viruses infecting the body politic through mechanisms of contagion and communicability" (Singer 1993, 27). It is not limited to actual illness or diseases but rather has "spread to areas far afield" (Singer 1993, 29). "In order to represent a phenomenon as socially undesirable, be it divorce, drug use, single motherhood, teenage pregnancy, one need only call it epidemic" (Singer 1993,

27). So, too, infidelity has been added to the list of contemporary sexual epidemics. As Singer argues, to label it as an epidemic not only "engages in a kind of rhetorical inflation" but also mobilizes a particular response. "An epidemic is a phenomenon that in its very representation calls for, indeed, seems to demand some form of managerial response, some mobilized effort to control." An epidemic of infidelity thus demands an intervention of control, a managerial response to minimize the risk of further contagion and contamination.

To call infidelity an epidemic is to set the stage for the urgency of both treatment and prevention. It requires that pleasures be disciplined. It requires that the very borders and boundaries that epidemics violate be protected. It demands "a new more prudential sexual aesthetic" that recognizes the life and death risks associated with undisciplined sexuality, and that places a new emphasis on constraint (Singer 1993, 114). As Singer argues, "there is a new emphasis on domestication and on a kind of restraint emblematized by the 'just say no' campaign," which is discussed in the next section. Just as the discourse of epidemic is extended beyond actual disease transmission, so too are the "just say no" campaigns extended beyond AIDS and drugs. The new cultural politics of adultery is just such a campaign. It is based first in prevention—in preventing the spread of this dangerous contagion of infidelity. But, if prevention fails, then it is also about treatment; infidelity can be treated with appropriate pseudo-medical intervention. As with these sexual epidemics generally, the family "is being repackaged as a prophylactic social device" (Singer 1993, 186). The sexually monogamous marriage is the new front line in the war on this epidemic. Both prevention and treatment start and end with individual husbands and wives as the new foot soldiers.

From Epidemic to Prevention and Treatment: Just Say No
In the film *Closer*, director Mike Nichols explores the destructive and corrosive nature of adultery through a narrative in which two couples violate the emotional and sexual intimacies of their relationships. Dan (Jude Law) and Alice (Natalie Portman), an unmarried couple, and Larry (Clive Owen) and Anna (Julia Roberts), a married couple, are engaged in a multiplicity of infidelities. Dan and Anna are attracted to each other before Anna even meets Larry, but they do not consummate their passions until after Anna and Larry marry. Larry and Alice engage in a barbed and ambivalent flirtation—it is unclear whether they are attracted to each other or are drawn together by a destructive and jealous energy produced by their partners' affair. Anna leaves

Larry, Dan leaves Alice, and Dan and Anna couple. During his postsepara-
tion devastation, Larry accidentally finds Alice at a high-end strip bar, where
they too engage in their own sexual and emotional infidelities. The mutual
infidelities are almost complete—but not without one more destructive turn.
Larry manipulates Anna into having sex with him "one last time" in exchange
for his signature on the divorce papers. Now, Anna is the double adulteress,
violating the sexual and emotional intimacy of her new relationship. Her
insistence that it was just meaningless sex rings hollow, as Dan is now the
jealous victim of adultery. He cannot get over it. Everyone has now lied and
cheated on everyone, and so begins the denouement of adultery and the move
toward reconstruction. Anna and Larry get back together. Dan and Alice try,
but Dan's insistence that Alice "tell the truth" about her infidelities produces a
final schism. Dan's desire for truth becomes simultaneously a test that pushes
her too far, and Alice leaves. And the final scenes reveal the lack of truth went
even further: Alice wasn't even Alice after all, and the only person she told
was Larry, who assumed she was simply performing her stripper non-truths.

Closer is a performance of the new politics of adultery. Each of the character's pursuit of desire produces deceit, jealousy, and destruction. Their failure
to just say no is held up as a kind of negative model of how not to live one's
life. There are however brief moments of insight into a parallel, more ethical way of being. In the scene where Dan confesses his affair, an emotionally
devastated Alice insists: "There's a moment, there's always a moment; I can
do this, I can give in to this or I can resist it" (Marber 1999). Despite attraction
and temptation, there is an ethical moment when you can still say no. It is an
acknowledgement that relationships will always be confronted by temptation,
but that an individual has the power to say no in the face of that temptation.
Alice is the voice of morality amidst a seeming ethical vacuum—where everyone gives in to their temptations. She alone insists that it is possible to just say
no, although she too ultimately performs her own multiple betrayals.

Closer is also a story about the possibility of redemption after failure. If individuals make the wrong choice—if they fall prey to the seductions of adulterous desire—they must then face another decision. Individuals can choose
to recommit themselves to their relationship. They can repudiate their adulterous relationship and seek absolution from their spouse by taking responsibility for their adulterous actions. Anna and Larry forgive each other for their
respective trespasses and move on. Dan and Alice do not. They remain frozen
in deceit and jealousy, where truth seeking on the road to redemption is not

possible. Alice refuses to tell the truth. Dan has an obsessive need to know. Any possibility of reestablishing trust is destroyed. The two couples represent the fork in the road after adultery: the violation of trust destroying the relationship versus forgiveness and recommitment to the relationship.

The dual emphasis on prevention and treatment is evident in the many cultural representations of adultery in television and film. It is seen on the afternoon talk shows, where adultery is a mainstay. Both *Oprah* and *Dr. Phil* have repeatedly featured marital infidelity, with a marked emphasis on the possibility of redemption after the fact. The *Oprah* show "Dr. Phil on Adultery" addresses the pervasiveness of adultery and the possibility of moving beyond it (2002). "Eighty percent of marriages are affected by infidelity. For the 35 percent of couples that stay together after infidelity, rebuilding a relationship and sex life can be difficult—but not impossible." Dr. Phil tells those who committed adultery: "You made a bad decision, so accept the responsibility." The road to redemption is all about taking responsibility—for one's actions and the consequences of those actions, particularly the emotional impact on one's spouse. In another appearance on *Oprah*, Dr. Phil has a segment entitled "Coping with the Aftermath of an Affair" ("Oprah's 2000 Time Capsule") in which he talks about moving forward with your life after an affair, and learning to trust again.

Sometimes, these shows are a performance in shaming. "How I Found Out My Husband Was Cheating" (2003), for example, is described as a show where "Betrayed women reveal the moment they found out, and the husbands answer the unanswerable—why did they cheat?" It includes a segment on "Confessions of Betrayal" where the men who have committed adultery talk about "why they strayed and risked everything." A whole show is dedicated to "Cheating Husbands Confess" (2004), where cheating husbands stand in the spotlight to reveal the "truth" about their decisions. The men speak, and the audience gasps in disapproval. It is a public shaming—a modern-day version of *The Scarlet Letter*, where they stand in public marked as bad citizens. Of course, in the modern version, it is an entirely voluntary decision—individuals decide for themselves to come forward and confess their sins on national television. Confession has long been part of the production of truth and the road to redemption, particularly in relation to sex (Foucault 1980). In the new cultural politics of adultery, the road to redemption similarly begins with the confession—first to one's spouse, but also to a broader authority of peers and experts who "judge, punish, forgive, console, and reconcile" (Foucault 1980, 62).

By confessing the truth of adultery, the adulterers can begin to move forward, either with one's old life or a new one. The shows produce these men as failed citizens, who are either lucky beyond belief that their wives have agreed to take them back, or rightly suffering the consequences of their actions since their wives divorced them. They serve as a warning, a harbinger of the road that lies ahead. The message is all about responsibility. Individuals need to take responsibility for their actions lest their unbridled passions lead them down this road to citizenship failure. The shaming of the other is all about the conduct of the self. Don't do as I did. Take responsibility for your actions and your marriage. These shows perform both prevention and treatment. Redemption is possible and begins with the confessional, with truth telling, as the first step towards rehabilitation. But, there is no guarantee—only 35 percent of the couples stay together—and therefore, the far better option is to not head down this road in the first place.

Dr. Phil's message is also prophylactic, dishing out advice of avoiding the behavior. For example, in his advice article entitled "Affair Proof Your Marriage," Dr. Phil writes that it is possible to "Inoculate yourself against infidelity by making sure you're attentive, involved and plugged in to your marriage." The discourse of preventing infection and contamination—of inoculation and vaccination —is never far from the surface. Since infidelities result from a breakdown in the intimacy and communication between the partners, he recommends that individuals "turn towards your partner—not away." Individuals must commit themselves to making their marriage a project:

> Work on your marriage every single day—not just during the bad times. Wake up each day and ask yourself, "What can I do today that will make my marriage better?" ("Affair Proof Your Marriage" drphil.com)

If your marriage is in a rut, get it out: "'Bored people are boring' says Dr. Phil. Find a passion, get energized, find some time together to rediscover the love and commitment you have for one another." In addition to working on the relationship, there is the requisite command to self-improvement: "Take care of yourself. Eat healthy, exercise, and look your best. Feeling good about yourself will radiate and your spouse will notice" ("Affair Proof Your Marriage" drphil.com). A marriage inoculated from infidelity is a marriage that begins with self-esteem and individual responsibility. Only individuals who feel good about themselves can commit themselves to feeling good about their relationships.

Both Oprah's and Dr. Phil's approach to marriage and infidelity fits within their more general approach of self-help as the path to the American Dream. As Alan Hunt has argued, "self-help operates through . . . the mobilization of self-esteem and self-respect." Both the *Oprah* and *Dr. Phil* shows are all about mobilizing these discourses of self-empowerment—self-esteem, self-respect, responsibility, and self-transformation. Individuals are called upon to better themselves—to lead better, happier, healthier, more fulfilled lives. Structural obstacles and public responsibility fade into the background. Occasionally, the difficult circumstances faced by an individual are brought into sharper relief but only to illustrate that individual initiative and perseverance can prevail. This is the self-help model of the Horatio Alger story; realizing the American Dream is only a "Live Your Best Life" *Oprah* workshop away. This self-help model is applied to the adultery context, allowing parties to a marriage to save their relationship in the aftermath of infidelity if they are prepared to take responsibility for their lives and their decisions and to commit themselves to the path of redemption. The model is also contained in the more prophylactic message: Avoid the path of infidelity by taking responsibility for your marriage.

Dr. Phil's advice—and the consequences of failing to follow it—is played out in a number of film and television representations of adultery. *We Don't Live Here Anymore* (2004), a film directed by John Curran, explores the dark underside of adulterous desires through a remarkably similar set of infidelities between two married couples. Jack (Mark Ruffalo) and Hank (Peter Krause) are colleagues, jogging partners, and best friends. But Jack is also sleeping with Hank's wife Edith (Naomi Watts). Hank is notoriously unfaithful, and Edith appears to have initiated the affair with Jack to get back at him. Jack, plagued by guilt, seems to encourage his own wife Terry (Laura Dern) into an affair with Hank. The film takes us inside Jack's tattered marriage with Terry. Terry drinks too much and housecleans too little. As one film critic described her, she is "a truly desperate housewife—frequently hung-over, mercurial, and domestically challenged . . . [but] also loving, passionate, and direct especially when she is trying to communicate with her passive aggressive spouse" (Knight 2004). She suspects that Jack is having an affair, but when she confronts him, he defensively tries to turn the tables, accusing her of infidelity with Hank. Terry and Jack fight—about the small details and overwhelming emotions that make up a marriage. The inside of Hank and Edith's marriage is rather harder to access; it is as if there is no inside, which is the very thing that leads Edith to her affair with Jack.

Like *Closer*, the story is one of attractions and lies, seductions and betrayals, and the inevitably corrosive consequences of these infidelities on a marriage. But in contrast to *Closer*, the stakes are higher in *We Don't Live Here Anymore*: There are three children involved. The narcissistic behavior of the parents is cast against the consequences for their children. There is a sense of claustrophobic dread that runs through the film. As A. O. Scott wrote in his *New York Times* review, "An uncanny suspense ripples through the movie. Some of its recurrent images—a railroad crossing, a rushing river—carry a premonition of mortal danger, and you watch nervously, certain that something terrible is going to happen" (Scott 2004). It is the message of danger, of inevitable destruction, that follows in the wake of these marital infidelities. Something terrible *is* going to happen—but it doesn't happen at a train crossing or a rushing river. A marriage or two is going to be ripped apart; children's lives are going to be devastated.

The film performs the two possible outcomes of adultery: destruction and redemption. Edith leaves Hank. Jack and Terry reconcile. It is a performance of citizenship failure in two parts. Both couples have failed to make their marriage a project; both couples have, in Dr. Phil's discourse, turned away from their marriages. But Edith and Hank have done so to a point of no return. Theirs is a relationship without communication. Hank has no emotional connection to his wife; he has no emotional connection to his daughter. He is narcissistic to the extreme, connected only to his writing and his desires. Theirs is not simply a clean house, it is a sterile one.

By contrast, Jack and Terry's relationship is emotionally fraught. Their mutual resentments, jealousy, hatreds, and loves are lived out loud. Their children hear them fighting. Their house is a mess, reflecting not simply Terry's housekeeping failure, but the state of their emotional lives. Emotions are strewn around their lives like their dirty laundry. While Jack and Terry are hardly model *Dr. Phil* citizens, their emotional connection to each other and their children is what provides them the life raft back from adultery. Jack literally looks over the edge—peering over a stone cliff from which his two young children are throwing stones into a rushing river below. He makes his choice to come back. Terry, who has already packed his bags, asks him whether his decision to return is simply about the children. She reassures him that they will be fine—she gives him an out. But, Jack says no, it is not simply about the children. It is his moment of redemption, of recommitting himself to his marriage project.

At the same time, Jack wants to know the details of Terry's affair. Where did they have sex? What kind of sex did they have? How did she feel? He cross-examines her with both a cold and removed indifference (he is after all having sex with Edith), and yet he is obsessed with all the excruciating sexual and emotional details. As with *Closer*, the confession plays multiple and contradictory roles: the first step in the path toward redemption—forgiveness requires knowledge and confession produces the truth of the adultery; but it is also another step in the infliction of pain and jealousy. The desire to know is about getting closer and pushing away, about the irrational obsession born of jealousy, about the space of emotional intimacy in marriage where all is to be revealed for better or for worse.

To tell the truth or not to tell the truth is an enduring moral dilemma for the adulterers: Is it the path back or the path out? *We Don't Live Here Anymore* explores the risks of both. But, reflecting the importance of confession in the new politics of adultery, the film appears to come down on the side of truth telling. Hank knew about Edith's affair all along: Her confession had no relational redemptive value. Hank himself never really confesses; that role is left to Terry, who in telling the truth to Jack opens up the space for their reconciliation. Jack's confession to Terry is a moment of crisis; the words "I love Edith" produce Terry's emotional collapse as she sees the very foundation of her marriage collapsing. She begs Jack not to do this: In the midst of the collapse, she still holds on to a crumbling space of emotional intimacy between them. When Jack does decide not to do this, when he peers over the side of the abyss and comes back, it is in very large part because of Terry's commitment to keep their space of intimacy alive. Truth telling is the only way back, but only if the couple is committed to the project of their marriage.

For Edith, on the other hand, her confession and Hank's virtual indifference constitute a moment of rupture. His lack of emotion, his inability to go to a space of emotional intimacy precisely because they do not have one, brings this lack to the surface in a way that Edith can no longer look away. To the extent that her affair was about getting even with Hank, about trying to make him feel jealousy or pain or just feel something, it was a failure. He appears to feel nothing. Once again, we have little direct access to the inside of their relationship. But, we see its absence when Hank tells Jack that the affair was good for his writing: He could focus on his writing because Jack was taking care of his wife. We see it in the final scenes, when Edith tells Hank that she's leaving, and he is mystified by her decision.

The void that is their marriage leaves her with no choice but to walk away. Edith exemplifies the citizenship failure that Dr. Phil counsels against: do not turn away from your marriage when there are problems. She made the wrong choice. Yet, her choice forces her to confront the fact that her marriage is not one in which her spouse is even remotely plugged in. Hank is not going to make their marriage a project. Her only choice then is to leave. And when she does leave, amidst the foreboding train crossing where something terrible might happen, her daughter smiles for the very first time in the film. It is redemption of a different sort: It is about Edith and her daughter's survival. She has worked hard at making her marriage work, she has worked hard on trying to get Hank to make their marriage work, and when that failed, she resorted to more desperate measures that also failed. It is Edith following Dr. Phil's advice about citizenship redemption: She has somewhat perversely earned her way out of the relationship. She has investigated every avenue of rehabilitation, and she is going to be able to look her daughter in the eye and say "I did it all."

We Don't Live Here Anymore is a contemporary morality tale about adultery—its symptoms, its causes, its consequences, and none of it is pretty. Despite the failings of its adulterous characters, not all of them are bad citizens. While warning against the inevitable destruction of adultery, it also tells a more sympathetic story about how to move on after it. Just like Dr. Phil and Oprah's discourse about adultery—it's better to avoid it, but if you don't, there is a way back; three of the characters in *We Don't Live Here Anymore* find a way to redeem their citizenship. Jack and Terry do it together within their marriage, and Edith does it alone by leaving her marriage. Imperfect citizens, yes, but not utterly failed. It is Hank who stands alone as a bad citizen. He fails to see how his selfish pursuit of pleasure undermined his family; he refused to do the work involved in committing himself to the project of his family or his marriage. Moreover, his adultery is contagious. He is responsible for his wife's infidelity, and he is responsible for Terry's adultery. He is a carrier of the infidelity virus, threatening to infect not only his own marriage but of all those around him. Hank is emblematic of a failed and dangerous citizen; his actions border on a kind of epidemiological sedition.

A more frivolous but not dissimilar depiction of adultery is seen in ABC's 2004 hit television series, *Desperate Housewives*. The comedy drama explores the dark underside of the lives of four housewives on Wisteria Lane. There is single mother Susan (Teri Hatcher), whose cheating husband left her for his younger secretary. Lynette (Felicity Huffman) is a high-powered career woman who temporarily joined the opt-out revolution to stay home with her four out-of-control children, verging on the edge of emotional collapse. Bree (Marcia Cross) is a tightly wound super mom, whose Martha Stewart ways are driving her family to the brink of insanity. And there is Gabrielle (Eva Longoria), a former model who married for money but now longs for passion and is involved in a steamy affair with her 17-year-old gardener. The show is narrated by a deceased fifth housewife who mysteriously killed herself after a day of "quietly polishing the routine of my perfect life."

Conservative commentators have condemned the show for its celebration of infidelity and sexual promiscuity. In the words of the American Decency Association, for example, "*Desperate Housewives'* constant barrage of sexual themes and normalization of adultery is one of the worst assaults upon the family" (American Decency Association 2004). But *Desperate Housewives* is no simple celebration or normalization of infidelity. Rather, it is a comedic representation of the new politics of adultery. Susan's divorce—and her emotional devastation—was caused by her husband's affair. Bree's husband's philandering not only results in a heart attack but the implosion of their marriage. The infidelity of these men is not celebrated but condemned. As for the female infidelity, while Gabrielle's affair may be, as one critic has suggested, the fodder of much water-cooler talk, it is also clearly represented as stepping well beyond the bounds of acceptability. She not only cheats on her husband, but she does so with a teenager. Gabrielle may be desperate; she may only be having the affair "to keep from blowing my brains out." But her adultery plus—adultery plus another heinous form of sexual activity, in this case, sex with a minor—invites shock and moral condemnation. She does not tell her friends because she knows they will disapprove. When the gardener's mother—another inhabitant of Wisteria Lane, finds out that her son is having an affair and mistakenly accuses Susan, Susan's moral indignation forces Gabrielle to confess. There is little ambivalence here—Gabrielle's affair is morally wrong.

Perhaps the most complicated story of infidelity is that of Bree's husband, Rex (Steve Culp). Rex's affair is represented as a citizenship failure: He is responsible for the failure of his marriage because of his choice to look outside to satisfy his admittedly fetishistic sexual needs. But Bree is not without responsibility. Her tightly wound obsessive ways have driven an emotional wedge between her family and herself. She is so busy committing herself to the image of Martha Stewart domesticity that she has failed to make her actual family a project. Rex gets points for trying. He tried to make his marriage—and their sexual relationship within the marriage—a project, by suggesting that they see a sexual surrogate. Bree reluctantly agrees to participate, but she falls short. She is unable to dedicate herself to their sexual relationship: In the midst of a sexual encounter, she is unable to stop herself from her obsessive need to clean. Yet, it is still Rex's decision to have an affair that crosses the moral line. His too is a kind of adultery plus—as if the infidelity alone is not enough, his affair is with a neighbor come s/m mistress who is only too willing to indulge Rex's fetishes. Rex pays dearly for his infidelity. He has a heart attack in the midst of one of his sexual rendezvous, which results in Bree discovering his affair. Bree agrees to nurse him back to health, but only so that she can then divorce him. His affair is enough to even get their son—who had previously blamed Bree for all their family's dysfunction—to side with his mother.

In each of these representations, the moment of adultery represents a crossing of the line; it is an unequivocal violation of the marital relationship, notwithstanding how dysfunctional the marriage might already have been. It is the line that once crossed unleashes the wave of relationship destruction. *Desperate Housewives* may be replete with adulterous affairs, but the message fits clearly within the new cultural politics of adultery. Like the films *Closer* and *We Don't Live Here Anymore*, it tells the stories of the consequences of emotional and sexual betrayal, albeit with a dark comedic effect.

The popularity of *Desperate Housewives* produced a series of media articles and stories about the show, some of which have highlighted the issue of female infidelity. CBS's *Early Show*, for example, featured a story entitled "When Women Cheat" (2005). The story provocatively opens with an implicit reference to the success of *Desperate Housewives*: "The adulterous woman used to get marked with a scarlet letter. Today, she gets a Golden Globe." Riding the wave of the *Newsweek* exposé of the new infidelity six months earlier, the story focuses on the reality of women's infidelity. It includes interviews with several experts, including gender studies professor Susan Shapiro Barash, who claims that "60% of married women will at some point in their marriage embark on an extramarital affair," and therapist Judy Kuriansky who discusses the motivation behind women's actions:

> The reasons that women cheat, similar to some of the reasons that men cheat, are that they are frustrated, and that they can! Women are increasingly more

emotionally secure, more financially secure, some of them, and they feel that they can do what they want and get their needs satisfied. ("When Women Cheat" 2005)

The story goes on with a reference back to *Desperate Housewives*:

> Infidelity is explained in a scene from *Desperate Housewives* as, "It's just sex! It's totally harmless."

> But for women especially, "It's just sex" is just unrealistic, according to Kuriansky.

> She explains, "The difference is, when women seek an affair, they may think they're looking for just sex, but as soon as the sex happens, their emotions get wrapped into it."

In the therapist's view, women are not capable of separating sex from emotion, and as a result, the sex becomes part of a far more complicated affair. And the clear message of the story is that infidelity results in marital breakdown. As one woman who had an affair says, "cheating women . . . don't think their husbands will leave them." But, the story tells us, "They do." The story ends with a Dr. Phil-like message on how to avoid infidelity and its inevitable consequences:

> If you want to avoid joining the ever-expanding unfaithful club—there's one key: communication.

> Kuriansky advises, "Sit down and have a conversation with your partner about what it is that you need emotionally, financially, socially and certainly sexually, that you can work out together. And either fix it, or forget it."

In this story, *Desperate Housewives* is used as a foil for articulating the new cultural politics of adultery. Infidelity unleashes the forces of destruction. The dialogue "It's just sex! It's totally harmless" is taken at face value to represent the message of the show, with which the therapist then disagrees. Yet, *Desperate Housewives* is itself a performance of the same politics of adultery. In fact, the CBS news story drops the context in which these words are uttered. The women, seated around a kitchen table in their coffee klatch, are reacting to the news of Susan's then husband's affair with his secretary. The words "its just sex" are ascribed to the adulterous husband, offered up as a pathetic justification for his behavior. The women collectively scoff, and one adds that the comment comes straight out of "the philanderer's handbook—page one." But, in a bizarre double reversal, the show's irony disappears in the CBS narrative, and its morality tale of adultery becomes a condoning of adultery that is in turn condemned. Yet, the bottom line message of *The Early Show* story is the same as that of *Desperate Housewives*: Infidelity is bad news.

The irony and morality tale underlying *Desperate Housewives* has not been lost on all cultural critics. Richard Goldstein, in an article enticingly entitled "Red Slut, Blue Slut," argues that while the show may be liberal on its surface, it is conservative at its core (Goldstein 2005). Goldstein describes the show as a mix of the "libidinous style of *Sex and the City* and combined it with the breathy excess of Reagan-era dramas like *Dallas* and *Dynasty*," perfect for these newly conservative times:

> Its characters inspire ridicule rather than empathy. Their transgressions are sinful rather than soulful. And a sense of imminent retribution hovers over Wisteria Lane like the *Satan ex machina* in a cautionary tale. (Goldstein 2005)

Goldstein continues:

> Religious conservatives are perfectly willing to be entertained by immorality; they only require that it be punished, at least eventually. As for wives who trespass against their husbands, bring 'em on—as long as they act like sluts rather than sexual adventurers. Such creatures are inevitable in a world where faith has been forgotten along with the knowledge of right and wrong. If that's your take on *Housewives*, it can be relished as a sendup of the polluted world. (Goldstein 2005)

Goldstein identifies the anti-adultery message of *Desperate Housewives*, although he associates it with a conservative politics. He explains the appeal of the show to liberal audiences through a very different lens of camp. While his identification of the moral ambiguity of the show and its appeal to those on both sides of the political spectrum is astute, limiting the adultery message to a conservative politics misses the broader cultural and political appeal of new politics of adultery. The new politics of adultery may have an obvious constituency with the conservative family values set. But, it is not limited to them. Rather, part of its discursive power lies in its appeal beyond the red/blue divide. Liberals too are being encouraged to take responsibility for their marriages, to understand the significance of the choices they make, and to avoid those actions that will destroy their relationships. It is part of the ethical appeal to the new ethical citizen. In this new ethnopolitics (Rose 2000), liberals in particular are being called upon, indeed, reconstituted, as "ethical creatures" capable of making ethical choices in their personal relationships.

The new cultural politics of adultery ultimately comes full circle back to the project of sex in marriage. The message of prevention and treatment includes the central idea of making one's marriage a project, and particularly, of making sex in marriage a project. The best way to immunize a marriage from the risk of infidelity is to work on the multiple dimensions of intimacy, including sexual intimacy. While the infidelity experts agree that infidelity is not simply about sex, they also seem to agree that a couple who works on their marriage need to be attentive to sex within their marriage. Good sexual citizenship still requires sexual monogamy. But the modality of its construction has changed. Channeling sex into marriage—as opposed to extramarital liaisons—is now the work of individual couples. Good citizens are those who manage the risk of infidelity and thereby help control the epidemic from spreading further within the body politic. Good citizens are those who make their relationship a project, who recognize the personal and social costs of infidelity and divorce, who in the face of the transformation of intimacy undertake the responsible and hard work of making their relationship work by working on their relationship.

Marriage and Divorce Reform as Self-Governance

Not everyone has abandoned the use of legal sanction in relation to marriage and divorce. Some conservatives have called upon the law to help reverse the divorce culture by returning to fault-based divorce and covenant marriage. Covenant marriage, first passed in Louisiana in 1997 and followed by Arizona in 1998 and Arkansas in 2001, allows individuals to choose between regular marriage and "covenant marriage." A covenant marriage is one in which the couples agree to limit the grounds of divorce. In Louisiana, for example, the covenant marriage option restricts divorce to fault-based grounds, including adultery, or a separation of two years (in contrast to a six month separation for regular marriage). Covenant marriage also requires that couples obtain premarital counseling, and marriage counseling prior to divorce. For example, the Louisiana law states that "couples agree to take all reasonable steps to preserve their marriage if marital difficulties arise, including marriage counseling" (La. Rev. Stat. Ann. S. 9:237(c)).

The return to fault-based divorce laws is primarily an attempt to stem marriage breakdown in the absence of a serious matrimonial offense, namely, to stop individuals from simply walking away from the marriages because they are no longer happy or emotionally fulfilled. Proponents of covenant marriage hope that a return to fault-based divorce, along with premarital counseling and a commitment to take all reasonable steps to preserve their marriages will reduce the rate and culture of divorce. Yet, within these more restrictive divorce laws, adultery is always retained as a ground for divorce. Covenant marriage laws reinforce the idea of marriage as a sexually monogamous relationship and that a violation of sexual exclusivity can result in a repudiation of the marriage. As Katherine Shaw Spaht, a leading proponent of covenant marriage, has written: "Adultery . . . has always been considered the most serious violation of a spouse's marital obligations. The possibility of the wife's adultery introducing a 'bastard' into the husband's blood line in combination with the sharing of one's sexual potential as an expression of the deepest human intimacy made adultery the most reprehensible of conduct within the marital relationship"(Shaw Spaht 1998, 114).

Covenant marriage in some ways signals a revival of the legal significance of adultery. While adultery remains available as a ground of divorce for regular marriages, in a more restrictive divorce regime it is likely to become a more frequently relied upon ground for divorce. However, covenant marriage is in many respects quite unlike the punitive adultery regimes of the past. Rather, these covenant marriage laws can be seen to be operating within the logic of individual choice and self-governance. Individuals are given the option of choosing between regular and covenant marriage. Individuals who choose a covenant marriage are making a choice to remove a choice. Beyond this, they are also making a choice to commit themselves to the project of their marriage. They are committing themselves "to take all reasonable steps" to save their marriage. Covenant marriage is about taking individual responsibility for managing and minimizing the risks of marriage. Within this politics of self-governance, adultery is a high-risk activity, at least for those who want to stay married. Adultery is a ground for immediate divorce. If you want to stay married, don't do it. If, on the other hand, you do not want to stay married, an unintended message of the law is "just do it." Because adultery is a ground for immediate divorce, the current marriage laws paradoxically create an incentive for the unhappy spouse to commit adultery. Either way, though, the responsibility for the future of the marriage lies squarely with the individual spouse, who is given a clear message that adultery can destroy even this higher form of marriage.

Covenant marriage is, then, not that different from the new politics of adultery. Notwithstanding its turn to law, it seeks to reduce divorce through responsibilization. Reflecting the new politics of adultery, covenant marriage seeks to stem the adulterous tides through self-governance. The assumptions informing divorce reform and covenant marriage are entirely consistent with the proliferation of cultural representations implicitly and explicitly condemning marital infidelity and insisting that the path to marital fidelity lies in self-control. Covenant marriage is constituted in and through this discourse of adultery and its production of good and bad citizens. Good citizens commit themselves to their marriages and to taking all reasonable steps to save their marriage. Conversely, bad citizens are those who commit adultery with little or no consideration of its consequences on spouses, children, and even on the adulterous other. Covenant marriage is simply one strategy of an increasingly pervasive cultural message that good citizens need to take responsibility for managing their sexual relationship risk.

The movement for divorce reform and covenant marriage exemplifies the new modality of self-regulation in contemporary sexual citizenship. Individuals are called upon through a choice of legal regime to participate in the "active and detailed shaping . . . of their daily lives in the name of their own pleasures, contentments, or fulfillments" (Rose 2000, 1402). Rather than a punitive regime intended to deter action through the threat of legal sanction, individuals are called upon to regulate their own actions in pursuit of their own happiness. While both the older and new regimes were and are constitutive of good and bad citizens (good = monogamous, bad = adulterous), the new regime brings a different kind of citizen into being. The good sexual citizen is now the subject who takes responsibility for their well-being, who manages their risks and promotes their personal and familial happiness. Good citizens should not have to be threatened by legal sanction to do so; they should want to do it themselves. They should choose a legal regime that commits them to making their relationship work. Moral regulation is now to be achieved through private choice—though one that is highly culturally and politically produced.

Conclusion: Adulterating Adultery

When asked what the single most important thing she wants people to know about infidelity, infidelity expert Shirley Glass says: "Boundaries. That it is possible to love somebody else, to be attracted to somebody else, even if you have a good marriage. . . . You have to conduct yourself by being aware of appropriate boundaries" (Glass 1998). Her major advice for preventing infidelity is therefore: *"Maintain appropriate walls and windows.* Keep the windows open at home. Put up privacy walls with others who could threaten your marriage" (Glass 1998). Adultery is all about failing to respect boundaries. It is framed as a border violation, and border patrol as the only way to prevent it. In this new politics of adultery, where the risk of infidelity is ubiquitous, good citizens must protect the borders of their marriage and, in so doing, protect the borders of their sexual citizenship.

The message is also one of self-discipline and self-conduct: Individuals must learn about these appropriate boundaries and govern themselves accordingly. Marriage has become a practice of self-governance; individuals are responsible for their own marriages and for the choices that they make within those marriages. But, as the chapter has argued, while self-governance may presuppose the freedom of the govern to act, it attempts to shape and direct the conduct of its subjects in and through this capacity. The self-governance of the politics of adultery is "deeply imbricated in public discourses and expert scrutiny" (Leckey). The transformation of intimacy has produced marriage as a more private affair, in which individuals may choose to enter and exit at will. The law will no longer stop them. However, the choices that individuals are encouraged to make are entirely another matter.

An army of experts has been deployed to tell people what choices they ought to be making. When they make the wrong choices, when their relationship flounders or fails, these private choices are subject to a new kind of public scrutiny. The experts may not be able to stop the divorce either. But, the discourse of infidelity is making these private choices a very public subject. Indeed, the experts, the books, the talk shows, with their rhetoric of epidemic and intervention, are suggestive of an expert disciplinary apparatus more akin to the early Foucault. But, this is an expert authority that is intricately tied to the "liberal aspirations of freedom, choice and identity" (Rose 1996, 97). It is part of a psychological expertise and "therapeutic ethics" that seeks "to free the self we truly are, to make it possible for us each to make a project of own our lives, to fulfill ourselves through the choices we make, and to shape our existence according to an ethics of autonomy" (Rose 1996, 97). It is a form of governance that produces the individual as free to choose and seeks to govern through the exercise of this free choice.

In the new politics of adultery, individuals are "free" to make good or bad choices, but the ethicality of these choices is prefigured. Good citizens will not have sex with other people. If they fail—if they do have sex with other people—then they are told to make certain choices and avoid others: confess, apologize and recommit to the relationship. Their citizenship will be redeemed. But, if they fail this second warning too, then their citizenship is irredeemable, and they become the unbecoming citizen. Good citizens commit themselves to the daily responsibility of working on their marriages and take all reasonable precautions by avoiding the seductions of infidelity. They protect the borders of their marriage. Bad citizens fail to do so. The choice is yours. The consequences are not.

But, borders are always permeable and foreclosure never complete. Although the politics of adultery attempts to fortify the walls around marriage by securing the private choices of individuals, the very message of the contemporary discourse of infidelity contemplates failure. The politics of adultery attempts to hold up failure as a warning to others—as a kind of modern-day public gallows where the adulterer is put on display through confessions of regret and unhappiness—but it cannot completely foreclose the alternative possibilities. Just like the covenant marriage laws create a perverse incentive to commit adultery in order to get a divorce, so too does the politics of adultery create the conditions for its own paradoxically undermining. It tells the story of infidelity over and over again. It tells of irresistible attractions and compelling seductions. These stories are a kind of pornographic text, replete with all the contradictions of such texts. Not unlike the explicit censorship discussed in the previous chapter, it speaks the very thing that it seeks to banish. The politics of adultery brings the narratives of infidelity—of illicit sexual desires, acts, and pleasures—into public discourse. While attempting to mark these desires, acts, and pleasures as unethical, the publicity of this discourse creates other interpretative possibilities. For example, if the risk of infidelity is so ubiquitous, if the seduction is so powerful, if so many women and men now engage in it, and if recovery is possible, maybe it isn't so bad after all. In other words, it is possible that the politics of adultery could further normalize adultery—the very thing that the politics is trying to undo. This is not the story that the politics of adultery is trying to tell, but the publicity of the discourse of infidelity cannot foreclose its interpretative possibility.

We also need to interrogate further the voyeuristic pleasures of the viewers or readers. The politics of adultery is intended for a viewing audience. Adulterers are held up for public viewing, shaming, and depending on their actions, redemption or denunciation. Whether it is *Dr. Phil* or *Oprah* or the entertainment gossip magazines, adultery has become a kind of commodity, to be consumed rather than practiced by the viewer. The affairs of celebrities continue to arouse fascination—everyone knows that Brad (Pitt) "cheated" on Jennifer (Aniston) with Angelina (Jolie) (although the question of whether they had sex is contested, the new politics of adultery makes it less significant). While this fascination is part and parcel of a more general obsession with the private lives of celebrities, there may be something quite unique to the voyeurism of the celebrity affair. It is a highly public performance of taboo and scandal, of the seductive and morally bankrupt lifestyles of the rich. We can judge, empathize, or envy as the mood takes us. And it may be that this is precisely what the politics of adultery leads us to do. We should not have affairs, but we can take a perverse delight in the affairs of others. It allows us to live and love a kind of vicarious adultery, while simultaneously condemning its non-ethicality. The performance of the cultural politics of adultery cannot foreclose these pleasures; indeed, it may be that the very discursive power of the politics of adultery traffics in them.

In a slightly different vein, Laura Kipnis, in her polemic on adultery, argues that the national obsession with adultery threatens to reveal a subversive truth, that is, the "toxic levels of everyday dissatisfaction, boredom, unhappiness and not-enoughness [that] are the functional norms in millions of lives and marriages" (Kipnis 2003, 190). Kipnis points to the extent to which the idea of marriage as hard work has captured our imaginations: "Yes, we all know that Good Marriages Take Work: we've been well tutored in the catechism of labour-intensive intimacy. Work, work, work" (Kipnis 2003, 18). The new politics of adultery—with its emphasis on preventing adultery through marriage as hard work—threatens to reveal just how unsatisfying marriage may be.

Indeed, many of the self-help books articulate not only work but dissatisfaction as a norm to be embraced. While the *Newsweek* exposé on women's infidelity closes with a reflection on the difficulties of marriage: "Who said being married and raising kids was easy?", others are more brutal. Iris Krasnow in her *New York Times* best-seller *Surrendering to Marriage: Husbands, Wives, and Other Imperfections* tells us not only that we have to work on our marriages, but also says of marriage: "It can be hell" (Krasnow 2001, 12). Throughout her book, as well as in her appearance on *Oprah*, Krasnow advises that we need to "accept and expect feelings of hate to be part of marriage." Her idea of surrendering to marriage is not one of a conservative surrender of wives to the will of their husbands, but rather, to the very idea that marriage is not a guarantee of happiness. "Being married happily ever after doesn't guarantee that we get to be happy. When we expect sustained happiness, we get sustained disappointment—or divorce." Indeed, for Krasnow, the key is to accept the imperfections of marriage. In so doing, she is tackling the expectations of happiness that accompanied the transformation of intimacy, and in turn the divorce revolution that followed in the wake of these unrealistic expectations. She not only echoes the idea that we need to make our marriage a project but also that we need to make *marriage* a verb. "Go on—surrender to your imperfect marriage. Admit that you love it more than you hate it. Keep your wedding promises of 'I do' and 'I will,' vows that you must, we all must, work ourselves to the bone to fulfill" (Krasnow 2001, 12). We come full circle then to the idea of the wedding vows as a work in progress; to the idea of marriage as something that you do over and over again. And to the new idea that it is not necessarily something that will make you happy.

This is hardly an unequivocally happy story about marriage. In its effort to produce a more realistic truth about marriage, it reveals its imperfections, its daily drudgery and boredom, its hatred and rage, its miseries. Indeed, it perfectly illustrates Kipnis's observation that the national obsession with marriage as hard work threatens to reveal the subversive truth about the toxicity of marriage. While trying to create less disappointment about marriage, and therefore less divorce, the message runs the risk of encouraging less marriage. If marriage is so hard, why do it? It is a message about marriage then, with multiple paradoxical interpretations.

These multiple interpretative possibilities highlight the gaps and fissures between the discourse of the new citizenship—the sexual citizen as privatized and self-disciplined in particular ways—and the subjective experiences of these projections. The effort to excavate a new cultural politics of adultery as a modality of this new sexual citizenship is not to suggest a direct relationship between ideal and experience, between icon and interiority. The articulation of new modalities in citizenship in law and culture does not guarantee that individuals will simply be reconstituted in its reflection. There are multiple locations of interpretation, resistance, contestation, and assimilation. The new politics of adultery and its modality of citizenship are bound to produce a range of unintended and contradictory consequences, with the possibilities of more or less adultery, more or less vicarious enjoyment in the adultery of others, and more or less enjoyment in the judgment of the adultery of others. Just as the politics of adultery was itself an unforeseeable consequence of the divorce revolution, so too might the contemporary obsession on self-disciplining adulterous desires produce a range of paradoxical and unforeseeable results. More self-discipline or less? Less legal surveillance or more? More adultery or less? The politics of adultery may well be transfiguring the multiple axes between self-discipline, legal regulation, and subjectivity in ways that remain unknowable. For the moment, it may only be possible to trace the parameters of its discourses and self-disciplining practices and to suggest some possibilities in its transformations of sexual citizenship.

3 Unbecoming Citizens

Welfare Queens, Deadbeat Dads, and
the Privatization of Dependency

I N *CLAUDINE* (1974), Diahann Carroll in an Oscar-nominated
performance, plays a mother of six children living in Harlem on
welfare. She falls in love with Roop Marshall, a garbage collector played by
James Earl Jones. The film tells a poignant story of their troubled relationship,
trying to find a space for their romance amidst a myriad of obstacles. Claudine struggles to raise her children, while working on the side as a maid. Her
boyfriend's presence also endangers her welfare eligibility, as surprise visits
by social workers threaten her family's already precarious economic survival.
The children present their own obstacles, with the older ones actively resisting Claudine's relationship and the younger ones unintentionally sabotaging
it in their desperate bid for fatherly attention. Roop has no desire to be a father again. He is estranged from his own biological children. But, this is not a
story of welfare fraud or sexual promiscuity or the evils of unmarried parenthood. In 1974, it was a story of the dignity of its protagonists who struggle to
survive, to raise children, and to find love. It reflected many of the political
struggles and aspirations of the moment: a welfare rights movement seeking
to establish the dignity of welfare recipients and the removal of the discrimi-
natory rules that undermined their rights, and a civil rights movement that
sought to eliminate the conditions of poverty and discrimination in which
African Americans continued to live.

The film challenged the emerging stereotypes of welfare recipients and the
creeping pathologization of African American families. Although Claudine is

a mother of six on welfare working in violation of the regime's eligibility rules and Roop is an absentee father with no relationship to his biological children, she is no welfare queen and he is no deadbeat dad. Indeed, in a heated exchange early in their relationship, the two characters play out the stereotypes that the film is intent on refuting. In response to a fairly aggressive question from Roop about how she ended up with six children at the age of 36, Claudine sarcastically retorted, "Haven't you heard about us ignorant black bitches always got to be laying up with some dude just grinding out having babies for the taxpayers to take care of. I get 30 bucks a piece for those kids. You know, I'm living like a queen on welfare." And in response to Claudine's critical questioning about not seeing his children, Roop angrily rejoins, "Well you know us black studs. No feelings. Knock 'em up, leave 'em. Heartless. Don't give a shit if the children starve." The stereotypes are already there: the welfare queen and the deadbeat dad, each pathologically deviant in their own unique way.

Claudine contested these stereotypes by telling a story about an African American mother's struggle to make ends meet, to take care of her children, and to carve out a space for a meaningful relationship. Claudine works hard to support her family—financially and emotionally. Roop is also hard-working and financially responsible. He financially supports his three biological children from whom he is estranged—although apparently, not enough for the welfare system. Roop is served for the willful neglect of his children, and his wages are garnished, which leads to an emotional breakdown of his relationship with Claudine. In his darkest hour, he simply cannot face taking on the financial burden of six more children. Despite his flight due to his fear of fatherhood commitment, Roop comes back, with more than a little help by Claudine's children. Claudine and Roop get married—or at least, they try to; their ceremony is interrupted by the police chasing Claudine's oldest son, a black activist who has just fled from a protest. In a darkly comedic ending, Roop, Claudine, and all her children are shown getting into a police van and then returning, triumphant, reconstituted as a family.

The story is one of struggle, hard work, and overcoming overwhelming obstacles: poverty, welfare, racism. Claudine's 16-year-old daughter gets pregnant. One of her adolescent sons wants to drop out of school. Claudine is faced with the prospect of her children repeating the cycles of poverty. Yet, she never gives in. Both Claudine and Roop have dreams and aspirations for a better life, and they are not afraid to fight to achieve them, despite all the obstacles in their way. In a reversal of the story that came to dominate the discourse of welfare politics, this is a story where one of the antagonists—the vil-lain—is the welfare authority. It is a white welfare worker, as symptomatic of an unfair welfare system that stands in the way of Claudine's ability to provide for her family, find love, and build her dreams. Claudine repeatedly stands up to the welfare worker, playing the game that she needs to play to maintain her benefits, while refusing to cede her dignity in the face of a system that is a constant affront to it. Roop wants to maintain his dignity by staying outside of the system, but his relationship with Claudine pulls him into its web, with no apparent benefit to Claudine, the children, or him. The film performed the injustice of the welfare system, with its obsessive bureaucratic concern over welfare fraud, putting form ahead of substance, procedure ahead of well-being, narrowing the lives and options of all who come before it.

But, the welfare stories and stereotypes that *Claudine* sought to challenge only continued to gain momentum. Through the 1970s, the welfare queen and deadbeat dad emerged as icons of bad citizenship. Welfare queens were either cheating the welfare system by working or too lazy to work. Deadbeat dads were sexually promiscuous and financially irresponsible, spawning and aban-doning leagues of children. These two new subjects were firmly entrenched within the popular imagination, as icons of failed citizenship and the disas-trous if brief experiment with the social welfare state. The welfare queen and the deadbeat dad became the symbols of all that had gone wrong with the American welfare state and as responsible for a broad range of social harms, from poverty and poor educational prospects to delinquency, substance abuse, and crime. Indeed, these subjects became the focal points in the attack on and eventual dismantling of welfare and in the production of a new ideal citizen. Their demonization created a strong social consensus on the need to reform welfare to break chronic dependency and to remake these outlaws into legitimate citizens. These unbecoming citizens required a new regula-tory regime to correct their deviant behavior, to break the cycle of welfare dependency, and to remake these subjects into self-reliant market actors and nuclear family members who could provide for their dependents.

By the time *Claudine* was released on DVD in 2003, new interpretative narratives were available. The ensuing years witnessed a dismantling of the welfare state. *Claudine* could now be seen as telling a story about the bad old days before welfare reform, where an overbearing bureaucracy under-mined individual initiative and family formation. It could be told through the lens of the need for welfare reform and as a gesture toward the success of this reform in the ensuing years. Under the old regime, Claudine's hard work was punished rather than rewarded. Her efforts to take responsibility for her children were undermined by intrusive welfare workers and an unresponsive welfare regime. Even her efforts toward forming a nuclear family and providing her children with a father were stymied by the misdirected surveillance of her intimate sexual relationships. Everything in the welfare regime encouraged responsible mothers like Claudine and hard-working potential fathers like Roop away from hard work and family formation. In this retold story of then, *Claudine* can be mapped onto the contested stories of welfare reform in America: neo-liberals, who in the intervening years have successfully pushed for workfare and market self-reliance in welfare reform, and neo-conservatives, who have successfully pushed for marriage promotion and responsible fatherhood.

This chapter engages with these contested stories of welfare reform and sexual citizenship in America. The first part looks at the contested stories of unbecoming citizens in the mainstream political discourses that animate welfare reform. It explores the ways in which neo-liberal and neo-conservative discourses produced the welfare queen and the deadbeat dad through the lens of their failure to abide by the privatized and self-disciplining codes of belonging, with particularly racialized and gendered narratives. These cultural icons were deployed by an ascending conservative political movement to assist in the dismantling of the limited American welfare state and in the articulation of new modalities of citizenship (Williams 1996). The welfare queen and the deadbeat dad were foils against which new and contested models of good citizenship could be advanced.[1] Their failure to conduct themselves according to the codes of good citizenship could justify the highly coercive approaches deployed against these unbecoming subjects, in the hopes of remaking them as appropriate self-disciplining citizens (Rose 2000). It exemplifies the authoritarian deployment of the rhetoric of self-governance; in the face of the failure of self-discipline, "the capacity for autonomous conduct can be developed only through compulsion, through the imposition of more or less extended periods of discipline"(Hindness 2001).

The second part shifts to the sphere of black popular culture and explores some of the ways in which these icons of failed citizenship continue to cast a long shadow on the cultural production of good citizens, particularly for African Americans. While the racialized images of African Americans as welfare queens and deadbeat dads are explicitly contested within this sphere, their legacy endures. From the familial controversies around hip-hop artists Lauryn Hill and P. Diddy to films such as *Baby Boy* and *Disappearing Acts*, the shadow of the welfare queen and the deadbeat dad looms large in the process of becoming and unbecoming citizens for the African American subject. Representations within black popular culture are engaging with a similar set of challenges to African American sexual citizenship, including the anxieties produced by relatively low marriage rates and relatively high single parenthood rates. Despite their explicit attempt to tell counter hegemonic narratives, these representations continue to bump up against the toxic legacy of the political attack of welfare queens and deadbeat dads. Sexual citizenship, in many of these narratives, can only be obtained through their disavowal in favor of a privatized and highly self-disciplined modality of belonging.

Welfare Queens, Social Welfare, and the New Sexual Citizen

African American women have never been held out in popular discourse as model citizens. Like all African Americans, their subjectivity is always perilously close to outlaw status (Austin 1994; Roberts 1996). But the arrival of the welfare queen in political and popular discourse marked a distinct assault on the citizenship of poor black women in America. It marked a new modality of unbecoming citizenship that built upon and reconfigured many racialized stereotypes long deployed against black women. The "welfare queen" arrived on the political scene with the "discovery" of a welfare crisis.

In the 1960s, the size and cost of AFDC soared.[2] The program grew from 3.5 million recipients in 1961 to 11 million in 1971 (Mink 1998, 51–52). The composition of welfare recipients changed significantly, as previously excluded single mothers—particularly, African American and never-married women—became entitled to AFDC (Brito 1999, 424; Handler 1987/1988, 488). Previously, the states had discretion under the ADC program (Aid to Dependent Children enacted in 1911, the precursor to AFDC, Aid to Families with Dependent Children, enacted in 1935) to set their own eligibility criteria, which were often used to exclude black mothers on "moral" grounds. Through the 1960s, due in part to the civil rights and the welfare rights movements, the number of black women receiving welfare benefits increased (Gillens 1999; Katz 2001; Williams 1996). While the number of black single mothers receiving AFDC has never exceeded 40 percent, their increased presence, alongside an apparent explosion in the size and costs of welfare, produced single black mothers as the new face of welfare.

The racialization of welfare was well underway in the conservative political discourse of the 1960s (Williams 1996) and was given further support with the publication of Daniel Patrick Moynihan's *Report on the Black Family* in 1965 tying poverty to the breakdown of the African American family. But, the term "welfare queen" was born in the 1970s with Ronald Reagan's infamous attacks on welfare fraud. In response to a story of a woman who had been convicted of $8,000 welfare fraud, Reagan repeatedly stated that "she had eighty names, thirty addresses, twelve Social Security cards" and that she drove her Cadillac to pick up her welfare check. While initially produced by the conservative attack on welfare fraud, her identity began to crystallize in political rhetoric and media representations as everything that was wrong with welfare dependency, pulling together a series of racial stereotypes. She was not simply a fraud, she was lazy, promiscuous, calculating, immoral. As Lisa Crooms describes: "The image of the Welfare Queen [is] that of a poor black mother who first became pregnant as a teenager. Her sexual irresponsibility resulted in her dropping out of high school and joining AFDC rolls. Rather than marry the child's father and make the best of the situation, she chose to remain single, to collect AFDC and to have more children by different fathers" (Crooms 1995, 622).

This image of welfare, alongside attention to increased expenditures, produced a political truth that welfare was "in crisis." Conservatives began a concerted and sustained attack on welfare dependency, with the welfare queen as its poster child. Fiscal and social conservatives shared a concern about moral hazard, that is, the idea that the availability of AFDC to poor single mothers reduced their incentives to avoid the costs of single motherhood and thereby created more dependents (McCluskey 2003, 807–808). It was the attack on welfare as undermining personal responsibility that helped to unite these divergent conservative factions (Williams 1996). But, a closer look at the discourses of citizenship reveal that neo-liberals and neo-conservatives, or fiscal and social conservatives, often diverged in their analysis of and prescriptions for the ills of welfare dependency. They had very different visions of good citizenship and, in turn, of how the welfare queen was a failed citizen.

One of the most influential voices in the attack on welfare was Charles Murray, who argued that the welfare state created an underclass of chronic welfare dependency (Murray 1984). According to Murray, the availability of welfare created perverse short-term economic incentives. Young women were no longer forced to shoulder the actual economic costs of bearing children out of wedlock. Rather, they might actually be financially better off having the children and going on welfare than not having children and remaining in low-paying employment. Murray's analysis was economic in nature and his prescription libertarian. The problem of welfare dependency could only be solved by abolishing welfare altogether. His work was influential well beyond his libertarian conclusion, with many of his ideas adopted by fiscal and social conservatives alike, deployed to promote rather different visions of welfare reform.

The neo-liberal strategy for welfare reform that animated the reforms of the 1970s and 1980s was heavily influenced by Murray's concern with reversing escalating costs of social welfare, eliminating moral hazard through marketized incentives and reconstituting welfare dependents into self-reliant market citizens. Welfare recipients had to be transformed into workers, and, in particular, single mothers dependent on welfare had to be transformed into employable self-sufficient workers within the paid labor force.[3] The citizenship failure of the welfare queen was cast in market terms: She was a bad citizen because she was choosing to not work, to not become economically self-reliant. It was an approach to welfare reform that envisioned the welfare queen in classic neo-liberal terms, albeit with a racialized twist. As Crooms describes, it was both informed by the assumption that poor black single mothers "lacked a conventional work ethic," although they were nonetheless "economically rational, treat[ing] pregnancy and childbirth as income-generating activities" (Crooms 2001, 104). The welfare queen was cast as a rational decision maker, who would make choices that maximized her self-interest. According to Murray's analysis of moral hazard, the existing structure of welfare made having children and going on welfare the rational and self-interest maximizing choice. These perverse incentives needed to be removed, so that the welfare queen would actually bear the full economic burden of her choices. As a rational, self-interest maximizer, she would then make different decisions; she would begin to self-discipline according to the dictates of the market.

Notwithstanding the discourse of the market citizen—of economic incentives, risk management, and individual self-reliance—the neo-liberal strategy did not disavow state regulation. The citizenship project of reconstituting dependent welfare mothers into self-reliant workers was one that involved extensive intervention into the intimate lives of its subjects and extensive intervention in the labor market. Initially, the strategies included a range of educational and training programs intended to make these women employable. Over time, however, the primary emphasis shifted from training to workfare, as women were required to participate in low-paying employment as a condition for welfare eligibility through increasingly coercive means. The moral hazard of welfare dependency—women having children and going on welfare instead of staying in the low-paying employment—would thereby be removed. Individual women would be forced to shoulder the costs of their high risk lifestyle, and low-paid work would be unavoidable. The new vision of good citizenship—self-reliant individual risk managers—rendered women's gendered roles all but invisible. Their dependency, once cast as a natural feature of their status as mothers, was reframed as a pathological dependency that needed to be fixed (Fraser & Gordon 1994). In this vision, the privatization of citizenship involved transferring responsibility for financial support from the state to the individual. It marked a transformation from social citizenship to market citizenship.

A very different vision of citizenship and the welfare queen was developed by social conservatives, whose views came to influence later rounds of welfare reform. For social conservatives, single mothers on welfare were responsible for spiraling rates of illegitimacy, which is in turn said to be America's single most devastating social problem (see for example, Whitehead 1993). The central goal of welfare reform is accordingly the reduction of illegitimacy by preventing nonmarital (particularly teenage) births and promoting marriage. Rather than transforming single mothers into employable market citizens, social conservatives seek to prevent single motherhood in the first place.[4] Any incentive in the welfare system to become single mothers needed to be removed.

But, social conservatives went beyond the neo-liberal idea of correcting the market distortion that had resulted from state intervention. It was not simply a matter of women getting jobs. Rather, they needed to be encouraged to not have children outside of marriage. The first line of defense should be sexual abstinence programs, discouraging women from having nonmarital sex. These programs are intended to intervene in women's intimate lives and assist them in making "better" choices. If abstinence fails, then women should be encouraged to marry the fathers of their children. Social conservative discourse, in accordance with its emphasis on rearticulating the traditional family and traditional gender norms therein, thus seeks to strengthen marriage and the two-parent family. The solution to moral hazard thus lies not in economic incentives but in moral regulation (McCluskey 2003, 823–825).

In this approach, the welfare queen is a failed citizen because she fails to sexually self-discipline, to choose marriage and to adopt appropriate gender roles as wife and mother within a traditional family. She is constructed through a discourse that pathologizes the black family: The failure of black women to marry means that they are responsible not only for their own poverty and that of their children, but for the multiple social and economic harms of the black community: delinquency, crime, drug addiction, violence. The welfare queen is responsible for raising generations of children who will simply reproduce the same pathologies and cycles of poverty, welfare dependency, crime, and societal dysfunction. In contrast to the neo-liberal vision, the welfare queen is not a rational decision maker. She makes bad decisions. She chooses to have premarital sex, to have children outside of marriage, and to not marry the father of her children. These are not only bad economic choices; they are bad *moral* choices. The citizenship failure of the welfare queen is thus cast in explicitly moral terms. She must be protected from her own moral failings. It is, moreover, a failed citizenship that is heavily sexualized. She is incapable of sexual control. She cannot be trusted to self-discipline. Deploying a series of racialized stereotypes of black women's sexuality, she is promiscuous, dangerous, seductive, out of control. To become a good citizen, her sexuality must be disciplined, harnessed, redirected to an appropriate site, namely, marriage.

Good citizenship requires a privatization of her dependency. But, the privatization of citizenship assumes a very different meaning than in the neo-liberal vision. In this social conservative approach, her financial dependency is to be transferred from the state to the family. Here, privatization marks a transformation from social citizenship to familialized citizenship. It is a form of privatization, however, that requires more than just making black men pay child support—it requires a restructuring of the black family. Unlike the neo-liberal approach to welfare reform that focused on the woman herself trying to remake her into an employable citizen, the social conservative approach implicitly invokes the absent father. If the welfare queen is to marry her way out of poverty and welfare dependency, she must have someone to marry—and that someone is supposed to be the father of her children. Ideally, she would marry before having children (sexual abstinence). If that fails, the objective is to get her to marry after the fact.

The promotion of marriage for women is intricately linked to the promotion of responsible fatherhood for men. Women need to be sold on the benefits of marriage and the two-parent family, while men need to be taught how to assume the role of the father within this family. The social conservative approach becomes an effort to redress both sides of the allegedly dysfunctional black family—matriarchal women who do not value the potential contribution of fathers and irresponsible men who do not know how to become fathers.

Correcting all these citizenship failures requires a heavy hand. A social conservative approach to welfare reform does not shy away from government intervention in the intimate lives of its citizens. For example, Lawrence Mead, an influential advocate of a new paternalism in welfare policy, has argued that the poor cannot be assumed to maximize their own self-interest or that of society (Mead 1997).[5] They must be made to do so through government direction and close supervision (Mead 1997, 2). In this understanding, citizenship cannot simply be left to the market, it must be cultivated by the state; individuals must be taught to self-discipline. It is illustrative of a different deployment of the ideas of self-governance than those seen in the politics of adultery discussed in Chapter 2. Here, the failure of individuals to self-discipline is deployed to justify a more coercive regulatory approach. As Nicholas Rose has argued in relation to welfare reforms in the United Kingdom: "[t]hose who refuse to become responsible and govern themselves ethically have also refused the offer to become members of our moral community. Hence, for them, harsh measures are entirely appropriate" (Rose 2000, 1407). The failure to abide by the appropriate code of work and family is deployed to justify a far more interventionist and coercive approach that aims to instill the norms of self-discipline and remake the outlier into the good citizen.

Federal Legislative Initiatives: From Fiscal to Social Conservative
The initial federal efforts to reform welfare and break the cycle of welfare dependency in the 1970s were animated by a neo-liberal vision of citizenship and its goal of reintegrating welfare recipients into the labor market. This new emphasis on work represented a shift in official welfare policy. From its inception in 1935 until the late 1960s, AFDC expected eligible single mothers with young children to stay home to provide child care.[6]

Beginning in the 1960s, however, attitudes about women's roles began to change with the dramatic increase in women's labor market participation.

Some public policy reformers began to argue that mothers on welfare should similarly be expected to work. Work requirements were first established with the 1967 Work Incentive Program, known as WIN (Social Security Amendment Act, 1967). In 1971, the program was replaced by WIN II, which introduced somewhat harsher work requirements and strengthened sanctions for noncompliance. While WIN had initially been voluntary for women, WIN II required that women with children over the age of 6 years participate in job training or employment programs in order to qualify for AFDC (Handler 1987/1988, 490). The amendments also shifted the focus from education and training to placement in entry-level programs. Neither WIN nor WIN II was particularly successful in reducing welfare dependency. In 1981, the Reagan administration amended welfare law to allow states to require welfare recipients to participate in Community Work Experience (CWEP), effectively a workfare program that would require recipients to work for public agencies in order to qualify for assistance (Diller 1998). The amendments also allowed a number of states to experiment with work-relief programs.

These work requirements reflected an emerging fiscal conservative vision of welfare reform that came to inform federal initiatives. The objective of these programs was to transform AFDC into a temporary assistance program that focused on rehabilitation through job training and employment. Welfare mothers whose dependency was once seen as a natural product of their roles as child care providers were being reconstituted as employable market citizens. This fiscal conservative impulse culminated in the Family Support Act of 1988, which aimed to integrate welfare recipients into the workforce by mandating that single mothers work or train for work as a condition of eligibility.

The central piece of this strategy was the Job Opportunities and Basic Skills program (JOBS) which required welfare recipients to work while also offering opportunities for education, job training, skills development, and child care. Recipients with children under the age of 3 were exempt from JOBS. The Family Support Act was designed to remake welfare dependents into responsible citizens through these work programs. As Representative Slathry stated in support of the bill: "The American taxpayer should be proud of this welfare reform legislation. It makes use of Federal funds by providing welfare recipients with the incentive to work and the education, training and support services needed to help them regain their place in society as productive, taxpaying citizens" (House Debates, Sept. 30, 1988).

In 1996, Congress passed the Personal Responsibility and Work Opportunity Reconciliation Act (PRWORA). The legislation, famously described by President Clinton as "ending welfare as we know it," ended the federal entitlement to AFDC and replaced it with block grants to the states known as Temporary Assistance to Needy Families (TANF). TANF established a five-year lifetime limit on welfare assistance and significantly toughened work requirements. Parents receiving assistance were required to engage in work after receiving benefits for no more than 24 months. The legislation gave states broad discretion in deciding how to spend the block grant, provided that the expenditures promoted any of the four purposes of the law. States could establish their own eligibility rules for assistance. They would, however, have to spend a certain percentage of state money for benefits and services for "needy families" with children, and they had to meet a set of work and participation rate requirements to avoid fiscal penalties. Most states developed time-limited assistance programs with an emphasis on work-related requirements. Many educational opportunities made available under federal welfare law were eliminated as TANF came to emphasize work over training (Diller 1998; Katz 2001, 326).

The work-first emphasis of PRWORA continued to promote the neo-liberal model of market citizenship. Government incentives believed to undermine individual self-sufficiency were removed, single mothers were reconstituted as employable citizens like any other, and the market was cast as the solution to welfare dependency (Katz 2001, 324–325). However, much of the political rhetoric around PRWORA—the stated objectives, the congressional findings, and the congressional debates—simultaneously reflected a social conservative vision of familial citizenship. Three of the four main objectives of TANF involve the promotion of traditional families.[7] PRWORA included a number of provisions designed to promote this social conservative vision of the traditional family. For example, the legislation included an illegitimacy bonus to states that show the greatest decline in out of wedlock births without an increase in abortion rates. It allocated $50 million a year for five years in block grants to states for abstinence-only education programs (PRWORA,§ 103).

These sexual abstinence programs were specifically defined in PRWORA as educational programs that teach the social, psychological, and health benefits of abstinence and the harms of sexual activity out of wedlock, including pregnancy, sexually transmitted diseases, and psychological harms (see § 710(b)(2)). It included teaching that "mutually faithful monogamous relationship in the context of marriage is the expected standard of human sexual activity." PRWORA also denied federal assistance to some minor parents. States are effectively precluded from spending TANF funds to provide assistance to unmarried, minor, custodial parents who do not participate in school or training rules and who do not live with a parent, guardian, or other relatives (Title 1, § 408(a)(5)). These various provisions in PRWORA reflect more of a social conservative vision of citizenship. Good citizenship involves marriage and two-parent families. Bad citizenship is not simply the failure to work but also nonmarital sex and illegitimacy.

PRWORA embraced both a neo-liberal emphasis on work and a social conservative emphasis on family as the solution to welfare dependency. As Anna Marie Smith has described, the legislation "expresses a remarkable hybrid discourse: it appropriates both the religious rights' moralistic emphasis on patriarchal and heterosexist 'family' values and the neo-conservative emphasis on downsizing government and exposing the impoverished individual to the corrective rigors of the market" (Katz 2001, 326; Smith 2001). Fiscal and social conservatives were able to unite under the sign of personal responsibility, yet their respective visions were measurably different. In the fiscal conservative vision, personal responsibility was cast in economic terms. Welfare queens were expected to transcend their economic dependence by becoming self-reliant market citizens. The problem was that the welfare state had undermined individual initiative and self-reliance, and the solution lay in restoring that initiative and allowing women to become completely self-sufficient. By contrast, in the social conservative vision, personal responsibility was cast in moral terms. Welfare queens were expected to modify their sexual and familial behavior. They were to avoid out-of-wedlock pregnancies, preferably by avoiding premarital sex and choosing marriage. The problem was that the welfare state had undermined the traditional family; the solution, then, lay in its restoration.

The social conservative vision of welfare reform and citizenship has become more evident in the recent debates surrounding the reauthorization of TANF.[8] Many believed that the family formation objectives of PRWORA had not been realized, and that it was time to put the promotion of marriage at the top of the reauthorization agenda (Horn 2001; Rector 2001).[9]

After a contentious multiyear battle in which several TANF reauthorization bills were debated by the Bush administration, the Senate, and the House, the Deficit Reduction Act of 2005 reauthorizing TANF through to

2010 was signed by President Bush on February 8, 2006. The TANF reauthorization provisions included the Healthy Marriage Promotion and Responsible Fatherhood Program, which allocates $150 million per fiscal year to
be spent on healthy marriage and responsibility fatherhood programs. The
provisions define "healthy marriage activities" as including a broad range
of programs promoting the value of marriage and marriage skills, including
public advertising campaigns, high school education, and premarital training courses as well as marriage enhancement and divorce reduction courses
and marriage mentoring for married couples (Deficit Reduction Act of 2005,
§ 7103(a)(2)(iii)). The idea underlying the new Healthy Marriage Promotion
program is that marriage is a way out of poverty and welfare dependency.
It can reduce the number of women who have children out of wedlock and
thereby reduce the number who turn to state assistance.

While these programs could come to have a highly coercive dimension—
they could become mandatory for women to receive welfare benefits—there
is a shift to a somewhat more self-disciplining discourse on welfare reform.
The idea is that these women have failed in the project of self-governance and
must be taught how to do so. Marriage promotion, through various forms of
education, counseling, and mentoring, is designed to teach these women to
become marriageable; it is training in the conduct of marriage. It is a form of
state-sponsored self-help, directed to the specifics of their citizenship failure,
namely, their sexual, familial, and relational conduct. It is also a highly coercive form of self-help: Failure to participate in the programs could result in a
termination of already limited benefits. These programs exemplify how self-
governance can be promoted in highly authoritarian ways and how law continues to play a significant role. Further, the failure to self-discipline—now in
the face of government programs specifically intended to help these women
remake themselves into good citizens—only further constitutes the single
mother on welfare as an unbecoming citizen.

This twist in the solution for welfare dependency is leading to a more general
promotion of marriage for welfare and non-welfare recipients alike. Many of
the marriage promotion programs do not require that the funds be specifically
directed towards TANF recipients or low-income populations. Rather, in this
welfarization of family law the welfare queen has been deployed as the poster
child for the evils of all forms of non-marriage—regardless of income (Brito
1999). The welfare queen becomes an icon not only for the dismantling of welfare, but also for a more general articulation of good—marital—citizenship.

The fiscal conservatism of earlier welfare reform has not disappeared. The basic structure of TANF remains intact, with its bloc grants, five-year entitlement limits, and work requirements. The emphasis on transforming welfare dependents into self-employed market citizens remains a central objective. The new social conservative emphasis on family formation is a supplement to the earlier fiscal conservative goals of individual self-sufficiency. In many respects, the initiatives are complementary. Fiscal conservatism is not so much opposed to shifting dependency from state to two-parent, opposite-sex family as it is agnostic. Its primary goal is to reduce welfare dependency, and its primary strategy is to increase the self-sufficiency of welfare dependents through an emphasis on market work. Similarly, social conservatism is not opposed to individual self-reliance and market work. Rather, it seeks to address what it views to be the cause of chronic welfare dependency—namely, illegitimacy and the decline of the traditional family.

There are also some significant differences between the neo-liberal and social conservative visions of citizenship. For fiscal conservatives, citizenship failure can be redressed through the market. By ensuring that women bear the costs of their decisions, they will make rational and self-interest maximizing decisions: they will delay childbirth; they will work; they will, in other words, self-discipline through the market. For social conservatives, citizenship failure requires state intervention. Their sexual and familial deviance is such that they cannot be trusted to make the right decisions. Nor can the market be assured to provide the self-discipline that these women need. The state must closely supervise and teach these women to become self-governing through sexual and familial morality. However, this difference is not quite as striking in practice as in principle. The fiscal conservative goal of reconstituting women into market citizens is no laissez-faire affair but requires considerable regulation. From training programs to workfare, more state intervention is required to correct past state intervention. Both neo-liberals and social conservatives seek to secure the self-governance of their citizens through various modes of regulation.

At a deeper level, there are contradictions between the visions of citizenship. For neo-liberals, market citizenship is cast in largely degendered terms: All good citizens must be self-reliant and must be responsible for financially supporting their children. Mothers, like fathers, must become self-reliant market citizens. For social conservatives, good citizenship is cast in more familial and gendered terms. Women are mothers, and their financial dependency should be directed toward a male breadwinner in a marital unit. Both seek to privatize and self-discipline citizenship, but their understanding of each diverges. For neo-liberals, privatization lies in the market, with its self-disciplinary codes, whereas for social conservatives, the private lies in the family and women must be taught to redirect their dependency and assume their gendered role therein.

Deadbeat Dads, Child Support, and the New Sexual Citizen

When the deadbeat dad first arrived on the scene, he was a creation of the divorce revolution. With the dramatic increase in divorce rates that accompanied no-fault divorce in the late 1960s and early 1970s, many women found themselves and their children economically impoverished following the breakdown of their marriages. These newly divorced women and their children presented a new claim on the welfare system—they had been married, they had children, they were appropriately dependent on their husbands, and then, they found themselves abandoned without financial support in the face of the divorce revolution. Like the widowed "deserving poor" of the past, these women similarly found themselves in financial need through no apparent moral wrongdoing of their own.

Rather than attacking these women for their welfare claims, a new political discourse began to emerge in the 1970s focusing on the culpability of the men who had abandoned them. The discursive power of this claim only intensified through the 1980s with the publication of various research studies of the economic impact of divorce. Lenore Weitzman's highly influential book, *The Divorce Revolution*, produced an alarming and much-cited statistic: One year after divorce, men experienced a 42 percent increase in their standard of living, while women and children experienced a 73 percent decrease (Weitzman 1985). While subsequent studies failed to substantiate these extreme numbers, many studies did illustrate a significant gender disparity in the economic consequences of divorce, with women and children bearing a disproportionate burden. These studies helped to produce the cultural image of the deadbeat dad—the selfish father who cavalierly abandons his children, buying sports cars and other luxury items while his children suffer.

The deadbeat dad was a very particular kind of bad citizen. Quite unlike the welfare queen, he was economically self-reliant and therefore already a market citizen. His citizenship failure lay in not supporting his dependents and the resulting shift of his financial responsibility onto the American tax-payer. He was an unbecoming citizen because he was not assuming his famil-ial responsibilities; and he was not incurring the costs of his own decisions. Further, the deadbeat dad was not targeted because he was responsible for the poverty of the welfare queen. Rather, he was targeted because he was respon-sible for the poverty of a more "worthy" class of dependents: divorced women and their children—or more specifically, white, previously middle-class and married women and their children.

This vision of the deadbeat dad as a market citizen who had failed in his familial responsibilities shaped the ensuing political responses. Beginning in the 1970s, an apparent consensus began to emerge from politicians of all stripes that parents should be responsible for supporting their children (Chambers 1995, 2588). Liberals and conservatives agreed that it was time to get tough on parents who tried to evade their obligations. Welfare dependency and state spending could be dramatically reduced by forcing fathers to take financial responsibility for their children following marriage breakdown. These fathers could afford to pay for their children—they were already self-reliant market citizens—all the state had to do was make them do so. Their citizenship fail-ure could be corrected and the cost of supporting dependents shifted to indi-vidual fathers who would have to bear the real costs of their lifestyle decision.

Social conservatives produced a very different understanding of father-hood, family, and citizenship. While also promoting personal responsibility, a social conservative vision of good citizenship is tied to rearticulating the traditional family. Deadbeat dads are bad citizens not simply because they have failed to assume the costs of their choices, but because they have made bad choices—they have abandoned their children through separation and divorce, producing an epidemic of single parenting and its resulting social harms. The citizenship failure of these fathers lies in their failure to live up to the moral standards of the traditional patriarchal family. Social conservatives would rather prevent fathers from becoming deadbeat in the first place. Mar-riage should be encouraged, and divorce should be discouraged, so that tra-ditional families can remain intact (Popenoe 1996, 222–223). Fathers must be more involved in the lives of their children not after a divorce, but during the marriage (Blankenhorn 1995; Horn et al. 1999). Fathers should be involved not only in financial provision but also as stable male role models for their chil-dren. Since child poverty and welfare dependency, alongside crime and other high-risk behaviors, are seen as caused by single-parent families, the solution is therefore to promote a traditional two-parent, marital family (Blankenhorn 1995; Popenoe 1996). Fatherhood, personal responsibility, and good citizenship are cast in explicitly moral terms—it is about rearticulating traditional gender roles within a traditional two-parent family as a way of reversing the moral decline of the family (Gavanas 2004).

This social conservative vision was not particularly influential in the reforms of the 1970s and 1980s. Reversing the trend toward no-fault divorce at the moment of its burgeoning was neither popular nor jurisdictionally possible at the level of federal politics. Social conservatives instead seemed to join in the neo-liberal chorus for more personal responsibility, through the enforcement of child support laws, notwithstanding a deeper ideological rift in their visions.

It is a vision of fatherhood and citizenship that does, however, come into its own in the 1990s and 2000s. Several material and discursive shifts occurred that allowed this vision to make gains. First, as tougher child support laws were put into place to crack down on noncustodial fathers, it became apparent that some fathers actually could not afford to pay. Many of these fathers, it turned out, were not self-reliant market citizens but actually could not afford to pay child support. Alongside an emergent fathers' rights movement that opposed the demonization of men and emphasized the importance of fathers in the lives of their children a discourse began to emerge that focused on remaking these men into self-reliant market citizens and involved, responsible fathers. Second, and equally important, the vision of the deadbeat dad was broadened to include the never-married dad, the men who fathered the children of the single women on welfare—which in the racialized stereotypes of the world of welfare meant African American men.

With this shift to the never-married African American father, and its whirlwind of stereotypes from sexual promiscuity and irresponsibility to violence and criminality, a whole new range of remedial possibilities began to emerge under the banner of promoting responsible fatherhood. Neo-liberals sought to correct the citizenship failure of these fathers in market terms: These fathers needed jobs. Social conservatives, in contrast, sought to transform this father into a family citizen, capable of assuming his position at the helm of the traditional family. According to social conservatives, these failed fathers could be remade into good citizens through marriage and appropriately gendered parenting training.

As with the welfare queen, both neo-liberal and social conservative approaches to the deadbeat dad seek to privatize citizenship; fathers and not the state should be supporting their children (Orloff & Monson 2002, 83). There is, however, a different emphasis in how to achieve this privatization. For the neo-liberal, privatization is understood in exclusively financial terms. The never-married father must be made capable of supporting his children through employment. Social conservatives, by contrast, seek to privatize citizenship through the rearticulation of the traditional family—privatization is understood in both financial and familial terms. They agree that fathers should financially support their children. But divorced fathers should not have divorced, and never-married fathers should get married. The privatization of financial responsibility must occur within the traditional two-parent family, where fathers must also become the moral leaders, providing appropriate gender role models for their children. These two approaches correspond to the two approaches within the responsible fatherhood movement that emerged in the 1990s: the fragile family approach that emphasizes making fathers employable and thereby capable of supporting their children and the pro-marriage approach that emphasizes making fathers marry the mothers of their children.

Legislative Initiatives: From Fiscal to Social, and Deadbeat Dad to Ir/Responsible Fatherhood

Initial federal efforts to strengthen child support enforcement were shaped by this neo-liberal vision of citizenship, with its goal of reducing federal spending on welfare (Krause 1990) and its understanding of deadbeat dads as economically self-sufficient market citizens who needed to be made to support their dependent children. In 1974, the federal government enacted the Child Support Act, creating Title IV-D of the Social Security Act, with a federal Office of Child Support Enforcement and requiring states receiving AFDC funds to establish child support offices to assist parents in establishing and enforcing child support obligations (Child Support Act, 1974). Title IV-D programs included locating absent parents, establishing paternity, and obtaining and enforcing child support orders. Custodial AFDC parents were required to assign their right to collect child support payments to the state, and child support collected on behalf of AFDC families was used to reimburse governments for welfare benefits paid to the family.

The primary goal of the Child Support Act was to reduce the federal government's spending on AFDC and thereby privatize the costs of dependency:

"the more child support collected, the less the cost of AFDC to the federal government"(Krause 1990; Morgan 1999, 708). This privatization of the costs of dependency was cast in the neo-liberal language of risk management and market citizenship, deploying good citizens to produce and shame bad ones. In the words of Senator Long, a leading sponsor of the legislation:

> Should our welfare system be made to support the children whose father cavalierly abandons them—or chooses not to marry the mother in the first place? Is it fair to ask the American taxpayer—who works hard to support his own family and to carry his own burden—to carry the burden of the deserting father as well? Perhaps we cannot stop the father from abandoning his children, but we can certainly improve the system by obtaining child support from him and thereby place the burden of caring for his children on his own shoulders where it belongs. We can—and we must—take the financial reward out of desertion. (Senator Long, as quoted in Harris at 634, 118 Cong. Rec. 8271 (1972))

Good citizens—the employed American taxpayer—should not be asked to shoulder the costs of decisions made by deadbeat fathers. Those costs needed to be imposed on individual fathers, and the financial incentive for abandonment would thereby be removed. The deadbeat father—the bad citizen—is understood in classic neo-liberal terms: a self-interested individual who makes rational, self-interest maximizing choices after assessing the costs and benefits. The problem with the old welfare regime was that the actual costs of supporting children were not imposed on this father. He therefore was able to make a self-interest maximizing decision and escape these costs. In the new regime, however, he may still decide to leave, but he cannot escape the costs. Financial responsibility—the hallmark of new good citizenship—is thereby ensured.

Despite the neo-liberal discourse of risk management and market citizenship, the privatization of public welfare in the new regime was to be accomplished through extensive government regulation. Shifting the costs from the public to the private sphere—from AFDC to individual fathers—required a broad regulatory network of both financial obligations and enforcement mechanisms. The project of reconstituting deadbeat dads into good citizens required an extensive intervention into the intimate lives of its subjects. As the legislative initiatives intensified, it became more readily apparent that this privatization of dependency would require more and more regulatory surveillance and control.

While the original program was limited to AFDC families, in 1984 Congress expanded the program to include all families eligible for child support with the Child Support Enforcement Amendment. Congress also broadened the scope of the law to include automatic wage withholding for overdue child support payments, impositions of liens against the property of defaulting parents, and the interception of federal and state tax refunds. The amendments further required states to develop advisory guidelines that could be used by courts in setting child support awards.

In 1988, Congress once again expanded the scope of its child support programs. The Family Support Act of 1988 required that all states implement mandatory presumptive child support guidelines by 1994. The legislation also created the U.S. Commission on Interstate Child Support to consider how the child support system could be further improved. The act provided for more immediate wage withholding, as well as a new focus on establishing paternity.

This increasing interest in establishing the paternity of children born out of wedlock signaled a shift in the identity of the deadbeat dad and marked the beginning of an effort to more explicitly relate him to the welfare queen. Women on welfare who had children out of wedlock were now being made to participate in the identification of the biological fathers of their children, in order to allow the state to broaden its effort to privatize the costs of dependency. Deadbeat dads were no longer only fathers who abandoned their children on divorce; rather, the category was being expanded to include fathers who never assumed responsibility for them in the first place. Rather than simply attempting to impose the costs of the decision to divorce on fathers, this expansion of the reach of child support would now also attempt to impose the costs of sex outside of marriage onto men.

With each expansion of the child support obligation and the enforcement mechanisms, the federal government attempted to ensure that the actual costs of supporting dependents were transferred to individual fathers. And with each expansion, the deadbeat father was further demonized. Each expansion meant that the one before had not been enough, that deadbeat fathers were continuing to evade their responsibility. Not only were they willing to violate the moral obligation to support their children, but now they were willing to violate an actual legal obligation as well. The deadbeat father would therefore have to be forced to incur the costs through increasingly coercive mechanisms. Indeed, a slightly different transformation was at work here. Deadbeat fathers were no longer simply failed citizens—now they were reconstituted as actual outlaws.

In 1992, Congress passed the Child Support Recovery Act intended to address problems associated with interstate child support enforcement by imposing criminal sanctions on noncustodial parents who willfully fail to pay child support obligations owed to a child living in another state. Criminalizing the evasion of child support represented a continuation of federal efforts to shift the cost of raising children from the federal government to parents through highly interventionist regulation. It also represented a significant development in the discursive production of the deadbeat bad from bad citizen to potential outlaw. Fathers who continued to evade their financial responsibilities were reconstituted as outlaws through the imposition of criminal sanctions.

In 1996, Congress passed the Personal Responsibility and Work Opportunity Reconciliation Act (PRWORA), discussed above, which again sought to intensify child support enforcement as part of welfare restructuring. To qualify for a block grant, a state must operate a Title IV-D child support enforcement program. Title III sets the new child support enforcement measures that states must implement to maintain eligibility, which included an expansion of paternity establishment, enhanced access to information and mass data collection, and increased enforcement remedies. The paternity provisions were once again designed to bring a larger number of potential parents within the scope of private child support obligations, while enhanced access to information, data systems, and remedies provide public mechanisms to enforce these private obligations. The debates on the child support provisions continued the theme of cracking down on deadbeat dads, enforcing personal responsibility, and saving money. Senator DeWine stated, for example, that the bill would strengthen the ability of states "to go after the delinquent and deadbeat parents":

> It is absolutely essential that we strengthen the ethic of personal responsibility in this way. We need to make it absolutely clear—America demands that parents be responsible for their children. Deadbeat parents cannot be allowed to walk away from their responsibilities. (Senate Debates on Conference Report on PRWORA of 1996, August 1, 1996)

These child support provisions were shaped by a neo-liberal vision of citizenship endeavoring to further privatize the costs of dependency (Brito

1999; Chambers 1995; Morgan 1999). Once again, good citizenship—personal responsibility—was deployed to produce and shame bad citizenship—personal irresponsibility. And once again, the regulatory net was broadened and intensified: more never-married fathers were included within the ambit of the deadbeat dad, and more regulatory surveillance was made possible.

While the neo-liberal vision of producing financially responsible fathers and privatizing the costs of dependency may have been dominant in the child support provisions, other provisions of PRWORA were marked by an emerging social conservative vision of fatherhood and citizenship. The stated purposes of the act included promoting marriage, responsible fatherhood and motherhood, and reducing illegitimacy. The findings portion of the act focused considerable attention on high rates of illegitimacy and its harms, including not only high rates of welfare dependency but also poor health, educational, and relationship prospects for their children. It distinguishes, for example, between divorced mothers and never-married ones, noting that "nearly 1/2 of the mothers who never married received AFDC while only 1/5 of divorced mothers received AFDC" (PRWORA, § 101). This implicit targeting of never-married fathers, alongside the identification of a broad range of harms associated with illegitimacy, represented a shift in the vision of the bad citizenship of deadbeat fathers. These fathers were not simply abdicating financial responsibility for their children, but their absence from their children's lives was now identified with other harms including poor educational prospects, higher incidence of abuse and neglect, and a future of welfare dependency and teenage pregnancies. The harm of bad fatherhood was no longer just about money.

This reconstitution of deadbeat dads also signaled a shift in the racialization of the category. While divorced fathers were constituted as overwhelmingly white, the shift to the sexual partners of the welfare queens began to include the African American man as a deadbeat dad and failed citizen. This broadening of the category, and its changing racialization, would eventually produce a shift in the remedial approach. Black men were not typically cast as self-reliant market citizens. The multiple dimensions of their pathologization in political discourse included their status as economic outlaws, as poverty stricken, as self-made members of the underclass. This identity shift would eventually produce a change in the understanding of their citizenship failure. These were not fathers who were simply refusing to pay. Their citizenship failure included the fact that they could not afford to pay. They were failed market citizens. Further, the harm of their citizenship failure was being explicitly linked to the pathologization of the black family—fatherlessness was contributing to the cycle of poverty, crime, and violence within the black community. These absent fathers needed to be brought back into the fold of the family—not simply to privatize the costs of dependency, but to reconstruct the broken black family, with the father at its helm.

A stronger social conservative approach to child support, fatherhood and family became evident in the fatherhood initiatives introduced and debated in Congress since the late 1990s. For example, the Fathers Count Act, passed by the House in 1999, but not the Senate, would have provided $155 million in grants for programs that promote marriage and responsible fatherhood. The objective of the act was, like the previous child support initiatives, to reduce welfare dependency by privatizing the costs of supporting families. However, the act took a very different approach to realizing this objective. Retreating from the demonizing rhetoric of deadbeat dads, the act sought to encourage fathers to become responsible for their children. Funding would be available for programs to teach parenting skills as well as to enhance employability through job training to allow fathers to fulfill their child support obligations.

Several distinct developments in the 1990s helped to account for this shift in emphasis from deadbeat dad to responsible fatherhood. First, there was increasing documentation of the financial realities and hardships of low-income fathers. As commentators observed, many of these fathers were better classified as "dead broke" rather than "dead beat" (Mincy & Sorenson 1998). In contrast to the image of the divorced father living high off the hog while abdicating his financial responsibility to his children, the studies demonstrated that many men were themselves poor and had little ability to pay anything more than nominal child support. Second, the responsible fatherhood movement successfully promoted its vision of fatherhood, family, and welfare dependency (see, e.g., Blankenhorn 1995; Horn 2001; Popenoe 1996). The new approach emphasized the importance of fathers in their children's lives.

While this importance was emphasized across socio-economic lines, there was a particular fatherhood message in the context of welfare and the poor black family. The problem of welfare dependency was recast as a problem of fatherlessness, which was in turn associated with a litany of social problems—delinquency, drug addiction, violence, and crime. As Lynne Haney and Miranda March have argued, liberals and conservatives alike seemed to agree on the "definition of the problem: The nuclear family was declining in African American communities, which resulted in generations of fatherless children" (Haney & March 2003, 466). Haney and March observe that the proponents of responsible fatherhood also agreed on "the general contours of a solution: to reconfigure the role of fathers in low-income communities" (Haney & March 2003, 466). Instead of coercive child support programs, proponents of responsible fatherhood "sought to transform these men into solid family members" (Haney & March 2003, 467).

The proponents of responsible fatherhood split into two distinct approaches (Gavanas 2004; Haney & March 2003). The fragile family approach focused on the financial vulnerability of these men. In this more neo-liberal approach, fathers could not be assumed to be market citizens. Much like welfare queens, they needed to be transformed into employable self-reliant individuals; they needed jobs. In this approach "the impediment to married fatherhood was not low-income fathers' moral or cultural ethos, but their inability to contribute materially. Without the ability to act as wage earners, these policy makers argued, men found it difficult to maintain a nuclear family form" (Haney & March 2003, 469).

The second pro-marriage approach focused on the moral vulnerabilities of these low-income fathers. In a distinctively social conservative approach, the problem was that these men did not value married fatherhood. In this approach, "The crisis of fatherhood was rooted in the ethos of the poor. The goal was to impose another definition of fatherhood on poor communities and to restore men to their rightful place as the fiscal and moral heads-of-household" (Haney & March 2003, 467). The crisis of fatherhood was part and parcel of the crisis of the African American family and needed to be fixed by restoring a married breadwinning father. While both approaches promote responsible fatherhood, in typical fiscal/social conservative distinction, one casts fatherhood in more financial terms, while the other casts it in more familial and moral terms.

The Fathers Count Act, as well as the other congressional initiatives around responsible fatherhood, represented a hybrid between the two visions of fatherhood, simultaneously providing funding for programs intended to help these fathers get jobs and programs intended to help these fathers assume their fatherly role within a male breadwinner, married family. The Healthy Marriage Promotion and Responsible Fatherhood Program of the Deficit Reduction Act reauthorizing TANF through 2010 allocates up to $50 million per year to be spent on responsible fatherhood activities. "Responsible fatherhood activities" are defined as programs that promote marriage (including the promotion of marriage and relationship skills, aggression management, and improving a family's ability to manage finances), encourage responsible fatherhood (including skills-based parenting education and encouraging child support payments), and foster economic stability by helping fathers improve their economic status through job training and career enhancement (Deficit Reduction Act, § 7103(a)(2)(C)(ii)). These responsible fatherhood provisions again represent a fiscal and social conservative hybrid, promoting both the ability of low-income fathers to pay child support and promoting a two-parent family, thereby avoiding the need for child support in the first place, both of which are seen to reduce welfare costs to the state.

These new initiatives represent a significant shift. They focus on the never-married, African American father: The problem is all about fathers who have never learned to be fathers. They seek to remedy the crisis of the African American family—by bringing these men back into the picture and restoring a two-parent family. Both seek to privatize dependency within marriage. While the neo-liberal approach seeks to do so through the promotion of market citizenship and contemplates a two-wage earning family, it nevertheless accepts married fatherhood as the ideal. Similarly, although the social conservative approach envisions achieving this ideal through the promotion of marriage, it also seeks to promote employed fathers who are capable of taking their place of privilege—financial and otherwise—at the helm of the family.

Further, both visions of responsible fatherhood adopt a language that is less demonizing and punitive. The project of transforming these irresponsible fathers into good citizens is increasingly about teaching these men to become better fathers through a range of skills training, counseling, and mentoring programs. One seeks to teach them job skills, the other marriage skills. But, as with the most recent initiatives on welfare mothers, both approaches are increasingly assuming a self-governance dimension. It is about teaching these men to self-discipline, about instructing them in the conduct of fatherly self-conduct. This is not to say that the child support regimes are any less coercive. Quite the contrary, the child support obligations and enforcement mechanisms at both the federal and state levels remain firmly in place and continue to be deployed against noncustodial fathers, criminalizing those who fail to self-discipline.

The citizenship failure of these irresponsible fathers is also a sexualized one. Much like the welfare queen, so too is the irresponsible father cast as a subject whose sexuality is dangerous, promiscuous, and out of control. The responsible fatherhood literature and programs sometimes comment on the need to readdress the prestige given to nonmarital sex by young, poor, "urban" (read "black") men. "Early sexual activity and 'babymaking' are viewed as a rite of passage within some groups of adolescent males" (Responsible Fatherhood website). The welfare reform legislation aims at getting these men to marry the mothers of their children—to transform irresponsible, unemployed, and unmarried fathers into responsible, employed, and married ones—intervening in other words, after the sex has already occurred.

However, the sexual abstinence programs—discussed in relation to welfare queens above—are also aimed at young men. The attempt to break the allegedly pathological cycle of poverty, illegitimacy, and crime within the black community includes an attempt to change the culture of male and female promiscuity; it is an effort to stop these young women and men from having sex in the first place. Bad citizenship is constructed in terms of sexual deviance, and good citizenship aims to harness sexuality by redirecting it to marriage. In contrast to some of the sexual citizens discussed in previous chapters, where nonmarital sex no longer operates as an exclusion to citizenship, an intensive surveillance of the sexuality of poor African Americans continues in which nonmarital sex remains a marker of bad citizenship. Good citizenship, for African Americans, demands the privatization of sex within marriage. But, it is a privatization that is to be achieved through highly public means. Indeed, the sex lives of these bad citizens were made into a public affair—their sex lives represented a virtual national crisis and its resolution, a national calling requiring highly intrusive public intervention.

Despite these many similarities and overlaps, there are also deeper contradictions between the visions of fatherhood and citizenship that parallel the divergent gendered visions for mothers. For neo-liberals, market citizenship is cast in less gendered terms. Fathers—just like mothers—must be made self-reliant market citizens who are capable of financially supporting their families. For social conservatives, familial citizenship is a highly gendered affair. Men must be trained in the male breadwinner model: For fathers, good citizenship involves assuming the financial and emotional leadership of the family. Fatherhood is a gendered role of financial provision and moral leadership that runs alongside motherhood as care-giving and financial dependence.

Both seek to privatize and self-discipline citizenship, but their understanding of privatization and the object of self-discipline diverge. For neo-liberals, the private lies in the market: It is about becoming a self-disciplining market citizen, able to support themselves and their children. For social conservatives, the private lies in the male breadwinner/female caregiver family. Fathers must be market citizens, but they must also self-discipline into their role at the helm of a gendered family.

The Legacy of Unbecoming Citizens Beyond Welfare

The privatization and self-disciplining of citizenship in welfare reform has helped produce a new modality of citizenship, which casts its shadow well beyond welfare recipients. The welfare queen and the deadbeat dad not only allowed for a dismantling of welfare but have become specters of bad citizenship, haunting all African Americans, regardless of income. Admittedly, the attack on welfare did not create the stereotypes; the racialized stereotypes already in circulation helped to produce the attack. But the attack on welfare did crystallize these stereotypes into iconic identities that continue to constitute the citizenship failure of African Americans. The privatization and self-disciplining of citizenship has produced and sustained an identity of failure: of familial pathology, sexual deviance, and economic dysfunction. Moreover, it is an identity of failure located in one central act: Children born outside of marriage. From Moynihan forward, illegitimacy has become the problem that needs to be fixed—it is the site of the pathology of the black family and the citizenship failure of both women and men. After three decades of sustained discursive and material attack, unmarried has been produced as a norm not to be for African American parents.

The story works, in part, because of its resonance with a material reality. Statistics confirm that there has been an increase in single-parent families, headed overwhelmingly by women, since the 1960s. This is true for black and non-Hispanic white families alike, although the numbers are considerably higher for African American families. In 1960, the number of African American children born outside of marriage was 7 percent. In 1980, it had increased to 36 percent, and in 1998, it was 63 percent. In 1960, the number of white children born outside of marriage was 2 percent, increasing to 8 percent in 1980, and 28 percent in 1998 (Sigle-Rushton & McLanahan 2002). For white children, "divorce has been the major pathway into single parenthood, accounting for

2/3 of the increase in single-parent families between 1960 and 1980." In contrast, for black children, nonmarital childbirth is the most important pathway (Sigle-Rushton & McLanahan 2002). By 2000, one in three children in the United States was born outside of marriage, and the proportion was twice as high among African American children (Ventura & Bachrach 2000). In 2002, 48 percent of all African American families were married couples; 43 percent were single-parent families headed by a woman, and 9 percent were single-parent families headed by a man. For white non-Hispanic families, 82 percent were married, 13 percent were headed by single mothers, and 5 percent were headed by single fathers (U.S. Census 2003).

Given these numbers, it is not surprising that unmarried childbirth within African American families has become a target not only of conservatives headstrong on dismantling welfare, but has also been identified as a problem by many within African American communities. Studies and programs directed toward fragile families and unmarried fathers abound. Intellectuals have debated the role of the family and the absence of fathers. William Julius Wilson, for example, has lamented the growth of single-mother families in the black communities, attributing the increase to the lack of marriageable, financially stable black men (Wilson 1987). While his focus is on the lack of economic opportunities for African American men, rather than marriage per se, Wilson's work has been the focus of critique by African American feminists for its attack on single mothers. Kimberle Crenshaw, for example, has argued that Wilson's need to "put black men back into the family" effectively posits female-headed families as "dysfunctional per se" (Austin 1994, 567; Crenshaw 1982, 165).

Even within the responsible fatherhood movement, there are deep disagreements over the nature of the solutions, with one faction focusing on economic opportunities and the other focusing on marriage. While Wilson's work parallels the fragile family side of the responsible fatherhood initiatives, emphasizing the need for economic opportunities, other more conservative voices within the African American community have taken a more morality-based, pro-marriage position. The emphasis on marriage as a solution has similarly been the subject of critique by a number of African American feminists. Perida Huda, for example, argues that this emphasis on marriage "as a solution to poverty is debilitating to the understanding of black single mother families as a deserving . . . family form" (Huda 2001). Both the nature of the problem and the proposed solutions are thus contested sites.

These concerns and contestations are reflected in a range of African American cultural representations, from films to song, which explore the issues of family, parenting, and relationships. The cultural representations of the black public sphere seek to tell powerful counter narratives to the stereotypes of the African American in mainstream culture and politics. Yet, many of these representations bump up against the legacy of the attack on the welfare queen and the deadbeat dad. In a kind of dialogic shadow boxing, these contemporary representations position their counter narratives against these discourses of welfare reform and failed citizenship.

The delegitimation of single motherhood and absent fatherhood forms part of the cultural and political landscape against which alternative stories are articulated. While not monolithic, many film and television representations within the family drama genre tell somewhat similar stories. Crushing poverty, systemic racism, and oppressive welfare bureaucracies often fade into the backdrop, while problems of privatization and self-governance are foregrounded. For women, the challenges are avoiding the perils of unmarried motherhood and trying to find a good man. For men, the challenges are taking responsibility—economically and morally—for one's self, one's partner, and one's children. The icons of bad citizenship produced in mainstream political discourse haunt these counter narratives, with their modality of unbecoming citizenship—of welfare queens and irresponsible fathers—casting their shadows in troubling ways over many cultural representations of African American families and the subjects who inhabit them.

Citizen Lauryn: In the Shadow of the Welfare Queen

> Woe this crazy circumstance
> I knew his life deserved a chance
> But everybody told me to be smart
> "Look at your career," they said
> "Lauryn, baby, use your head"
> But instead I chose to use my heart.
> *"To Zion," Lauryn Hill*

When Lauryn Hill released her first solo neo-soul R&B album *The Miseducation of Lauryn Hill* in September 1998, it went directly to number one on the Billboard Top 200 chart. She became the first solo female artist to sell more than 400,000 units in the first week. Hill was nominated for eleven Grammy awards and took home five, including album of the year, best new artist, and best female R&B vocal performance. The album went triple platinum.

But Hill's fame and fortune were not enough to insulate her from the scandal and controversy that erupted around her life. Hill was an unmarried mother of two children—her son Zion born in 1997 and her daughter Selah Louise born in 1998, shortly after the release of her best-selling album. The children's father is Rohan Marley, Bob Marley's son, with whom Hill lives. Her album included "To Zion," a love song to her young son, whom she chose to have notwithstanding the advice and criticism of many around her. But her personal choice was one that became deeply loaded with the legacy of single motherhood for African American women. Her unwed status became the focus of controversy in some quarters of the African American community, with many claiming that she was a terrible role model for young women. The controversy peaked after her appearance on the Essence Awards in June 1999, where Hill gave a heartfelt acceptance speech. "I want to let young people know that it is not a burden to love Him, and to represent Him, and to be who you are, as fly and as hot and as whatever, and to still love God and to serve Him. It's not a contradiction" (Dickerson 1999).

Media outlets, from radio call-in shows to Internet sites, witnessed an outpouring of outrage. The Electronic Urban Reporter, a black entertainment website, ran a special section on the e-mails that the site received (Dickerson 1999). The basic message was that many disapproved of her lifestyle—of her sexy dressing, her out of wedlock children, and her nonmarital cohabitation with their father. One e-mail stated, "Lauryn's lifestyle doesn't match her sermons. If she's gonna shack up (and in her parents' home, no less) with her man and her two babies, that's her business, but Lauryn's crossing the line when she gets on every available TV screen talking about how 'holy' she is. God is not in that mess" (quoted in Dickerson 1999). Another wrote: "If Lauryn Hill weren't famous, but instead worked the register at [McDonald's], black folks would be the first people saying what a poor role model she is and how she needs to get her life together" (Dickerson 1999).

Hill's fame, financial security, and stable live-in relationship with her children's father was not enough to immunize her from the allegations that she was perpetuating the negative stereotypes of black women as unmarried, promiscuous, single mothers. The concerns typically raised about single mothers either on welfare or working at poverty level wages simply did not apply to her. She did not live in poverty. She was not in fact raising her children as a single mother, but in a two-parent albeit unmarried family. Yet, her critics attempted to paint her with the same brushstroke. On one hand, the controversy could be seen as a microcosm of the broader culture wars, situated within the African American community. Hill's convergence of a sexualized and religious identity produced a typical conservative reaction. Yet, the controversy cannot be understood outside the context of the racialized stereotypes of African American women. So far-reaching has the stereotype of the welfare queen become that even those very few black women who reach the apex of success are still at risk of being caught in its shadow. In an act of intra-community contestation and self-regulation, some within the African American community sought to distance themselves from the specter of bad citizenship. Their own redemption as citizens required the repudiation of an identity that had been projected onto their bodies. In a gesture of preemption, some within the community sought to exorcise their body politic of its overly sexualized identity. Lauryn Hill became every bit as dangerous as the welfare queen—perhaps even more so since she could have chosen otherwise.

The idea of choice is significant. Hill's song, a moving tribute to the joys of having and raising a child, is a kind of pro-choice/pro-life anthem. As black feminist critics of reproductive rights struggles have long insisted, for African American women, the problem is not simply one of the right to choose an abortion (Roberts 1999). It is the right to choose more generally—the freedom to choose to have children as much as the freedom to not have them. Black women's role in caring for their own children—in contrast to caring for the children of others—has not been socially valued or even recognized (Roberts 1999). And in the decades since the assault of welfare queens began, the reproductive and care-giving role of African Americans has only been further vilified. The power of Lauryn Hill's tribute to her son lies in this legacy. Her choice to have her son, when all those around her told her not to, is a powerful statement of resistance to the denial of this right. And it is a celebration of the decision that she made. "Now the joy of my world is in Zion."

This is a difficult, paradoxical, and powerful position for an African American woman. Even some of Hill's supporters, like hip-hop feminist Joan Morgan, have expressed ambivalence over this choice. On the one hand, Morgan is unequivocal in her defense of Hill in the moment of the controversy:

> You can't put the weight of the black community on Lauryn. There was no Lauryn Hill when I was in high school, yet me and my two friends were the only ones who didn't get pregnant. Lauryn's a positive influence, if anything.

Teenagers see her with her man by her side and solid ground under her feet. Why can't that be the influence she has? (Morgan quoted in Dickerson 1999)

Yet, elsewhere she has expressed her misgivings over the proliferation of single motherhood amongst the black middle class (Morgan 1999).

This cultural controversy was reproduced in a life imitating art imitating life way. In *Disappearing Acts* (2000), a film based on the novel by Terry McMillan, Zora (Sanaa Lathan) is a music teacher who aspires to be a successful singer songwriter. She falls in love with Franklin (Wesley Snipes), a construction worker who dreams of owning his own business. Along the bumpy road of their relationship, Zora gets pregnant and decides to have the baby. But her producer warns her of dire consequences: She will never finish her demo, and her singing career will come to naught. Her response: "But Lauryn Hill has two children." Here, Hill is held up as a symbol of possibility; fame and family need not be contradictory, even for a single black mother. Yet, Hill remains an unrealizable possibility. It turns out that Zora's efforts to make it in the music industry, and to be a single mother, are more difficult than she had imagined. Her producer drops her. Ultimately, the narrative resolution to this dramatic tension is commitment—implicitly marriage—but mostly, monogamous commitment, responsible fatherhood. The Lauryn Hill controversy cameo is deployed as an unrealizable ideal, as that which many young black women may aspire to, yet in "real life" turns out to be both undesirable and unattainable.

Or is it? In the film, Zora does become a mother and a successful singer-songwriter. And despite the trials and tribulations in their relationship, Franklin and Zora end up together. In fact, the film parallels the actual life of Lauryn Hill, who despite the controversy over her "single" motherhood, is a successful singer-songwriter who lives with her children's father. Zora, like Lauryn, worked hard against the odds to pursue her dreams that in the end included not only a successful songwriter career, but also motherhood and the love of a good man.

Disappearing Acts is a story that refuses the association of African American women with the welfare queen; yet it is a story that bumps up against its legacy. Zora's sexual citizenship is produced as privatized and self-disciplined. She is fiercely independent and economically self-sufficient. She works hard on her self, on her career, and on her relationship. The meaning and implication of her pending unmarried motherhood is contested: Is it the end of her career, or can it be managed, through the same ethic of hard work and responsibility that characterizes Zora's life? Contested yes, but also one ultimately resolved in favor of responsibilization. Zora is prepared to go the road of motherhood alone. But it is not her first choice, and she is also prepared to do the hard work that her relationship with Franklin requires.

Disappearing Acts, like Lauryn Hill's real life, is a story deeply implicated in the contestations over African American motherhood within the black public sphere. For some, unmarried motherhood remains a proxy for the citizenship failure of African American women; it is the undoing, or unbecoming, of any chance of their citizenship. Yet for others, this proxy is unpacked, if only a little. *Disappearing Acts* ends not with marriage but with commitment to a two-parent family. It is a counter narrative that seeks to shift the ground from marital status to the material reality of the lives lived. It is a counter narrative reflected in the discourse of Lauryn Hill's supporters who in the midst of the controversy tried to focus attention on the fact that she was a model of responsibilized citizenship. As one supportive commentator observed, "You have to look at her whole life, not just the babies, who, by the way, she is pointing to God and a model Christian life. She has support from a good man, a loving family, independent means" (quoted in Dickerson 1999). While the significance of marital status is contested, the underlying modality of good citizenship as privatized and self-disciplined is rather less so.

The controversy around Lauryn Hill is not the first, nor is it likely the last, attack on the single motherhood of an accomplished and financially secure African American woman. [10] But, it illustrates how the focus on illegitimacy as citizenship failure continues to be deeply racialized. Contrast the obsession about single parenting within the African American community with an increasing, albeit begrudging, acceptance of single parenting for some white women. While the cultural controversy produced by the Murphy Brown television character in the 1980s suggested that illegitimacy was still a highly contested act for all women, the ensuing decades have seen a proliferation of high profile white single mothers as well as cultural representations of white single motherhood. For example, in a 2001 article entitled, "The New Single Moms and How They Do It," *US Weekly* highlighted several famous "single mothers." It focused on Camryn Manheim, an Emmy Award-winning actress, but also included brief bios of other recent single moms, including Jodie Foster, Calista Flockhart, Diane Keaton, Rosie O'Donnell, Katie Couric, and Nicole Kidman. Quoting Aretha Franklin, the article proclaimed that "sisters are doing it for themselves." Ironically, there were no "sisters" on the list—not one African American woman was among the list of celebrity single moms.

The same exclusive focus on white single motherhood is found in the proliferation of cultural representations of single motherhood. In the 2001–2002 season of *Friends*, Rachel, the character played by Jennifer Aniston, became a single mother. In the same season, Miranda in *Sex and the City* also decided to become a single mother. Some commentators have argued that there is a particular story being told in these representations of single mothers. Robin Silbergleid has argued that these cultural representations are characterized by a strong heteronarrative, in which the story of single motherhood is contained within a dominant structure of heterosexual romance and family (Silbergleid 2002). For example, in *Friends*, although Rachel and her long-time love interest Ross are not married, it is clear from the moment she decides to keep the baby that the child will have two involved parents (Silbergleid 2002). In fact, the baby narrative helps to keep Rachel and Ross united, initially as friends and parents in a way that sustains their unstated love. The series finale finally sees Rachel and Ross reunited—heterosexual romance and the traditional nuclear family prevail. A similar story reigns in *Sex and the City*. Steve, the father and Miranda's ambivalent love interest, is from the beginning very involved with their child, and ultimately they marry. The missing man is never really missing: In the end, the family is formally united in marriage.

While the citizenship of some of these white single mothers may be contained within a heteronarrative where marriage provides the resolution, it is possible to provide an alternative reading. In both *Friends* and *Sex and the City*, there is a moment where the possibility of single motherhood is affirmed. It is a choice that women can make; it is a viable family form. Both Rachel and Miranda struggle with the choices that face them and decide for themselves to become single mothers, without any guarantee of male involvement, let alone marriage. While the fathers become involved, for a while both Rachel and Miranda inhabit the identity of single mothers by choice.

Nor are there always happy romantic endings to the real-life stories of actresses like Camryn Manheim or Diane Keaton, who have never married. These are single mothers whose fame and/or fortune provided some immunization from the accusation of citizenship failure. Their motherhood may be controversial, but they have come a long way from Dan Quayle's attack on Murphy Brown's single motherhood. Indeed, they are able to create a discursive space to inhabit a positive identity: single mothers by choice.

It is difficult to say the same for African American single mothers—fame and fortune notwithstanding—where single motherhood by choice continues to be constituted as pathological. Even the contested narratives of Lauryn Hill and *Disappearing Acts* are, at most, carving out a space of unmarried motherhood with a father close at hand. They may be unmarried, but they are not parenting alone. The specter of bad citizenship produced in the context of poor black women continues to haunt all black women regardless of income. Single parenthood—going it alone—is not produced as a legitimate choice for any African American woman; it remains heavily tainted with the markers of unbecoming citizenship.

Some have suggested that the message in recent cultural representations goes beyond a continued delegitimation of single motherhood. Makani Themba, for example, sees evidence of an attack on independent African American career women (Themba 1998). From the film and subsequent television series *Soul Food* to the book *The Sistahs' Rules*, Themba argues that the new message is that "real women have husbands."

Soul Food tells the story of three adult sisters struggling to maintain their relationship after the death of the family matriarch. The eldest is a fiercely independent lawyer, the middle sister is a stay-at-home mother, and the youngest is struggling with her place somewhere in-between. But, as Themba describes, the stay-at-home mother is happy, the career woman is miserable, and the middle sister learns which pole to move toward. All three sisters are married, but the career sister alienates her husband by working too hard at work and not hard enough at home.

The Sistahs' Rules by Denene Millner is a best-selling dating advice book on how African American women can get a good man, replete with information about not being too aggressive or independent. Themba sees in these and other cultural representations directed at African American women a rearticulation of a traditional 1950s nuclear family with a stay-at-home mother, only this time, directed at the African American family. This new message is not only promoting marriage but also traditional gender roles of marriage, for women and men. If women are being encouraged to return to the domestic sphere, it is because men are being encouraged to take their "'rightful' place as king of the castle and wage earner" (Themba 1998). This emergent cultural representation of black women is a social conservative variant of the shadow cast by the failed citizenship of the welfare queen; the rearticulation of the African American family and African American manhood requires that she be remade in the image of the appropriately dependent housewife.

The stories are powerful counter narratives to the racialized stereotypes of African American women: The women of *Soul Food* are no welfare queens. As good mothers, committed wives—even an unsatisfied lawyer— these women are inhabiting spheres long denied African American women. Yet, the stories are being told in the shadow of the legacy of these unbecoming citizens. The women of *Soul Food* are all married—their citizenship appropriately privatized either within the family or the market and self-disciplined. They work hard to take care of themselves and their families; and when they don't, or when they work on the wrong part of their lives (work over family), they pay the price. It is another powerful—and contested—image in black popular culture in which single motherhood is not only not an option, but where the sexual citizenship of African American women is represented as privatized, self-disciplined, and reconstituted in highly gendered terms.

P. Diddy, Baby Daddies, and the
Shadow of Irresponsible Fatherhood

In September 2004, a Westchester County Family Court judge ordered Sean Combs—aka hip-hop mogul P. Diddy—to pay $35,000 a month child support as well as nearly $400,000 in arrears and $60,000 in attorneys' fees to his ex-girlfriend, Misa Hylton-Brim for the support of their child, Justin. P. Diddy appealed the decision, and in April 2005 the New York Supreme Court reversed the lower court decision in part, reducing his support payments by $12,000. However, at $21,782 per month, the New York Supreme Court's support order represents a significant increase from the $5,000 per month that he had been paying in child support. In an interview with the Associated Press, the hip-hop mogul vowed to appeal, saying the case was an attack on his character. "It's not about money. I don't care how much money I have," he said. "If you come at me and say I don't take care of my child, I'm going to take care of that to the end" (Associated Press, May 24, 2005). P. Diddy emphasized that he did support his child: "I do take care of my child to my fullest, that's something that should be rewarded. It's not something that should be handled this way."

The mother of the child, Hylton-Brim said that she brought the case because of an inequity in what P. Diddy was paying to his girlfriend, Kim Porter, the mother of his second child, Christian. However, P. Diddy said reports that he pays Porter about $30,000 a month were untrue. "She gets $12,000 a month. [But] she pays for everything," including health care, he said. In addition to child support, P. Diddy said that he also pays for his son Justin's health insurance, tuition, vacations, clothes, and other items, totaling approximately $120,000 per year. Diddy's lawyer had previously stated that Hylton-Brim was effectively seeking adult support. "This is not about child support, it's about adult support," said Stephen Gassman. "Any increase in support will be likely utilized to enhance [Hylton-Brim] and her other two children's lifestyles." (*New York Daily News* Oct. 5, 2004).

The order for child support, one of the largest in New York history, needs to be put in the context of P. Diddy's wealth: His 2002 federal tax return put his income at $16 million. It is, in this respect, not unlike other high-income child support cases where custodial parents seek what may appear to be exorbitant amounts of money to support children with luxurious lifestyles. It is not uncommon in these cases for the high-income payor parent to resist the claim as exorbitant and to suggest that the demand will unduly benefit the lifestyle of the custodial parent. But, there is more going on in this case. A host of racialized icons and assumptions swirl around the controversy, making it as something other than a mere high-income earner child support dispute. P. Diddy claims that the case is not a question of money but of reputation; he is fighting against the stain on his reputation caused by the allegation that he does not support his child. It is the allegation of irresponsible fatherhood that he seems most concerned to discredit. P. Diddy is, in effect, shadow boxing the demons of bad citizenship for African American men.

P. Diddy is one of the most successful performers and producers in the world of hip-hop, often described as one of hip-hop's moguls. He is, in many respects, the model of the American Dream; a self-made man, starting from nothing, and moving up and out of the ghetto into fame and fortune. He is a self-made market citizen, a highly successful entrepreneur, and a pop culture icon.

But, that is not all that he is. As an African American man, his citizenship remains precarious at best, constituted by a multitude of negative characteristics, made all the worse by his rapper identity. The racialized stereotypes of rappers as criminal, violent, sexually promiscuous, crass consumers all threaten his claim to good citizenship. In this case, it is the shadow of irresponsible fatherhood that looms over his citizenship. P. Diddy is at risk of bad citizenship according to the racialized script of irresponsibility: because, like all African American men, he has produced children out of wedlock and not married the mothers of his children; because, like all African American men, he is not financially supporting them; because, like all African American men, he indulges his own crass and selfish needs rather than taking care of his children.

Not unlike the Lauryn Hill controversy, the icons of bad citizenship born of poverty and welfare dependency threaten even those who have more than transcended that demographic. P. Diddy is still at risk of bad citizenship, even though he is more than financially self-sufficient, even though he has achieved extraordinary wealth, and even though he supports his children at a very high income level.

It is this racialized sting of the allegation of irresponsible fatherhood that animates P. Diddy's articulation of the harm to his reputation. But, the defense then deploys its own racialized allegations. P. Diddy's lawyer's comments that the claim is really one of adult support, enhancing the lifestyle of Hylton-Brim and her other two children, sets up a different set of racial and gendered stereotypes. The implication is that Hylton-Brim is attempting to live off the proceeds of P. Diddy, to enhance her lifestyle—behavior typical of "baby mamas." The lawyer mentions that she has two other children. The unstated but obvious fact is that they have other fathers, that she is not married, that she is a baby mama to others as well, that she is a sexually promiscuous African American woman trying to use her children to support herself. Not unlike the welfare queen, she is a new kind of African American woman—the "hoochie mama"—trying to rely on wealthy black men instead of the state to support her. Just like the welfare queen, she coldly calculates using her children for economic support and engages in excessive and crass consumption (how else to explain the need for so much money?).

For P. Diddy, then, a high-income child support dispute is not framed simply as a glimpse into the excessive lives of the rich and famous, but also, as a baby mama drama. Indeed, one media story opened with the words: "The baby mama drama just won't stop for P. Diddy" (*Chicago Tribune* 2005). This is an explicitly racialized framing device, invoking the images of single black mothers seeking support from absent black fathers and of the endless conflict that ensues between them. In the discursive trappings of the new politics of irresponsible fatherhood, the very allegation of failure to pay child support, alongside the endless conflict with the child's mother, sets a series of racialized images into play, which coalesce to produce P. Diddy as an irresponsible father, well beyond the welfare dependency and poverty context.

P. Diddy's baby mama drama is suggestive of how far the icon of irresponsible fatherhood now casts its shadow of bad citizenship over black popular culture. Responsible fatherhood and marriage are all the rage. From the film *Soul Food* (1997) to John Singleton's drama *Baby Boy* (2001) to Cheryl Dunye's comedy *My Baby's Daddy* (2004), films by African Americans are often populated with women who work hard and want to marry and men who must learn to become responsible fathers. It is a cultural trend that reflects an anxiety born of a very real set of demographics—of the disproportionately high number of single-parent families and absent fathers within the African American community.

These representations all seek to tell powerful counter narratives to the racialized stories of mainstream welfare discourse that more accurately reflect the lives and challenges of African Americans. For example, none of the mothers in these films are on welfare—they all work hard to financially support their families and take care of their children. But, the challenge is often framed as transforming absent fathers into present ones—of getting these men to form nuclear families and committing themselves to the project of raising their children. Allusions are made to the economic insecurity of African American men, such as the difficulty of finding secure employment, particularly for those with criminal records. In *Soul Food*, for example, the youngest sister's husband cannot find work because of his criminal record, despite his best efforts to go straight. But the economic problems are often resolved or resolvable, and the real problem is framed as getting these men to settle down into the role of responsible fatherhood. These are stories of privatization and self-governance; African American men must learn to take responsibility for their actions, their lives, and ultimately their families.

In *Baby Boy* (2001) writer and director John Singleton explores the inner trials and tribulations of Jody, a 20-year-old African American man living in South Central LA, with two children by two women, and who still lives in his mother's house. The film is a not particularly subtle reflection on the infantilization of black men. It opens with the image of Jody sleeping in his mother's womb, with a voiceover explaining that young black men are infantilized. The men themselves refer to their girlfriends as "mama," their friends as "boys," and their homes as their "cribs."

Against this thematic backdrop, the film explores one young man's struggle to grow up. Jody has a relationship with both of the mothers of his children. He appears to be in love with Yvette, who supports herself and her child, and to have sex occasionally with Peanut, who lives at home and appears to be supported by her fairly well-to-do family. But, he is unable to take responsibility for either of his children. He continues to live the life of a young man, a teenager who does not work, who does not support himself or his family.

All of this changes when his mother's new boyfriend Mel, an ex-con, moves into the house. Mel is tough and unapologetically sexual, but now he's on the straight and narrow, running his own landscaping business. Mel represents the wrong road that Jody might still take and the right one to which he aspires. But Jody refuses any fatherly advice, and simply resents the new Oedipal presence. His mother Juanita tells Jody that she has a right to her own life and that he needs to grow up and move out. At the same time, Yvette begins to tire of Jody's irresponsible and cheating ways. It all comes to a head when Yvette's menacing ex-boyfriend gets out of jail and arrives on her doorstep, threatening the nuclear family that could be. Jody is finally faced to grow up, to take responsibility, to save his family. He becomes a responsible father—to one of his children at least. The film's last scene is of Jody and a pregnant Yvette with their child in the park; they are married, Jody has become a responsible father, and the nuclear family is now complete.

Singleton has made a film that seriously explores the complexities of African American masculinity, against a backdrop of violence, unemployment, and the other challenges of inner-city life. Its protagonist is represented as both sympathetic and exasperating; he's a good guy, but he just cannot quite get his act together. "I do what I do, but I'm good," Jody says to Yvette. His irresponsible acts—his infidelities, his inability to move out of his mother's house, his unemployment, his failure to support his children—are not excused but part of the narrative that he must confront. Singleton is unrelenting in his story about infantilization and the need for young black men to grow up. "Growing up," in this narrative, means taking responsibility for one's life, one's decisions, and the consequences of one's decisions. In Jody's context, it means taking responsibility for himself and his children; it means embracing responsible fatherhood.

There is a certain tension in the resolution, in so far as Jody embraces fatherhood for only one of his children; Peanut and her child are nowhere to be seen in the final scene of fatherly and familial responsibility. But, it is nevertheless a resolution all about growing up by taking responsibility and embracing the ideals of responsible fatherhood.

It is, in this respect, a surprisingly simple solution for a complex set of challenges by a filmmaker who does not shy away from engaging the broader systemic challenges of racism, poverty, and violence. His earlier film, *Boyz n the Hood* (1991), for example, was all about the challenges of violence facing young men in the ghetto of South Central LA. Even in *Baby Boy*, Singleton keeps the oppressive reality of poverty and violence in sharp relief throughout much of the film, until the narrative resolution where it fades into the backdrop. As Patricia Hill Collins has observed, "Singleton's solution of having Jody leave boyhood behind by marrying one of his baby mamas is far too simple. In the end, we see this new family happy, playing in the park, and awaiting the arrival of another baby. In real life, no neat formulas exist that provide the instant happy ending of *Baby Boy*" (Hill Collins 2004, 212). The story is resolved through self-governance and responsibilization, through Jody taking responsibility for his life and for his family. It is a narrative not that far removed from the message of responsible fatherhood programs: Through marriage and/or employment and a heavy dose of self-actualization, absent fathers can be transformed into present ones, and the broken family can be fixed.

Baby Boy is not alone in its filmic representation of responsible fatherhood. *My Baby's Daddy*, by filmmaker Cheryl Dunye, is a comedic exploration of the struggles of three men to come to terms with their role as unmarried fathers: two black, one Hispanic. It deploys all the comedic tropes of men with utterly no idea of how to care for babies: not wanting to change diapers, discomfort with breast milk, unable to adequately watch over the babies because of their ongoing selfish pursuits of other women. But after a near crisis they are forced to clean up their act, and they become responsible fathers. The film preaches the message of responsible fatherhood, of men who are forced to grow up and take responsibility for their new roles as fathers. While the film allows for various ways to become responsible fathers, not always marrying the mother of the child, it does insist that each of the men must change himself and take responsibility for himself and his children. It is a film that was poorly received and critically panned, yet it is worth noting, if only because of the message articulated by an otherwise serious filmmaker.[11] And the message is unrelenting: Absent and clueless unmarried fathers must and can be transformed into present and responsible ones.

These films tell contested narratives of self-governance, of the need of African American men to step up and transform themselves into responsible, privatized, and self-disciplining citizens. While often telling an empathetic story of these fathers against a backdrop of the very real challenges of poverty, unemployment, violence, and racism, the narrative resolutions bump up against the icons of bad citizenship produced by welfare discourse. The script of failed citizenship and in turn of its redemption has permeated the black cultural sphere. Like the responsible fatherhood programs more generally, the role of marriage is contested in these films, but committed fatherhood is not. Responsible fatherhood—stepping up to take responsibility morally and financially—is the *sine qua non* of their citizenship eligibility. It is a script with resonance in the material reality of African American families, with its disproportionate number of single mothers and absent fathers.

But it is also a script that even in its most sympathetic cultural performances is one that risks falling into an overly simplistic resolution. Irresponsible fathers can become citizens by taking individual responsibility, by marrying and/or committing to the mothers of their children and becoming present in the lives of their children. The process of unbecoming can be undone through a fairly simple act. And yet, as P. Diddy's baby mama dramas suggest, it may not be quite so simple. African American men—regardless of their financial success and fatherly responsibility—continue to run the risk of unbecoming citizens by virtue of the very script that demands that they become market and familial citizens. Becoming a citizen for the unmarried African American parent remains an elusive challenge, even for those who appear to have otherwise met the criteria of citizenship.

Conclusion

These representations of motherhood and fatherhood are among the many contested images of African American citizenship in black popular culture. Films, television, and music engage with a broad range of themes from gang violence to hip-hop culture, and from the sexual objectification of women to romantic chick flicks. Yet within the family drama genre, the challenges of single parenthood are a recurrent theme. Single motherhood and absent fatherhood are presented as identities better avoided. The lead characters are presented with choices, but the normativity of these choices is prefigured: Committed, two-parent families are the best way.

These cultural representations can be read in the register of self-governing citizenship, that is, as part of a technology of governance through regulated and accountable choices of citizens (White & Hunt 2000). In contrast to the highly authoritarian welfare regimes that govern with a heavy state hand—albeit with a view to attaining self-governance of the affected population—this is a form of governing through the "responsibilized and educated anxieties and aspirations of individuals" (Rose 1999, 88). The characters in these films engage in "sustained and intense self-scrutiny" (Hunt 1999, 218) on their path to self-realization, and in the end choose committed parenthood. Like *Claudine*, the narratives of these films contest the racialized stereotypes and myths of African Americans as welfare queens and deadbeat dads. Yet, they are repeatedly confronting these images: In the counter narrative, they are the identities that African Americans are not.

Indeed, *Claudine* was in many respects a harbinger of the films to come. While it stands alone as a film about the dignity of a single mother on welfare, it can be viewed with more thematic continuity as a film about privatized self-governance. Claudine struggles for self-sufficient market citizenship and responsible family citizenship. She works hard to support herself and her family, and she works hard on her relationship, in the face of an intrusive welfare bureaucracy that undermines both her enterprising initiative and her efforts toward family formation.

While Claudine claims her entitlement to welfare, in a kind of Marshallian social citizenship discourse reflected in the welfare rights movement of the day, this dimension of the narrative has been eclipsed by the intervening years of welfare reform and African American self-governance. Today, *Claudine* can be retold in several of the registers of welfare reform and African American sexual citizenship, from the neo-liberal insistence of individual initiative and market citizenship, to the social conservative emphasis on marriage and responsible parenthood. But, like the black cultural representations more generally, *Claudine* is engaged in a dialogic relationship, engaging and contesting these discourses and the shadows of the welfare queen and the deadbeat dad. It can be retold as a story of responsibilization—of both Claudine and Roop taking responsibility for their lives, their decisions, and their families. Not unlike the counter narratives of *Disappearing Acts* or *Baby Boy*, the narrative resolution is provided through a highly individualized solution of responsibilization and familialization, notwithstanding the broader critique of racism and the welfare state contained within the film. Hard work, marriage, and responsible parenthood—the hallmarks of a privatized and self-disciplined citizenship—are held out as the solution, as the path to belonging.

4 Queer as Citizens

I N *KISSING JESSICA STEIN*, two 20-something straight girls—one curious, the other frustrated with the dating scene in New York—decide to give lesbian love a shot. And it works, at least for a while: They date, fall in love, and move in together; even Jessica's mother accepts her daughter's choice. The film is a story about exploring sexuality and accepting yourself for what you are or what you choose to become. It is a story about acceptance—self-acceptance, family acceptance, and community acceptance. And it is, in part, a story about normalizing lesbian sexuality—if not the erasure of difference, then at least its reduction to a matter of personal taste.

By contrast, the American version of the television show *Queer as Folk* follows the sexual exploits of a group of gay men who are unapologetically eroticized. They have sex—lots of it—with many sexual partners. They are pleasure seekers—sex and drugs and the throbbing beat of techno-pop. At least initially, they have no time for monogamy, marriage, or military service. The show openly mocks assimilation—disparaging everything from gay marriage to gay designer reality shows—for their heterosexual normativity. It is a story about sexual difference, about bodies saturated with sex, and about the difference that this sex makes.

Both of these cultural productions tell stories about sexual citizenship. *Kissing Jessica Stein* can be told as a story about citizenship as normalization. It is a story of assimilation in which the heterosexual requirement of membership is relaxed, but in which individuals can still live happily—if not ever after—in monogamous couplings, surrounded by loving families. By contrast, *Queer as Folk* can be told as a story about sexual citizenship that refuses normalization and assimilation. These are gay men who celebrate their sexual difference and their outlaw status. These are the contrasting stories, the fault lines of contemporary debates about sexual citizenship for gay men and lesbians: stories about assimilation versus subalternity, about the privileges of inclusion versus its normalizing costs.

Some tell the story as a progress narrative in which gay men and lesbians are in the process of becoming full and equal members of the polity, with increasing access to the panoply of rights and obligations of citizenship. Others tell a darker narrative about the costs of membership, with citizenship coming at the expense of transgression.

It is a debate that is all too well rehearsed in the context of gay marriage. Advocates of same-sex marriage argue that inclusion in this important social and legal institution is fundamental to the full citizenship of gay men and lesbians. It provides access to legal rights and responsibilities as well as to broader cultural discourses and practices of belonging. Opponents from within gay and lesbian communities argue that same-sex marriage will be normalizing and domesticating, undermining and excluding the more subversive dimensions of queer identities (Warner 1999). The debate performs an either/or of being for or against same-sex marriage, and for or against inclusion in citizenship as it is currently constituted. It is a debate that can be mapped rather neatly on *Kissing Jessica Stein* and *Queer as Folk*: assimilation versus transgression, monogamous loving relationships versus multiple libertine sex.

But, it is a debate that misses the messiness, ambivalence and multiplicity of the inclusions and exclusions of citizenship. As performed, the debate utterly fails to capture the multiple readings that need to be brought to bear to the stories of inclusion and exclusion. *Kissing Jessica Stein* may be told in the register of assimilation. But, it can also be told as a story about the fluidity of sexuality. In an exchange with her two gay best friends, one accuses Helen of trying on lesbianism like a new fashion and reprimands Helen for the idea that she can just choose her sexuality. But, the other friend is more open-minded, encouraging Helen in her new pursuits. The vision of sexuality that infuses the film is one of the fluidity of sexuality, in which attraction and intimacy are not reducible to stable identity categories. *Kissing Jessica Stein* is then also a story of the socially constructed nature of sexuality, a story that challenges the more essentialist approaches that posit sexuality as a fixed category of identity. Jessica and Helen have a fluid sexuality, and their identities are not derived from these sexualities. The sexual politics of the film has a "more queer" sensibility, destabilizing the lines between heterosexual and homosexual, suggesting those lines are more porous and less important than those policing the borders would suggest. The private intimacies of Jessica and Helen are morphed into a more public transgression of stable sexual categories.

Similarly, *Queer as Folk* can be told as a "less queer" story. As Michael explains in the opening narration of the pilot, "The thing you need to know is, it's all about sex." Gay male identity is conflated with sex—public, anonymous, excessive sex. Straight folks are discussed with derision, representing all that these queer boys are not. Despite its name, *Queer as Folk* runs contrary to a queer politics. It does not challenge gay and lesbian identity categories, nor does it attempt to displace the hetero/homo binary. It posits an essentialized gay identity, a fixed identity constituted in and through sex, constructing itself in opposition to heterosexuality.

Nor is *Queer as Folk* unapologetically transgressive of established borders. The gay men in *Queer as Folk* are consumers. Brian's apartment is exquisitely modern, adorned with all the accoutrements of stylish living. His car, his clothes, his cell phone are always the best, the latest, the most beautiful. While the others in the posse are not as rich, they are no less consumption oriented. Indeed, these gay men inhabit a universe of private enterprise: from the glitzy bars to the small comic shop to the online live sex site, the gay counter public is a deeply marketized space. In *Queer as Folk*, the gay male subject comes into being as a privatized consumer of these sexualized spaces and services. Over the show's five seasons, many of its characters come to embrace the very issues that they initially mocked, like monogamy and marriage. *Kissing Jessica Stein* turns out to be open to a more queer reading, and *Queer as Folk* to a rather less one.

These rereadings suggest that struggles for sexual citizenship are more ambivalent than the fault lines of the debate would suggest. Some scholars have tried to make this point, arguing that inclusion within citizenship contains elements of both normalization and subversion (Stychin 2003; Weeks 1997, 1999). Others have suggested that the fault lines of the debate are themselves foreclosing. Judith Butler, for example, has argued that to be for or against gay marriage, gay rights, or inclusion within citizenship is to engage the framework of normalcy and deviance, of legitimacy and illegitimacy, that forecloses other ways of thinking about the sexual field (Butler 2004). In its dichotomized performance, the fault lines of the citizenship debate, particularly as it plays out in the context of same-sex marriage, fails to interrogate the transformations occurring in the process of becoming. Gay and lesbian subjects are in the process of becoming citizens. This process may be incomplete and uneven. But, it is a process that is underway. The sides of the debate fail to capture the multiplicities and contradictions of this process of becoming.

In attempting to move beyond the stultifying binaries of the same-sex marriage debate, Butler suggests that there are "middle zones and hybrid formations" between legitimacy and illegitimacy: "nonplaces . . . are not sites of enunciation, but shifts in the topography from which a questionably audible claim emerges: the claim of the not-yet-subject and the nearly recognizable" (Butler 2004, 108). In this spirit, this chapter seeks to reveal the ambivalences in the middle grounds and hybrid spaces of citizenship, particularly in the multiple spaces of the border. I use the ambivalence of border crossing as an entry point into the same-sex marriage debate, in an attempt to displace the dichotomous performance of either/or. I approach same-sex marriage as a zone of ambivalence and multiplicity, arguing that as same-sex marriage becomes part of the present, the marriage debate is no longer productive. Same-sex marriage needs to be approached through the temporality of the present, as a new moment in the process of becoming, constituting new modalities of citizenship and new borders. Rather than arguing for or against citizenship for gay and lesbian subjects, I explore some of the discursive and material realities and ambiguities of the process of becoming citizens. What happens at the borders of citizenship? As some gay and lesbian subjects cross the border into legitimate citizenship, how are those subjects transformed? In what ways are gay men and lesbians becoming subject to new forms of self-governance as they come inside marriage? How is citizenship transformed? And how is the border itself transformed? How porous is the border, and what anxieties are produced by such fluidity? How do these anxieties produce a desire for more intense border patrol? What is opened and what is closed at these border crossings?

Same-Sex Marriage and the Zones of Ambivalence

Same-sex marriage has not been produced as a zone of ambivalence. Indeed, it may be among the least ambivalent zones in the public sphere. There are two positions: for or against. Social conservatives are against it. Progressive liberals are for it. In a parallel debate, gay and lesbian mainstream rights advocates are for it. Queer activists are against it. The debate has raged, and the dichoto-mies have been performed over and again. As Judith Butler has argued, it is a debate that forces a foreclosure of the spaces in between, of the questions that cannot be asked, because if one is not for it, one is against it (Butler 2004).

Further, it is a debate with a temporal dislocation: It assumes same-sex marriage as the future and debates the desirability of this future. But, same-sex marriage is no longer only of the future; it inhabits the present. Same-sex marriage now is—uneven, ambivalent, fragile—but it is.[1] Gay and lesbian subjects are getting married in the here and now. Indeed, gay and lesbian mar-riages are now in the past—as the ceremony fades into the day-to-day realities of marital practices, or further, into the shadows of divorce. The marriage debate must accordingly shift its focus from the future to the present, from what will be to what is starting to become. Same-sex marriage is not what it once was, as gay and lesbian subjects cross the borders into marriage and into citizenship. No longer the antithesis of gay and lesbian, what has marriage become? What have gay and lesbian become?

This process of becoming the present is found in the transformations within *Queer as Folk*. The representation of the gay and lesbian subjects is not static. While it may have begun as a performance of radical gay sexuality, in favor of sexual multiplicity and against sexual monogamy and marriage, its characters have changed over time. Michael—the one who brought us the foundational narrative—"The thing you need to know is, it's all about sex"— enters into a monogamous relationship with Ben. Michael and Ben begin to displace Melanie and Lindsay, the lesbian couple, as the models of familial domesticity. They are not only monogamous, but they assume all of the trap-pings of a privatized, self-disciplining domesticity. Michael and Ben become the foster parents of a troubled teenager, Hunter. In the process, they must transform themselves into the folds of respectability, ever ready for the visit of the social worker. Their apartment, although small, is impeccably tidy. Theirs is not the average family—Ben and foster son Hunter are HIV posi-tive. Their worries traverse the gay/straight spectrum, with self-discipline extending from domestic aesthetics to getting Hunter to school on time, to ensuring the diets, exercise, and mentality to keep the disease at bay.

In a dramatic shift from the show's earlier performance of gay politics, the fourth season ends with Michael and Ben getting married. They travel to Toronto, Canada, along with the gang, for the purpose of cycling back to Pittsburgh as part of the Liberty Ride, a fundraiser for a local hospice. On route to Toronto, Ben proposes and Michael—initially ambivalent—accepts. They go to City Hall, and in front of friends and family (Michael's mother Debbie is ever-present), exchange their wedding vows. But, not without the performance of the marriage debate. During his moment of doubt, Michael tells Brian that Ben has proposed, and the two argue.

BRIAN: We're queer. We don't need marriage. We don't need the sanction of dickless politicians and pederast priests. We fuck who we want to, when we want to. That is our God-given right.

MICHAEL: But it's also our God-given right to have everything that straight people have. Because we're every bit as much human as they are.

Not only does Michael overcome his doubt, but Brian puts his politics aside to make sure that the newlyweds are given a proper celebration. The marriage debate is performed, and although Brian does not change his views, he does respect and embrace his best friend's choice.

Their debate reveals something of the transformations that occur in the process of becoming citizens. As the gay subject comes to be incorporated into some of the institutions and practices of citizenship, a new range of choices confront this subject:

BRIAN: . . . And since when did you ever have the least interest in getting married?

MICHAEL: I didn't. But not because I didn't want to, but because I never thought I could. It wasn't a story I told myself like straight kids did—you know, that someday I'd meet that special person and we'd fall in love and have a big wedding. It was never real for me. And all the stuff started happening in Massachusetts and California and here. . . .

For Michael, law enters into the cultural realm, creating a narrative that was not possible before. The process of becoming brings into existence a range of possibilities and choices that were previously unthinkable: Now, marriage is thinkable, if not entirely legally accessible. With these new choices comes a further transformation of identity: Michael embraces an identity antithetical to his identity but a few years earlier. Crossing borders begets new borders.

The episode performs a multiplicity of border crossings, including a literal one. As the Liberty Ride comes to the Canada/U.S. border, Ben and Michael have their first newlywed encounter with the U.S. state, as they attempt to cross the border as a married couple. The U.S. federal government does not recognize same-sex marriage and therefore refuses to allow them to submit a single custom's card. The process of crossing the territorial border is simultaneously a recrossing of the social citizenship border; they are cast back into noncitizens, or less than full citizens, as they are reconstituted as unmarried. As the subjects cross the territorial border, their marriage is effectively annulled. Yet, the cultural reality of their marriage does cross the border—the couple wears their wedding rings, they made their commitment, they know in their hearts that their marriage is real.

While the territorial border survives intact, the cultural border between gay/straight, married/not married undergoes its own transformation. Ben and Michael live in a cultural space somewhere in between married and not married. They imagine and make audible a new identity—the gay married citizen—and a new practice of citizenship—two men performing marriage. It is an identity and practice that can be viewed through Brian's assimilationist lens: queers mimicking the most normalizing dimensions of heteronormativity. But, it can also be viewed through a lens of the multiple changes that accompany the process of becoming. Ben and Michael may be highly domesticated subjects, but they refuse to be de-eroticized. The final scene of the marriage episode closes on newlyweds Michael and Ben having sex with a lingering shot of the wedding bands on their fingers. A jarring punk version of "Over the Rainbow" plays in the background. On one hand, the scene can be read as the most normalized gay sex ever represented—it is not only marital sex, it is the scene of consummation, the very thing that makes a marriage real, transforming it from contract to status.

Yet, in an extraordinary transformation of the representation of gay sex as promiscuous, threatening, disrupting the social order here, in a double reversal, gay sex makes gay marriage real. In this scene, the gay subject/citizen refuses its de-eroticized modality. Not unlike the transformation of sodomite to citizen in the film *Wilde* and the Supreme Court ruling in *Lawrence v. Texas*, citizenship is accomplished not through an erasure of the act of sodomy but, rather, in and through it. This performance of sodomy—sodomy as consummation—pushes at the edges of domesticated citizenship. Gay marriage is no longer sexually anesthetized; rather, in this representation, it includes sexual desire. One of the producers, Daniel Lipman, says of this scene:

What happened was the music forced you to hear the song that you've heard a zillion times in a new way. The lyrics, what they're saying, is "somewhere over the rainbow, birds can fly, why can't I?" and what you see are the two men who are married, who have rings. Basically, they are saying "we are here, gay marriage is here, and whatever happens, ultimately, you're going to have to recognize it, world." And you look at that in a new way with the song.

Alongside the jarring music, the viewer is asked to reimagine a world in which gay marriage simply is. The music also forces the viewer to reimagine a world in which gay marriage includes sex. It is a new look not only at gay marriage, but also at gay sex: gay sex as domesticated within marriage but not erased, and gay sex as a site of celebration, erotic desire, and relational commitment.

This consummation scene represents another in-between space, a middle zone between marriage and non-marriage, between legitimate and illegitimate citizenship. Gay sex is domesticated, yet the heterosexual core of marital sex is displaced. Gay marital sex is performed publicly, as it simultaneously privatizes that desire. The subjects are transformed, the border is transformed, the practices of citizenship are transformed in ways both more and less radical than a dichotomized same-sex marriage debate can capture.

The marriage episodes also witness a series of border crossings in the underlying gender politics of the show. The gay/lesbian opposition played out in earlier seasons of *Queer as Folk* is now further complicated. It is no longer simply the heteronormativized lesbians who embrace familial domesticity, but it becomes part of the potential identity of the gay male citizen. Yet, there is arguably still an underlying opposition: Just as the gay men do weddings better (recall that they saved Mel and Lindsay's wedding), so too do the gay men do familial domesticity better. The domestication of Ben and Michael within the bonds of sexual matrimony occurs at precisely the same time as Melanie and Lindsay—once the models of a much disparaged familialized domesticity—are coming undone. The season ends with Mel and Lindsay separating because of Lindsay's affair with a man. Becoming citizens sets them up for citizenship failure. Mel and Lindsay have stumbled on the terrain of citizenship. They are bad citizens—not by being outside of marriage, but by failing within its terms.

These marriage episodes at the fourth season of *Queer as Folk* mark a moment in the process of becoming, in which gay and lesbian subjects have crossed a particular set of borders into legitimate citizenship and begun to engage, in ways both aspirational and oppositional, with the terrain of marriage. Marriage is no longer represented as the antithesis of gay identity but as a possible choice of citizenship.

It is also represented as involving a range of risks of citizenship once reserved for heterosexuals. Same-sex marriage is no longer simply aspirational or, conversely, something to be against. As it becomes part of the sexual field, part of the terrain of sexual citizenship, gay and lesbian subjects will now have to negotiate its multiple normativities and regulatory practices. Consummation and adultery, once exclusively heterosexual terms, will themselves be transformed by the entrance of these new citizens and so, too, will these new citizens be transformed by their entry into a world that includes consummation and adultery, in ways that remain as yet unknown.

Real Marriage in Real Time

The legal recognition of same-sex marriage in the United States remains at an early stage, with some courts beginning to redraw the borders of marriage to include same-sex couples, while most others continue to reinforce its opposite-sex borders. The constitutional challenges that dominate the contemporary legal and political terrain invoke all of the hopes and fears of border crossings and border patrol. While many same-sex couples are attempting to cross the borders of marriage into legitimate social citizenship, social conservatives are attempting to resurrect heterosexuality, if not as a thick border of all components of citizenship then at least for this fundamental social institution.

Legal recognition although uneven and fragile, has begun, with the first legal same-sex marriages in the United States being celebrated in Massachusetts in May 2004. Since that time, the constitutional challenges continue apace, with lower courts in Washington State, New York, and California striking down the prohibition on same-sex marriage. Appellate courts in both Washington and New York have since overruled the lower courts and, alongside courts in New Jersey, Arizona, and Indiana, have upheld the constitutionality of the traditional opposite-sex definition of marriage. The legal battles continue with most of these lower court opinions under appeal, with new challenges arising in other states, and with yet other states attempting to pass constitutional amendments prohibiting the recognition of same-sex marriage.

While the courts obviously divide on the basic question of the legitimacy of same-sex marriage, they also diverge on the underlying question of the nature of marriage. These challenges force the courts to address the question of the nature of marriage in order to decide whether it can or should accommodate same-sex couples. The courts on both sides are engaged in a form of border patrol of the institution of marriage. One side seeks to maintain more traditional borders of marriage, while the other seeks to expand those borders. Yet, in so doing, both are engaged in a process of reconstituting marriage, its subjects, and its borders.

On one side are the cases that seek to maintain the heterosexual definition of marriage. Often, the reasoning is simply at the definitional level: Marriage is and has always been defined as the union of one man and one woman; therefore, it is by its definitional nature heterosexual. In *Lewis v. Harris*, for example, the New Jersey Superior Court wrote that "the prohibition on same-sex marriage is not so much a limitation on the right to marriage, but a defining element of that right accepted for generations" (*Lewis v. Harris* 2003, 13).[2] In terms of the equal protection analysis, the court concludes that as a result of this opposite-sex definition of marriage, same-sex couples are not similarly situated to opposite-sex couples. "Individuals who wish to enter into mixed gender marriage seek access to the historically defined concept of marriage. The plaintiffs, on the other hand, are in a class of individuals who wish to alter the fundamental nature of marriage itself." In the court's view, "the differences between these classes are stark" (*Lewis*, 23). The very definition of marriage as heterosexual is used to preempt an equality challenge from anyone who is not included within the definition. In other words, the heterosexual border of marriage is used to defend the heterosexual border of marriage.

The courts upholding the opposite-sex definition of marriage also typically discuss the link among marriage, procreation, and childrearing. While most courts no longer assert procreation as the essence of marriage, they nevertheless conclude that the state's interest in promoting procreation and childrearing in marriage is an important and legitimate one that justifies the restriction on same-sex marriage. The courts focus on the fact that only heterosexual couples can procreate "naturally," namely, through sexual intercourse between the couple. They admit that the line-drawing exercise is imprecise, insofar as heterosexual couples that do not or cannot procreate can still marry. However, the courts typically excuse this lack of precision, in that the lack of "mathematical nicety" does not necessarily invalidate the line drawing. As the court stated in *Standhardt*, "the fact that the line could be drawn differently is a matter for legislative rather than judicial consideration" (*Standhardt*, 463).

There is a perceptible shift in the discourse about reproduction in these cases. At one time the idea of procreation was reserved for heterosexuals;

same-sex couples were simply excluded from the idea of having and raising children. However, the courts increasingly, if begrudgingly, recognize that same-sex couples are having and raising children. In *Morrison v. Sandler*, the Indiana Court of Appeals noted that same-sex parents are successfully raising children. In *Standhardt*, the Arizona Court of Appeals observed that "children in same-sex families could benefit from the stability offered by same-sex marriage." In this legal discourse, the same-sex family has arrived, to a large extent, normalized. Same-sex couples are parents, indeed perfectly good parents, who could benefit from the additional stability of marriage. These courts conclude that it is nevertheless entirely legitimate for state legislatures to draw the border line around marriage in such a way as to promote "responsible procreation." Because heterosexual couples are the only couples who can procreate just by having sex, it is entirely appropriate for the state to promote marriage for these couples as a way to promote responsible procreation.

There is, however, a twist in the court's effort to reassert the heterosexual borders of marriage. In *Morrison*, the court relied on this idea of responsible procreation as a justification for the opposite-sex definition of marriage. In so doing, the court noted not only that same-sex couples are having and raising children, but further, that they do not need to be encouraged to procreate responsibly in the same way that heterosexual couples do. The court focuses on the "key differences" in how most opposite-sex couples and all same-sex couples become parents.

> Becoming a parent by using "artificial" reproduction methods is frequently costly and time-consuming. Adopting children is much the same. Those persons wanting to have children by assisted reproduction or adoption are, by necessity, heavily invested, financially and emotionally, in those processes. Those processes also require a great deal of foresight and planning. "Natural" procreation, on the other hand, may occur only between opposite-sex couples and with no foresight or planning. All that is required is one instance of sexual intercourse with a man for a woman to become pregnant. (*Morrison*, 24)

Given the state's legitimate interest in ensuring "that children are raised in stable environments," the court reasons that there is less concern about same-sex couples than about opposite-sex couples:

> Those persons who have invested the significant time, effort, and expense associated with assisted reproduction or adoption may be seen as very likely to be able to provide such an environment, with or without the "protections" of

marriage, because of the high level of financial and emotional commitment exerted in conceiving or adopting a child or children in the first place. By contrast, procreation by "natural" reproduction may occur without any thought for the future. (*Morrison*, 24)

It is only opposite-sex couples who can "reproduce on their own by having sex with little to no contemplation of the consequences" and who therefore need to be encouraged to get and stay married. Same-sex couples do not need to be encouraged to procreate responsibly; they already do so. The court goes to some length to emphasize this distinction:

> We are using the term "responsible procreation" to mean the procreation and raising of children by persons who have contemplated, and are well-suited for, the required commitment and challenges of child-rearing. . . . Again, same-sex or opposite-sex couples who adopt or use assisted reproduction technologies may be presumed to have, by necessity, thoroughly contemplated such challenges before investing the time, money, and effort needed to adopt or use reproductive technology. Opposite-sex couples who can reproduce "naturally" need not, and often do not, engage in such contemplation before having intercourse. (*Morrison*, 24, note 13)

According to the court then, same-sex couples are responsible parents, who contemplate the many challenges of parenting before embarking on it and who are well-suited for its commitment. In this remarkable inversion of the gay/straight stability/instability dichotomy, it is now same-sex parents who are, by their very path to parenthood, stable, whereas heterosexual parents are not necessarily so. It is opposite-sex couples who may have irresponsible sex and as a result irresponsible childbirth. Without marriage to bind the mother and father together, "heterosexual intercourse, procreation, and child care are largely disconnected processes, would be chaotic" (*Morrison*, 26, quoting from Cordy dissent in *Goodridge*). Marriage is required for "formally binding the husband-father to his wife and child, and imposing on him the responsibilities of fatherhood" (*Morrison*, 26) and to prevent the chaos of irresponsible heterosexual procreation. In this narrative, it is straight couples who are at risk of citizenship failure and who need marriage to keep them in line. Same-sex parents may be excluded from marriage, but they are produced as good parents, as good familialized citizens who do not present the same perpetual risk of sexualized citizenship failure.

Some critics might suggest that this reasoning in *Morrison* is disingenuous, that the court is simply deploying traditional arguments about procreation and marriage dressed up in a slightly more acceptable rhetoric. There may well be instrumentalism in the court's reasoning. We should nevertheless take this rhetoric seriously, insofar as it says something about dominant discourses within which citizenship and gay and lesbian subjects are being constituted. And in taking this judicial discourse seriously, there is a discernible change in the citizenship status of gay and lesbian subjects. Gay and lesbian subjectivity is no longer based on vilification and outlaw status, but on a different kind of border drawing in which same-sex couples are partially included within the bounds of respectable citizenship, notwithstanding their exclusion from marriage. It is reflective of the process of becoming—no longer fully excluded, yet not yet fully embraced.

Moreover, this process of becoming has begun to change the discourse. It is beginning to change the way in which courts engage in the exercise of border patrol and the way in which these subjects are being constituted. It captures the ambivalences of this process of becoming, or perhaps more accurately in this case, the irony of inclusion through exclusion. The heterosexual border of marriage is defended but in a way that nevertheless recognizes that gay and lesbian subjects are crossing the borders of familialized citizenship. The act of exclusion is accomplished through an act of normalization.

This discursive shift and its begrudging acknowledgment of limited citizenship are evident in the most vociferous opposition to same-sex marriage, namely, the efforts to pass constitutional amendments prohibiting same-sex marriage. The debates around the Federal Marriage Amendment(FMA), an amendment to the U.S. Constitution prohibiting the legal recognition of same-sex marriage, are marked by this tension between increasing citizenship recognition and border patrol. Quite unlike the debates around same-sex marriage with the passage of the Defense of Marriage Act (DOMA) in 1996, the debates around the FMA are increasingly cast in a language that recognizes the citizenship of gay and lesbian subjects. In the DOMA debates, one of the themes was an explicit moral disapproval of homosexuality; the proponents had little reservation about expressing their support of the act in the language of moral disapprobation. But, ten years later, the discourse had shifted. While some themes have continued—the importance of tradition, the family, and the protection of children—the moral condemnation of homosexuality is no longer as readily apparent.

In contrast, one of the major themes to emerge in the FMA debates is a denial of discrimination against gay and lesbian subjects. Many supporters of the FMA who testified before the various congressional subcommittees emphasized this nondiscrimination argument, suggesting that the counter argument was not only wrong, but offensive. Senator Cornyn, for example, told the Senate Committee on the Judiciary that "it is offensive for anyone to charge supporters of traditional marriage with bigotry." Similarly, he stated that it is a "myth . . . that proponents of traditional marriage are 'writing discrimination into the Constitution.' This argument is both curious and offensive" (March 23, 2004).

Underlying this denouncement of the critics of the FMA is the idea that it is no longer justifiable to discriminate against gay and lesbian subjects. Even the proponents of the FMA must deny this discrimination. This argument was made succinctly by Senator Orrin Hatch, a leading supporter of the FMA, during the Senate debates: "No one wants to discriminate against gays . . . simply put, we want to preserve traditional marriage." But, Senator Hatch went even further, asserting "Our attempt to protect traditional marriage laws has nothing to do with the private choices of gay and lesbian *citizens*" (Hatch 2004, emphasis added). Discrimination is not acceptable precisely because gay and lesbian subjects are now recognized as citizens. Therefore, the opponents of same-sex marriage must now find a way to finesse the discrimination inherent in prohibition, through denial and a rhetoric of outrage.

The FMA is an effort to resurrect the heterosexuality of the marriage borders and to limit the sexual citizenship of gay and lesbian subjects. However, even this most virulent of border defenses is being articulated in the discourse of citizenship. It is an example of how the process of becoming has transformed the discursive terrain of citizenship. As gay and lesbian subjects cross borders for some purposes, as they unbecome sexual outlaws, the language of border patrol itself changes. Social conservative opponents of same-sex marriage must appropriate the discourse of those who have sought to advance the citizenship rights of gay and lesbian subjects. As in cases like *Morrison*, exclusion is being sought through a discourse of normalization and partial inclusion.

On the other side of the debate are the cases that have struck down the prohibition on same-sex marriage as violating state constitutions—*Baker* and *Goodridge*, and the lower courts in *Hernandez, Marriage Cases* (California), *Anderson,* and *Castle* (some of which have been overruled)—which provide a very different answer to the question of the nature of marriage: an answer that begins to redefine the legal understanding of marriage. In the challenges that allow same-sex marriage, marriage is increasingly defined in the language of commitment and intimacy. For example, in *Hernandez*, the New York Supreme Court stated:

> As a society, we recognize that the decision of whether and whom to marry is life transforming. It is a unique expression of a private bond and profound love between a couple, and a life dream shared by many in our culture. It is also society's most significant public proclamation of commitment to another person for life. With marriage comes not only legal and financial benefits, but also the supportive community of family and friends who witness and celebrate a couple's devotion to one another, at the time of the wedding and through the anniversaries that follow. Simply put, marriage is viewed by society as the utmost expression of a couple's commitment and love. (*Hernandez* 2005, 609)[3]

The language of commitment emerges as the central defining feature of marriage. As the New York court further states, "Marriage, as it is understood today, is both a partnership of two loving equals who choose to commit themselves to each other and their children" (*Hernandez*, 609). The court in *Goodridge*, while discussing many legal dimensions of civil marriage, similarly emphasizes the centrality of commitment as the essence of marriage: "Civil marriage is at once a deeply personal commitment to another human being and a highly public celebration of the ideals of mutuality, companionship, intimacy, fidelity and family" (*Goodridge*, 594). The essence of marriage as commitment is again emphasized by the court in specifically rejecting the idea that marriage is about procreation: "It is the exclusive and permanent commitment of the marriage partners to one another, not the begetting of children, that is the sine qua non of civil marriage" (*Goodridge*, 961).

The idea of marriage as commitment is a redefinition consistent with what Anthony Giddens and others have called the "transformation of intimacy" (Beck 1999; Giddens 1992). Marriage has changed from a lifelong status to an individualized and voluntary relationship intended to promote the emotional well-being of its parties (Giddens 1992). It is based on individual choice and individual fulfillment; entry and exit is governed by individual choice rather than lifelong commitment. In this transformation, marriage is no longer a lifelong commitment for reproduction, childrearing, and social stability but rather a relationship of emotional intimacy. Giddens describes it as a "pure relationship"—a relationship that is "entered into for its own sake, for what can be derived by each person from a sustained association with another; and which is continued only insofar as it is thought by both parties to deliver enough satisfactions for each individual to stay within it" (Giddens 1992, 58). It is based on the idea of confluent love or an "opening oneself out to the other"; its continuation depends on the ability to sustain intimacy (Giddens 1992, 61). As Giddens further argues, pure relationships and confluent love have "no specific connection to heterosexuality" (63).

This transformation of intimacy is evident in the pro same-sex marriage cases where marriage is redefined as no longer about procreation and channeling sexuality but rather about voluntary commitment and emotional intimacy. The incorporation of same-sex couples into the institution has precipitated a transformation in the articulated definition of the institution. Admittedly, these changes to the definition of marriage have not been caused by same-sex marriage, but reflect broader social transformations in the relationships of intimacy through the latter part of the twentieth century. It is these broader transformations of intimacy that produce same-sex marriage as imaginable, as a meaningful idea. Nonetheless, it is in these constitutional challenges that many of these inchoate changes to social understandings of marriage are being legally articulated. It is in the moment of border crossing, of same-sex couples being included in the institution of marriage, that marriage must be explicitly redefined.

This is not, however, to suggest a winner in the same-sex marriage debates. While same-sex marriage does seem to have a transformative dimension, it is not unambivalently so. If marriage is being redefined as commitment, it is important to ask, Commitment to what? At an obvious level, it is commitment of two people to each other. But, what is the nature of this commitment? What is its purpose, and what is its effect? As the court states in *Goodridge*: "Marriage anchors an ordered society by encouraging stable relationships over transient ones. It is central to the way the Commonwealth identifies individuals, provides for the orderly distribution of property, ensures that children and adults are cared for and supported whenever possible from private rather than public funds, and tracks important epidemiological and demographic data" (*Goodridge*, 954).

In the pro same-sex marriage decisions, marriage is all about social stability through the orderly distribution of rights and responsibilities, the privatization of dependency, and raising children. Commitment involves the commitment not simply of two people to each other, but a commitment of those two people to live with each other and the world around them in a particular way. It is an economic commitment to assume mutual rights and responsibilities, to financially support each other and their children. It is a sexual and emotional commitment to monogamy and fidelity, a commitment to each other to the exclusion of all others. It is a commitment that is, at least in principle, lifelong. Despite the rejection of marriage as in essence about procreation, this emphasis on stability, monogamy, and fidelity has a strikingly similar effect; marriage is produced as including stable and responsible procreation in monogamous relationships. Unpacking the commitment suggests that it is a vision of marriage that is not that different from the one articulated in the anti same-sex marriage decisions. It is a commitment to having and raising children in a stable, two-parent, monogamous family, admittedly with a nonheterosexual twist. It is a commitment to the very vision of marriage that queer scholars have critiqued, that is, a highly privatized, domesticated, normalized vision of human relationships.

While same-sex marriage forces the articulation of a significant transformation in marriage, it is simultaneously performed through the rearticulation of many of its more conventional dimensions. Even in the pro same-sex marriage decisions, the borders of marriage are being carefully managed. As the court in *Goodridge* states: "Certainly our decision today marks a significant change in the definition of marriage as it has been inherited from the common law, and understood by many societies for centuries. *But it does not disturb the fundamental value of marriage in our society*" (*Goodridge*, 965, emphasis added). Rather, in the court's words:

> . . . the plaintiffs seek only to be married, not to undermine the institution of civil marriage. They do not want marriage to be abolished. They do not attack the binary nature of marriage, the consanguinity provisions, or any of the other gate-keeping provisions of the marriage licensing law. (*Goodridge*, 965)

The court is engaged in a performance of border patrol not unlike those of Justice Kennedy in the *Lawrence* decision discussed in Chapter 1. When gay and lesbian subjects cross the borders, whether from criminal sodomite to sexual citizen or same-sex couple to married citizen, the anxieties of border crossings must be managed. Just as Kennedy is able to shift the homosexual from bad to good citizen by carefully ensuring that the borders between good and bad citizenship are carefully maintained, so too does the *Goodridge* court allow a border crossing by carefully propping up the borders of marriage. The court concludes, "That same sex couples are willing to embrace marriage's solemn obligations of exclusivity, mutual support, and commitment to one another is a testament to the enduring place of marriage in our laws and in the human spirit" (*Goodridge*, 965). Despite the border crossing, marriage is the same as it ever was.

Of course, marriage is *not* the same as it ever was—it has changed in ways that are significant, and it has been maintained in ways that are significant. In the moment of assuaging fears of border chaos, the court emphasizes continuity and downplays the extent to which same-sex marriage not only brings new subjects into marriage but also forces the articulation of the new understanding of marriage as commitment. The court can accomplish this emphasis on continuity in part because this new understanding of marriage already carries considerable resonance. The transformation of intimacy has already produced a change in societal understandings of the nature of marriage; it no longer sounds jarring to hear marriage described in these words, even for those who oppose same-sex marriage.

The gay and lesbian subjects who cross the marriage border are being reconstituted in ambivalent terms. In these border crossing cases, gay and lesbian subjects are often explicitly rearticulated in the language of good citizenship. Indeed, in some cases they are being constituted as the new model citizens. Although subsequently overruled in *Anderson*, the Washington Superior Court struck down the prohibition on same-sex marriage, the same-sex couples seeking to marry were framed in the language of heroic citizenship:

> The characteristics embodied by these plaintiffs are ones that our society and the institution of marriage need more of not less. Let the plaintiffs stand as inspiration for all those citizens, homosexual and heterosexual, who may follow their path. (*Anderson*, 12)

The same-sex couples are held up as a model of citizenship that all should follow. The court further articulates their particular citizenship virtues:

> Their lives reflect hard work, professional achievement, religious faith and willingness to stand up for their beliefs. They are law-abiding, taxpaying, model citizens.
>
> They include exemplary parents, adoptive parents, foster parents and grandparents. They know well what it means to make a commitment and honor it . . .

there is no worthwhile institution that they would dishonor, much less destroy. (*Anderson,* 12)

Not unlike the Fab Five of *Queer Eye for the Straight Guy,* gay and lesbian subjects are the new model citizens, the heroic citizens, standing for all that is valued in American citizenship. In an extraordinary reversal of the more traditional terms of heterosexual sexual citizenship, gay men and lesbians are here becoming the most becoming of citizens.

These two sides of the same-sex marriage debate have more in common that may initially meet the eye. Both are encountering the constitutive tension of citizenship and border control. Citizenship requires borders; it demands an inside and an outside, with clear lines of demarcation between the two. Porous borders cannot be protected, so border crossings—the inclusion of the previously excluded into citizenship—must necessarily be accompanied by a propping up of the crossed borders. While one side seeks to maintain heterosexuality as a thick border, the other seeks to maintain the borders of marriage by redefining it in the language of intimacy and solidarity.

Further, both sides increasingly share a language of the citizenship of gay and lesbian subjects. As gay and lesbian subjects become citizens—or at least unbecome outlaws—they can no longer be vilified in the moral discourse that only a few years ago was still politically viable. And it is this process of becoming that creates the very anxiety of border control. Both sides are producing and responding to anxieties about border control, which in turn reconstitute the borders and the citizens who cross them.

Governance Inside Marriage

As same-sex couples come inside marriage, they will become—or will seek to become—subject to its regulatory practices. The inside of marriage is a site of multiple forms of legal regulation and self-governance. It involves not only a set of legal rights and responsibilities, but also a broad set of societal expectations and practices of self-conduct. As they cross the border into marriage, same-sex couples will begin to face a new set of citizenship norms. They, too, now face societal judgment for practices unbecoming of a citizen. Like Melanie and Lindsay, the lesbian couple in *Queer as Folk,* or Bette and Tina on *The L Word,* these same-sex couples now face a new set of risks of citizenship failure: adultery, relationship breakdown, divorce.

Quite predictably, divorce has emerged as one of the first sites of contestation from inside of marriage. A few of the couples who either entered civil unions in Vermont or marriages in Massachusetts or Canada have since sought a dissolution of their civil union or their divorce. For residents of Vermont or Massachusetts, this is a relatively straightforward legal matter. For residents of other states who came to Vermont or Massachusetts to be civilly unioned or wed, respectively, exit is a complicated affair. Under the Vermont Civil Unions Act, a person must be a resident of Vermont for one year in order to apply for dissolution of their civil union in Vermont courts. The Connecticut Civil Unions Act of 2005 has a similar residency requirement. Couples who marry in Massachusetts or Canada also face a one-year residency requirement to obtain a divorce. [4]

Same-sex couples who traveled to marry or enter a civil union face considerable legal difficulties in the event of relationship breakdown. Many states refuse to recognize the validity of the same-sex marriage and therefore refuse to extend the rights and responsibilities otherwise associated with marriage to these couples. This non-recognition includes divorce: If there is no valid marriage, then there is no marriage to dissolve. Same-sex couples who seek to dissolve their civil union or obtain a divorce in their resident state must then confront a new set of border crossing issues: Do their civil unions or marriages cross state borders? Can they get a divorce in a state that recognizes neither civil unions nor same-sex marriages? As a result, the early divorce cases are arising as a variation on the cultural border crossing cases; they are all about the validity of the union or marriage.

To date, most of the interstate cases involve attempts to dissolve Vermont civil unions. Some cases have recognized the validity of the civil union, while others have refused to do so. [5]

Like the constitutional challenges, these cases are all about establishing the validity of the civil union or the marriage in order to dissolve it. But unlike the constitutional challenges, the plaintiffs in these cases are no longer heroic citizens, performing the virtues of stable, privatized citizenship, but rather are now failed citizens. They are forced to relitigate their marriages at the moment of marriage failure. Their failure is held up for a kind of public viewing.

While the new politics of adultery and the more general societal backlash against divorce are attempting to shame opposite-sex divorcing couples, these same-sex cases are not actually about divorce. Unlike the anti-divorce movement, the publicity of these cases is not about trying to keep these couples married. Rather, these cases are about whether the couples were ever married in the first place. As one woman who sought a dissolution of her Vermont civil union in New Jersey explained, "I would not invalidate our civil union by agreeing that it didn't count" (*Anderson*).

Some social conservatives have been quick to jump on the bandwagon of these divorce cases, not only as a way of relitigating the invalidity of the initial border crossing, but also as a way of performatively ridiculing the very idea of same-sex commitment and stability. For example, in the face of one of the first applications for same-sex divorce in Massachusetts, one same-sex marriage opponent stated that it simply confirmed that gay couples are not equipped for marriage: "We're not surprised," said Kris Mineau, president of the Massachusetts Family Institute, which is fighting for a constitutional amendment to ban gay marriage. "Particularly among male homosexuals, the promiscuity is just phenomenal" (Peter 2004). After the Iowa divorce, Congressman Steve King, who is one of the plaintiffs in the appeal opposing the recognition of the marriage, made the following statement: "Unicorns, leprechauns, gay marriages in Iowa—these are all things you will never find because they just don't exist. But perhaps Judge Neary would grant divorces to unicorns and leprechauns too" (King 2003).

These early divorce cases are more like the border crossing constitutional challenges than they are about the governance of the inside of marriage. Yet, the fact that they are about divorce—about marital failure and a form of citizenship failure—begins to raise the specter of this type of governance. Same-sex couples will be increasingly subject to the same set of cultural norms and practices as opposite-sex couples, including the mandate to make their relationships a project of self-governance and to take all reasonable steps to minimize the risk of relationship breakdown. They, too, will be called upon to become responsible risk managers, who recognize the fragility of relationships and will take all reasonable steps to minimize the risk of relationship breakdown, including immunizing their relationship from the epidemic of adultery.

Some of these messages of self-regulation have begun to appear in the cultural domain of same-sex marriage. In the marriage episodes of *Queer as Folk*, where the marriage of Ben and Michael is accompanied by the separation of Melanie and Lindsay, we begin to see this idea that entrance into marriage includes exposure to a new set of relational risks including infidelity and divorce. Mel and Lindsay have stumbled on the new citizenship terrain. Having become sexual citizens, they now represent a rather unbecoming facet of it: infidelity, failure to work on their relationship before and after it, and separation notwithstanding the presence of very young children. Theirs is a failed sexual citizenship, within the new politics of adultery and the pushback on divorce.

Lindsay's affair plays out many of the fears of the new politics of adultery. It is a woman choosing to have an affair; she has the affair at work; she fails to resist at the moment when she could have just said no; and, contrary to the therapeutic model of deliverance, she is not sufficiently contrite and apologetic in its aftermath to allow for treatment. Mel too, however, is unable to commit herself to the course of treatment; she is unable to forgive Lindsay and unwilling to do the work on the path of forgiveness. Lindsay's affair is made all the worse by its timing. Melanie is pregnant with what was supposed to be the couple's second child. Lindsay has not only jeopardized her relationship; she has jeopardized the well-being of her family and her family-to-be. She has callously put her sexual self-interest in front of the interests of their children—born and unborn. While in the new politics of adultery, sexual infidelity always represents a citizenship failure, the familial circumstances of the couple heightens the nature of the infraction.

There is a further twist in Lindsay's infidelity, insofar as her affair is with a man. This makes her infidelity both more and less transgressive. On the one hand, she has engaged in heterosexual sexual intercourse and has therefore committed adultery by the strictest of legal definitions. On the other hand, her affair with a man raises questions about her sexuality. After all these years, is Lindsay really a heterosexual, a reading that would fit within the show's performance of a fairly rigid gay/straight dichotomy. Or, does her sexual desire begin to displace that dichotomous sexuality, creating the possibility of a more fluid sexuality? To what extent are Mel and Lindsay separating because Lindsay has had sex with a man or because Lindsay has had sex with another person? Is the violation a specifically lesbian one? Or is it simply a marital exclusivity one?

This sexual ambivalence plays back into the new politics of adultery. If the violation is that Lindsay had sex with a man, then there are several interpretive possibilities. One reading is that Lindsay is a heterosexual woman. Although she has failed in her relationship, it was untrue from the beginning. Lindsay would be analogous to the *Oprah* and *Dr. Phil* stories of husbands who realize that they are gay or transsexuals. In *Oprah*'s "My Husband Is Gay" or *Dr. Phil*'s "Extreme Marriages," the infidel husband is treated differently from those who have heterosexual affairs. The infidelity is condemned, but the dissolution of the relationship is treated with a kind of inevitability.

The major mistake that these husbands made was a failure of self-discovery: They failed themselves and their families by not recognizing their gay essence before they married. The infidelity is not the major story but a kind of subplot leading to an inevitable conclusion. [6]

In a second reading, Lindsay is bisexual. This is a much more complicated terrain, in which the risk of infidelity is exponentially higher. Bisexuality, in popular discourse, is often associated with non-monogamy; bisexuals are only really bisexual if they have relationships with women and men at the same time (Klesse 2005). It is associated with a kind of failure in self-discipline; bisexuals are individuals who cannot even commit themselves to a single gender, not to mention a single person. If Lindsay is bisexual, her relationship then faces a heightened risk of infidelity and a diminished capacity for self-discipline. In order to protect her relationship and her children from the chaos of adultery, Lindsay will have to work at least twice as hard as a straight woman to ensure that she does not fall prey to the seductions of adulterous desire. On the flip side, the problem for Mel is that she must be able to work to forgive Lindsay. But, unlike the more run-of-the-mill heterosexual victim of adultery, she must be able to forgive the fact that Lindsay had sex with a man. She must now recognize and embrace the possibility of bisexual adultery: The risk is higher, and the ability to forgive potentially more difficult. The generic risks and harms of violating marital exclusivity are thereby heightened, making the possibility of treatment even more challenging.

In a third reading, Lindsay is a lesbian who has sex with men. After Lindsay's sexual encounter with the artist Sam, Melanie becomes suspicious and confronts Lindsay. Lindsay does not deny the affair, but instead insists that it "reconfirmed for me that this is who I am. That my life is with you and Gus. And the baby. That I still choose you." Melanie, unable to forgive Lindsay, continues to focus on the fact that she had sex with a man and that she cannot be a lesbian.

MELANIE: I know which team I play on. It's not a choice or a preference. It's who I am. It's who I've always been. A rug muncher, a muff diver, a cunt lapper, a bull, a lezzie, a dyke.

LINDSAY: What do you think I am?

MELANIE: Don't ask me to make up your mind for you. You have to do that all by yourself.

LINDSAY: I'm a lesbian.

MELANIE: Not if you're having sex with a man, honey.

Lindsay insists on her identity as a lesbian, while Melanie denies her quali-
fications. Lesbian becomes a site of contestation. Is it defined exclusively in
terms of sexual desire and sexual practice? Is it a category foreclosed by one
sexual encounter to the contrary? Lindsay acted out her desire for Sam but
argues that it only reconfirmed her identity as a lesbian. It is an acknowledgment and simultaneous denial of a category of lesbians: lesbians who have sex
with men.

The category of lesbians who have sex with men is one that begins to con-
fuse the gay/straight dichotomy, while remaining framed within it. It still insists on the identity of lesbian, yet it refuses to define it exclusively in terms
of sexual desire and practice. It also raises the possibilities of a more fluid notion of sexuality—one defined in less absolutist terms. Lindsay's affair is, in
one reading, reminiscent of the sexuality of *Kissing Jessica Stein* in which attraction and intimacy are not reducible to stable identity categories. Yet, even
with this reading, with its more fluid and contested notions of sexuality, there
is no narrative ambivalence over the infidelity: Lindsay cheated. She violated
the terms of their marriage. She put her relationship at risk, and she seriously
compromised the best interests of the children of the marriage.

In the final season, Melanie and Lindsay reconcile. They looked over the
edge of their relationship abyss and, against the odds, they came back. They
become part of the mysterious 35 percent of couples who survive infidelity (although there are no known statistics about same-sex couples and infidelity).
Melanie is able to forgive Lindsay; she recommits herself to the relationship
and to the process of rebuilding trust and intimacy. It is part of the complicated story of treatment and relationship redemption in the new politics of
adultery. It is not enough for the guilty party to simply seek forgiveness; the
other party must be prepared to engage in the equally difficult work of forgiveness and reconstruction.

Despite these ambivalences and the fairy tale ending, the message is consistent with the new politics of adultery: Extramarital sex is dangerous, corrosive, destructive. It will ruin your relationship. Gay or straight, don't do it. It
is a story that runs counter to the nonmonogamous narrative that characterized some of the other gay relationships in *Queer as Folk*. Brian, in particular,
long insisted that monogamy is for heterosexuals. Yet, even Brian and Justin
have their rules: no kissing on the mouth, no repeat partners. They, too, have
their lines for protecting the emotional intimacy of their relationship. It may
be a far cry from the new politics of adultery, which condemns any and all

forms of sexual interaction with another. But, they have their own version of fidelity. Brian and Justin are juxtaposed with Michael and Ben, who are more traditionally monogamous. In one of the episodes of the fourth season, Ben is shown facing down an adulterous seduction, and in keeping with his promise of sexual and emotional exclusivity to Michael, just says no. Ben performs the ethical moment of the new politics of adultery, the moment where resistance is possible. In contrast, Lindsay did not. While Brian may still be opposing the normativity of this new sexual citizenship, Ben is becoming a good citizen within its discursive frame. Lindsay is not. The ideas of the new politics of adultery can thus be found creeping into the show's narratives, despite the ambivalent performance of the citizenship debates.

Queer as Folk is not alone in these representations. The L Word, Showtime's lesbian version of Queer as Folk, explores the romantic and sexual exploits of a group of rather fashionable lesbian friends living in Los Angeles. Amongst the many characters are Bette (Jennifer Beals) and Tina (Laurel Holloman), who in the first season are the long-term lesbian couple trying to have a baby. But, before the season is over, the not-so-stable-after-all couple is rocked by infidelity: Bette has a passionate affair with Candace, the sexy carpenter helping her with her gallery's art installation. Tina discovers the affair through an intimate touch exchanged between Bette and Candace. The couple has an emotional confrontation, ending in tearful sex. But, the damage is done, and the season ends with Tina leaving. She takes refuge at her friend Alice's apartment, where she is shown in tears, her wedding ring removed.

Much of the second season focuses on their separation. Tina and Bette are shown with their lawyers, arguing over the terms of their "divorce" and their division of property. Yet, throughout the legal conflicts, Bette desperately wants to get back together. She tries to apologize, privately and publicly, in hope of reconciliation. But, her efforts are rebuffed by Tina, who becomes involved with another woman, Helena. The plot is further complicated by the fact that Tina is now pregnant, with a baby that she and Bette had planned to have together. Eventually, after much work on Bette's part, the couple reconciles, and Tina moves back home for the birth of their child.

Bette's infidelity is loaded with many of the messages of the new politics of adultery. It is costly and destructive. It could have been resisted but it isn't. It is with a woman who works for her. It is a woman having the affair. Moreover, it is a manifestation of an underlying crisis of intimacy: The couple has been drifting apart for several months. But, it is the infidelity itself—the ultimate act of betrayal—that pushes the couple over the edge into relationship break-down. While treatment may be possible, it is never guaranteed, and in this case, Tina is initially unable and unwilling to forgive Bette. Bette is devastated by the breakup, all the more so by the fact that she is ultimately responsible for it. She replays the affair in her mind, trying in her words, to figure out "the moment that I could have said no" (episode 203). Resistance is possible and would have been the better option. But, ultimately, she does the hard work of contrition and apology, and Tina eventually forgives her. In the third season, it becomes clear that Bette has learned her lesson. When confronted with the possible seduction of a beautiful senator, to whom she is obviously attracted, Bette walks away.

Queer as Folk and The L Word are illustrative of the kind of self-governance to which same-sex couples may be increasingly subject. Being inside marriage means being subject to its regime of responsibilization. It means taking re-sponsibility for one's marriage and taking all necessary precautions against its failure. As with the predominantly heterosexual context of the new poli-tics of adultery discussed in Chapter 2, this is a kind of governance that may be increasingly performed on a cultural rather than a legal terrain. While it may be a while before same-sex couples begin to appear on Dr. Phil, self-help guides for same-sex couples are beginning to appear, some of which specifi-cally highlight the challenges of sexual exclusivity for a culture that has at times self-consciously celebrated nonmonogamy. For example, in an article posted on the National Center for Lesbian Rights website, lesbians are ad-vised on how to survive infidelity (Huntington). Some of the advice is lesbian specific, noting for example that lesbians are more likely to have affairs than straight couples: "Well, whereas straight men and women have best friends, comrades and confidants of the same sex who they are not attracted to, lesbi-ans are almost always best friends with a potential mate." However, the treat-ment advice directly parallels that directed at heterosexual married couples in the new politics of adultery: "complete honesty," severing any and all contact with the third party, taking responsibility, and getting "to work and fix[ing] your relationship" (Huntington). Such self-help guides are likely only the be-ginning of a multiplicity of cultural representations that will subject gay and lesbian subjects to these new citizenship norms.

This politics of adultery may begin to be performed in law. In Vermont and Connecticut, civil unions can be dissolved on the same grounds as mar-riages, which in both states include adultery. In Massachusetts, grounds for divorce also include adultery.[7] We may then reasonably expect it to appear in law. As same-sex couples marry and divorce, there will eventually be adultery cases. A Melanie will seek a divorce from a Lindsay on the basis of adultery, which will in turn require that the legal definition of adultery be revisited. Or, in another interesting twist, a Bette and Tina, or a Michael and Ben will seek to get married under the new covenant marriage laws, subjecting themselves to a higher form of marriage and a more stringent set of divorce grounds. Legal regulation may no longer be the central form of regulation, but it may still be called upon from time to time to participate in it.

The politics of adultery is but one example of how the inside of marriage will subject gay and lesbian subjects to a new form of governance. It is an example of how inclusion within citizenship transforms the subjects, and in the language of its critics, subjects them to a regime of normalization.

When same-sex relationships are recognized—legally or culturally—same-sex couples become subject to the demands of responsibilization. They, too, will be called upon to take responsibility for their relationships, to make their relationships a project, and to work hard on them to make them work. Citizenship success within this newfound recognition lies in the choices of individuals. Good citizens will choose to work hard to manage the risks to their relationships. If the going gets tough, they will choose to work harder, calling in the experts if necessary. And if they fail, they will be subject to the regime's normative judgments of unbecoming citizenship.

Queer Eye Beyond the Gay/Straight Guy

In *Queer Eye for the Straight Guy*, five gay men come to the rescue of a disheveled straight man. They descend upon his house like an aesthetic swat team and engage in "a playful deconstruction of the subject's current lifestyle" (QueerEye.com). Carson, the fashion stylist, savages his clothes closet—making fun of his style and throwing out clothes by the pound. Thom, the interior designer, disparages the décor or lack thereof and begins the process of purging furniture, lamps, and other sundry items that have seen better days. Ted, the food and wine guy, tackles the kitchen and parodies the food in the fridge. Kyan, the beauty guru, zeros in on the obscenities of the bathroom, focusing on the filth and the lack of grooming products. And Jai, the culture guy, tries to figure out their straight guy's cultural edge, anxiety, or aspirations.

Having established his multiple fashion and aesthetic crimes, the Fab Five set out to "build a better straight man." They take him shopping and begin a makeover. All the while, the banter is playful—simultaneously teasing and supportive. The Fab Five try to get a sense of their straight man—his likes and dislikes, his comforts and aspirations. They listen to him. While they make him over, they try to do so in a way that respects his inner sense of self. And they listen in particular to his romantic goals: He wants to be a better boyfriend or husband; he wants to change for the love in his life; or if he is single, he wants to bring love into his life. Throughout the show, both his inner self and his romantic aspirations are the referent points for the Fab Five's transformation.

After the shopping makeover, they bring him home, where Thom has performed his miraculous decorating makeover; rooms are completely transformed with new furniture, carpets, and artwork. Kyan takes their straight man to the bathroom where he is shown how to use his new grooming products. Ted takes him to the kitchen, where he gets a cooking lesson. Carson orchestrates the fashion show and tells him what to wear for his special evening. Jai gives him a little chat on the cultural part of his evening, often focusing on how to make his girlfriend/wife/family/friend feel special. The Fab Five depart, but their cameras stay behind to watch their straight man prepare for his special evening. As he grooms, dresses, and cooks, the Fab Five retire with martinis in hand to their living room, where they gather around the television to watch their straight man. The girlfriend/wife/family/friend arrives, and the straight man performs his new self, with the Fab Five all the while engaging in a sportslike commentary on his successes and failures.

The show is a shopping fest, highlighting the newest trends and brand names in fashion, home design, grooming, food, and culture. It is a performance in marketized citizenship, where status and identity is produced through consumption. The goal of the Fab Five is to increase their straight men's cultural capital, by teaching him to make better consumer choices, all the while remaining true to his social origins (Bordieu 1984). But, the show is about more than consumer citizenship and its brand names. It works because of the synergy between the Fab Five—the constant witty repartee, the mild sexual banter, all with a gay twist. And it works because of the synergy between the Fab Five and their straight man. While they engage in relentless teasing, it is done with a kind of earnest sensitivity; they care about their straight guy, they want to make him a better straight man, they want him to succeed. They are experts in the arts of self-transformation and self-governance, and they only succeed if he succeeds, if he learns to take better care of his domestic life.

Some have criticized the show for playing into gay stereotypes (Sawyer 2003). Others suggest that the show transcends those stereotypes. It is a debate not unlike same-sex marriage with positions for or against; is it assimilation or transgression. And not unlike the marriage debate, it is a debate that misses the broader discursive significance of the Fab Five as the new models of citizenship. As media critic Jack Myers has observed, "Queer Eye takes the stereotypical gay character and elevates him to iconic status" (Myers 2003). Queer Eye is not simply illustrative of gay men crossing the borders into legitimate citizenship; rather these five gay men have become heroic citizens. They come to the rescue of domesticity, heterosexuality, and masculinity.

Their straight men are utterly incapable of caring for their domestic sphere. They do not know how to dress, groom, decorate, or cook. These lost arts of the domestic sphere—once the preserve of women—are resuscitated through an increasing emphasis on domestic arts and domestic divas in much popular culture. It is seen, for example, in the explosion of the home decorating and cooking channels and in the proliferation of glossy decorating, food, and wine books and magazines on the domestic arts, all dedicated to improving cultural capital by refining consumption.

While Queer Eye is not alone in its attention to the aesthetics of domestic consumption and self-conduct, it does so in a rather unique way. Queer Eye is all about the role of gay men as experts in this resuscitation. As some of its detractors have pointed out, gay men have long been associated with the domestic arts—they are the decorators, the fashionistas, the stylists—now, these gay men are specifically coming to the rescue of the straight guy in this domestic sphere. With changing gender relationships, heterosexual men can no longer simply rely on women—as mothers or wives—to maintain the domestic sphere.

These men sometimes live alone—never married, newly divorced, or widowed. Or they live with women who themselves seem to have lost the art of the domestic. With this once invisible work of the domestic sphere—decorating, cooking, dressing, and grooming—no longer being performed by women, the domestic is collapsing into utter disarray, at precisely the same time as greater emphasis is being placed on the domestic as a site of cultural capital and aesthetic self-governance. These men are desperately in need of training in the lost arts of the domestic.

This is not simply about straight men taking on the aesthetic of the domestic. This is about gay men coming to the rescue of heterosexuality. The straight guys are men who do not have a girlfriend or wife, or who have a girlfriend who will not move in with them, or who have a wife who is at her wits end. These are heterosexual men whose failure in the domestic sphere is threatening their ability to attract, marry, and/or keep a partner. The masculinity that these straight men have been performing is a failed one: It is operating to repel—or at least not sexually excite—the very women that they want to attract. As one commentator has observed, beneath all of its queerness, *Queer Eye* embraces the very traditional ideal of heterosexual romance: "In its best moments, it's about rekindling romance for the person who makes us want to be better people—it's about understanding and empathy, and the Fab Five are the guiding spirits to that ideal" (Shimes 2003).

The Fab Five do their work by privileging heterosexual masculinity, while simultaneously remaking it. From the moment they arrive at their subject's house, they playfully point out his failures, making fun of his dreadful clothes, appalling kitchen, even more appalling bathroom. It is a performance in the failure of a kind of masculinity. Yet, they are not out to destroy masculinity, but to perfect it. They are, in their own words, "building a better straight man." It is by placing heterosexual masculinity in this privileged position—as that which is in need of rescue—and by positioning the Fab Five as the knights in shining armor, that *Queer Eye* is able to accomplish a reversal in the terms of citizenship success and failure. Straight men are failing. Gay men can help them. It is this positioning that allows for a reconfiguration in the relationship between them. The gay men become the experts in performing heterosexual masculinity, as they teach the straight guy to perform it better.

Ironically, this rescue is accomplished through a ritualized performance of the gay/straight dichotomy. This relationship is of course the very premise of the show. The opening sequence depicts a street corner at the intersection of Gay and Straight. The show's tension works because of its reversal of the traditional antipathy of straight men to homosexuality. Straight men must displace their discomfort with gay men in favor of trust. And the Fab Five are as gay as gay can be. They perform their sexuality, through a diluted sexualized banter with one another other and their straight guy. This sexual banter does not let the viewer—or the straight man—forget that these are men who are attracted to men. While Carson, the fashion guy, may be the most screamingly effeminate, each of them perform their sexuality.

The straight guys are similarly confidently—if ineffectually—heterosexual. They play poker or collect baseball paraphernalia; they wear rock and roll t-shirts or NASCAR hats. There is no mistaking the differences between gay and straight.

Yet, the gay/straight opposition is simultaneously reconfigured. Not only are gay men cast as the heroes of straight men, but the very border dividing them is destabilized. The straight men must be prepared to accept the sexuality of the Fab Five, to be the focus of its attention albeit for a few brief days with considerable pecuniary benefit, but nonetheless in a kind of public spotlight where the presence of their sexuality cannot be avoided. The very difference capable of producing cataclysmic violence is here downgraded and reconfigured as a kind of ironic, playful cleavage. United in the pursuit of a better masculinity, the erotic is both more and less important. The gay/straight relationship is reconstituted, with gay men as experts in all things male, and with straight men as the willing receptacles of their knowledge.

The mainstreaming of gay characters on prime-time television, and the queering of cultural citizenship, is, paradoxically, performed through a simultaneous deconstruction of the very categories that bring gay/straight into being. Becoming citizens means becoming both more and less gay, as the category of gay becomes less stable. Gay/straight required clear borders. But as gay crosses into citizenship, the borders become more porous and more ambiguous.

Queer Eye bears more than a slight resemblance to same-sex marriage. It delivers a message about the importance of marriage. It tells us that good citizens must make their marriage—or their relationship or their relationship in prospect—a project. They must learn to work hard on their relationship by working first on themselves. The queer boys of *Queer Eye* are the heroic citizens who will lead this renewal of the domestic and help save heterosexuality from imminent collapse, just as same-sex couples are cast as heroic citizens who are committed to the fundamental importance of the institution of marriage. *Queer Eye* and same-sex marriage are both arguments for marriage and the intimate sphere: these are important, indeed absolutely crucial, sites for our personal happiness and self-fulfillment.

In both *Queer Eye* and same-sex marriage, the queering of citizenship begins to blur the boundaries that produced gay and straight, citizen and non-citizen, hero and outlaw. They both help reveal the extent to which the transformations in the modalities of sexual citizenship require an analysis that moves beyond a focus on the multiple instantiations of heteronormativity. The

sexing, privatizing, and self-disciplining of citizenship is occurring in many
ways not captured by a focus on a gay/straight divide, in the multiple contestations of sexual citizenship between and among straight citizens, and in the
ways in which these same contestations and forms of governance are extending to the gay citizen.

The debates about both *Queer Eye* and same-sex marriage also raise questions about who is policing the borders of citizenship. We have seen the extent
to which social conservatives are attempting to resurrect heterosexuality as
a thick border. We have also seen the extent to which many courts entrusted
with border patrol allow border crossings only by reinforcing the idea of
clearly delineated borders. But, there are also ways in which those inside gay
or queer politics are engaged in varying forms of border patrol. For example,
the debate about *Queer Eye* involves the question of representability: who gets
to be represented and what qualifies as a gay stereotype.

Its critics suggest that the Fab Five are simply gay caricatures, reinforcing negative stereotypes of gay identity as queens, designers, and decorators.
Underlying this critique is the idea that these gay stereotypes harked back to
a day of exclusion (or at best, limited inclusion as decorating consultations)
and that they are best left behind as gay and lesbian subjects cross the borders
into citizenship. There is an implicit policing of the borders of citizenship
here, with only some gay and lesbian subjects entitled to cross, lest the other
less respectable subjects undermine the legitimacy of those newly inscribed
citizens. It may encourage border crossing (for some); it nevertheless seeks to
police that border.

The queer critique of same-sex marriage is one that arguably engages in its
own form of border control. In asserting that same-sex marriage is normalizing of gay and lesbian identity, there is a way in which this queer critique has
the paradoxical effect of propping up the very gay/straight dichotomy that it
so often seeks to deconstruct. The very identity of queer seems to be predicated on its exclusion; its radical and subversive nature is dependent on remaining on the outside. The idea here is that if gay and lesbian subjects cross
the borders into citizenship, and become assimilated into its many norms and
practices, they will lose their radical edge.

While queer theory is extremely critical of the essentialist notions of identity that inform much gay and lesbian politics, including the movement toward same-sex marriage, there is a way in which their defense of the outside,
the outlaw, the beyond has the effect of reinforcing a gay/straight opposition,

with gays/queers on the outside and straights on the inside of citizenship. The queer side of the same-sex marriage debate appears to be oddly vested in the very border and its underlying dichotomies that it asserts to be an artifice. In a reversal of the claim that marriage excludes the queer, this critique can be read as insisting on its own exclusion.

Queer After Gay

Six Feet Under, HBO's award-winning offbeat drama, tells the story of the lives, loves, and losses of the Fisher family, who own and operate a funeral home in Los Angeles. The show begins with the death of the patriarch, Nathaniel Fisher, which sets the stage for his two sons, Nate (Peter Krause) and David (Michael C. Hall) to take over the family business. Among the cast of characters are their mother Ruth (Frances Conroy), their teenage sister Claire (Lauren Ambrose), and a revolving door of their girlfriends, boyfriends, and spouses. The dysfunctionality of the Fisher family is set against the arbitrary nature of death, with the regular cast supplemented in each show by corpses, grieving families, and visiting ghosts. The show's sardonic humor explores the emotional melodramas and repressed desires of each of the characters, as they fumble through their daily existence, surrounded by death.

David, like the other main characters of *Six Feet Under*, is on an emotional journey, trying to come to terms with his internal demons. But, David's particular struggle begins, and ends, with the fact that he is gay. Throughout the first season, David struggles with his closeted sexual identity and his on-again off-again relationship with boyfriend Keith. He eventually comes out to his family, but his self-loathing continues, with recurrent relationship crises and confrontations. Along the way, the show explores the ups and downs of David and Keith's same-sex relationship, from negotiating monogamy to adopting children.

David's brother Nate—heterosexual to his core—struggles with his own demons—an inability to commit to a relationship, wavering between Brenda and Lisa (he marries each one in due course). Nate never conquers his demons; his first wife dies, and he is about to leave his pregnant second wife when he suddenly dies. Nor does he find solace in death, coming back to taunt Brenda. It is David who triumphs. It is David and Keith whose relationship survives, who adopt children, who buy the funeral home, redecorate it, and live happily, if not "ever after," in it. It is the same-sex couple who overcome their adversities, their demons in themselves and each other, and who negotiate the treacherous terrain of a marriagelike relationship.

Six Feet Under is not a gay show in the style of *Queer as Folk*, *The L Word*, or even *Queer Eye for the Straight Guy*. It is a quirky family drama, which has a gay man as one of the central characters. It is a kind of postidentity politics cultural representation, where gay characters begin to be mainstreamed into a broader narrative. It is a new kind of mainstreaming, in which gay characters have crossed the borders into representation in a way that begins to explore their multidimensionality rather than simply their gayness. While their gayness was an important part of their emotional and relational struggles, it was not their whole story.

David and Keith's relationship is tumultuous. They fight and bicker. At times, it is simply a representation of the daily discord of intimacy; other times, it is a manifestation of deeper psychic wounds. They go to couples therapy to work on their relationship and to work on themselves. As self-disciplining selves, they seek to manage the risks of their relationship. Their relationship is also sexual. From the beginning to the end, David and Keith—like all the characters—have sex. Despite their move toward, and episodic repulsion from, domesticity, David and Keith are deeply sexual beings. They watch porn. They have hot passionate sex together. Sometimes, they have sex with other men. But, even as they move toward monogamy, their conjugal lives affirm the sexual. Their citizenship is not achieved at the expense of sex, but rather, is affirmed on the terrain of the sexual, alongside the familial and the domestic.

Six Feet Under represents a reversal in the heterosexual conventions of sexual citizenship. After six seasons it is the same-sex couple that emerges triumphant in life, even if unable to avoid the vicissitudes of death. It is the same-sex couple that embraces domesticity, that seriously undertakes couples counseling to work on their relationship, and that buys and manages the family business. It is the same-sex couple that succeeds in all the markers of good citizenship: domesticated sexual citizenship, market citizenship, and self-disciplining citizenship.

They are not alone; the Fab Five too have emerged as new model citizens. But unlike the gay men of *Queer Eye*, David and Keith are avowedly sexual. Their citizenship may have circumscribed sex to the domestic sphere, but in that sphere, the sex is represented and affirmed. In many ways, David and Keith evoke the zeitgeist of the present. As same-sex marriage becomes a reality, as gay and lesbian couples cross the border into this dimension of citizenship, new realities are produced; new things are happening that are simply not captured by a debate that argues for or against. Borders are being crossed, moved, defended, and reconstituted. Citizens are being made, contested, and remade. It is a process within which some gay men can even emerge as heroic citizens; their avowedly sexual citizenship coupled with domesticity, markets, and self-discipline. And as they cross the borders, so too are the borders transformed. To the extent that queer citizenship is beginning to disrupt and unsettle the borders between gay and straight, queer critique needs to move beyond its focus on the heteronormative if it is to capture the emerging modalities and ambivalence of inclusion and exclusion. Just like in *Six Feet Under*, gay/straight is coming undone.

Conclusion

Up Against Sexual Citizenship

IN THE PRECEDING CHAPTERS, I have explored the contours of an emerging modality of sexual citizenship—a citizenship that may be overtly sexed, but simultaneously privatized and self-disciplined. Citizenship is increasingly sexed up: It incorporates once abject sexualities and once deviant sexual practices. Sexual discourses now saturate the public sphere, as the subject of political contestation and cultural representation. Some commentators welcome and celebrate this transformation. Brian McNair, for example, celebrates the "pornographication" of mainstream cultural representations as a democratic affirmation of diverse sexualities (McNair 2003). Many others lament this transformation, in a range of contested discourses. Queer critics focus on the loss of the radicality of outsider status, while more conservative critics bemoan the loss of a more confined sexuality. I have tried to bracket the normativity of these claims, focusing instead on what happens when the borders of sexual citizenship are contested and crossed, when outsiders become citizens, and when new outsider and insider identities are produced and regulated.

Membership may have its privileges, but it also has its costs, reconstituting the identities of those once excluded and subjecting these newly inscribed members to new regimes of governance. But recognizing the costs of inclusion should not be taken as argument against citizenship, for exclusion too has its costs. The contemporary terms of sexual citizenship are that which those inside and outside are up against, whether a given subject desires inclusion or not. Some may desire belonging but resist its terms; others may seek to maintain the otherness of their exclusion. Yet others may wish to maintain belonging in a counter public but are compelled into the broader terms of citizenship. The postures may be infinite, desirous of some inclusion but not others. But, the subject remains constituted by the terms of this citizenship: good, bad, becoming, unbecoming, or something in between.

The chapters have approached the legal and cultural regulation of sex and sexuality through the lens of citizenship. One might legitimately ask whether much of the analysis has proceeded in its absence? Could the analysis have been told in another alternative register, such as rights or recognition? Undoubtedly, it could. But, there is I believe a value added to the register of citizenship. The idea of citizenship directs analytic attention to questions of belonging and borders. While it has traditionally been focused on the relationship between the individual and the state and thereby runs the risk of reinforcing an overly narrow focus on the juridical and political dimensions of belonging, in its more recent instantiations, citizenship has been deployed to capture a broader range of social practices of belonging. I have explored both the legal and cultural representations of these practices of belonging, with a sharp focus on borders, border crossing, and border anxieties. I have linked issues of sex and sexuality with citizenship through this register of practices of belonging.

My point has been to highlight how sexual practices are a central dimension of contemporary citizenship. This is not a novel claim. From the practices of the ancient Greeks to the proliferation of public discourses of sex from the seventeenth century forward to the articulation of the American nation, sex has long been implicated in citizenship (Cott 2000; Foucault 1985). It is rather a claim about the particular modalities of contemporary citizenship, in which sexual discourses have saturated the public sphere in more explicit ways. As neo-liberal citizenship has become more about self-governance, this responsibilized citizenship includes an explicitly sexual dimension; individuals are called upon to make the right choices about sex, managing sexual risks through self-discipline. Like freedom more generally, sexual freedom has become a terrain to be managed (Foucault 1980, 1985; Rose 1999). Belonging is not achieved at the expense of freedom per se, but rather, in and through its proper exercise. Sexual citizenship is produced and realized by managing the multitudinous possibilities and making the right sexual choices.

The register of citizenship also focuses attention on the anxieties of border crossing. As the chapters have explored, the process of becoming sexual citizens, of subjects crossing the boundary from outlaw to citizen, is a process accompanied by deep anxieties about border control. Citizenship requires borders, and borders require exclusion; a border is only meaningful if there is also a subject, a non-citizen, to exclude or a bad citizen to punish. The preceding chapters have focused on a few of the excluded, the unbecoming, the failed citizen.

Future analyses of sexual citizenship will need to continue to address the ongoing questions of exclusion. Whose identities remain constituted in and through sexual practices that produce them as outsiders? For example, those whose sexualities implicate non-consensuality remain firmly embedded on the outside, constituted and regulated as outlaws. Rapists and child sexual abusers are outlaws par excellence. Their sexual practices and desires make them pathological deviants, whose aberrant sexualities must be disciplined through highly interventionist and coercive means. But, consensuality has not emerged as the new bright line between citizen and outlaw. The preceding chapters have focused on relatively uncontested consensual sex—sex in which the consent of the parties has not been at issue—and explored ways in which these consensual sexual practices may still produce failed or unbecoming citizens.[1] From sodomy to indecency, premarital sex to adultery, s/m sex to commercial sex workers, consent does not operate as an automatic citizenship sanction.

Future analyses of sexual citizenship will need to continue to address the question of which subjects are joining the sexually excluded. Whose identities are in the process of unbecoming? Which subjects are being produced as outsiders through their sexual practices and sexual choices? And how are borders, geographic and/or metaphorical, implicated in these ongoing processes of abjection? For example, while some gay and lesbian subjects are incorporated into the folds of legitimate citizenship, others are abjected. There is, for example, the demonization of the crystal meth-using gay man who has promiscuous, unprotected sex allegedly spreading a new HIV super-virus (Franke 2005). Some gay and AIDS activists have explicitly denounced these subjects and their unsafe sexual practices, in language that resound in the new modalities of citizenship. Larry Kramer, for example, playwright and long-time gay activist, expressed his outrage that gay men are killing each other: "We are murderers, murdering each other" (Kramer, quoted in France 2005). He elaborated: "If intelligent, smart people are unwilling to take responsibility 100 percent for their own dicks, I don't know how you stop the killing."

The denunciation is articulated in the discourse of responsibilization. These gay men are failing to take responsibility for their sexual practices and to manage the risks to their health. These are gay men who refuse to self-discipline and who are becoming a threat to the health of the body politic and to the citizenship of gay men. One gay man—Patient Zero, who is alleged to have been the source of the super-virus and to have spread it far and wide through unsafe sex—is held out for particular vilification. Kramer is blunt in his condemnation of Patient Zero: "This guy is a total and utter asshole" (France 2005, quoting Kramer). "What happens is, this is what people think gay people are like. Now we can't move forward, we can't get to our place in the sun, because of stupid assholes like this." Patient Zero is a failed citizen, an outlaw citizen not only for failing to sexually self-discipline but also for compromising the newfound belonging of responsible gay subjects.

Even without the super-virus (which has been contested and refuted), a new sexual outlaw is being produced through a particular combination of discourses on crystal meth drug use, promiscuous sexual practice, and an increase in HIV transmission within the gay community. One anonymous gay man quoted in a news story said, "The difference between sex with crystal and sex without it is like the difference between Technicolor and black-and-white" (quoted in Specter 2005). He continued, "Once you have sex with crystal, it's hard to imagine having it any other way." Both the crystal meth and the sex on it are addictive. And dangerous. The drug not only removes inhibitions but also common sense, and unprotected sex is said to invariably follow in its wake (Specter 2005).

There are, in this new outlaw, then intersecting discourses of failure: drug addiction, sexual addiction, and unsafe sexual practices. Each is a failure to self-discipline; together they are a recipe for self-destruction. Once again, Larry Kramer, speaking in the high morality of subjects desperately seeking to maintain a precarious inclusion, writes: "You want to kill yourself? Go kill yourself. I'm sorry. It takes hard work to behave like an adult. It takes discipline. . . . Grow up. Behave responsibly. Fight for your rights. Take care of yourself and each other" (quoted in France 2005). Citizenship demands responsibility. And the failure of a gay man to behave responsibly becomes a risk to the citizenship of all gay men. Yet, the exclusion of these subjects may be necessary for the inclusion of others. It is a performance of border, a reassurance that the terms of belonging remain in place.

The very real politics of border crossings and the anxieties of border patrol will require the future analyses of sexual citizenship to extend beyond the figurative borders of social belonging to the literal geographic borders of more traditional invocations of citizenship. The preceding chapters have focused on figurative borders and the practices of belonging within a national polity, assuming formal legal membership rather than interrogating it. But, the norms and practices of contemporary sexual citizenship are also implicated in crossing borders and obtaining this formal legal status. Immigration scholars have highlighted the role of sex and sexuality in citizenship, from gay asylum cases (Hanna 2005; Morgan 2006) to work permits for exotic dancers (Macklin 2003). Marriage, for example, has long been relevant in the ability of subjects to cross borders, with immigration law allowing at least some citizens to sponsor foreigners for the purposes of marriage. This immigration practice has in turn created anxieties about potentially fraudulent marriages, that is, about whether the marriages are "real" or simply entered into for the purposes of attaining American citizenship.

Marriage remains a site of contestation and anxiety in contemporary citizenship practices and transnational border crossings. One example is the practice of mail order brides. Finding brides from other places is hardly new to American life: "Picture brides" and arranged marriages were common through much of American history. But, the modern mail order bride industry is said to be different, with the proliferation of companies on the Internet that seek to match Western men with brides predominantly from Asian and former Soviet countries. [2] Although the statistics are contested, estimates suggest that between 100,000 and 150,000 women advertise annually, and between 2,000 and ? such marriages are begun in the United States each year (Scholes 1998).

The practice has been steeped in controversy since it first garnered public attention. Initially, anxiety swirled around the potential for marriage fraud: order brides did not want to enter into legitimate marriages, but simply want an avenue to American citizenship. The first attempt to regulate the ? ing industry, the Immigration Fraud Amendments Act of 1986, was directed toward protecting men from such marriage fraud. The law set requirements for sponsoring a spouse for permanent residency, including that the couple remain married for two years before allowing them to petition for a ? status; this would follow an INS investigation of the legitimacy of the marriage.

This focus of anxiety began to shift in the 1990s. Alongside an increased visibility of issues of violence against women, the practice of mail order brides came into the public spotlight as a result of several cases of abuse and murder of women who had been mail order brides. In 1995, a 25-year-old Filipina woman was killed in a Seattle courthouse by the man she had married through the mail order bride industry. Her death came while she was seeking a divorce, ten days after immigrating to the United States. Publicity around the murder led to the introduction in Congress of a bill authorizing a study of the international matchmaking industry, which was subsequently enacted as part of the Illegal Immigration Reform and Immigrant Responsibility Act of 1996. This new law carefully straddled the conflicting concerns of marriage fraud and domestic abuse. As one commentator pointed out, it was "a model of bipartisan balancing, . . . every reference to abuse of immigrants by U.S. Citizens or permanent residents was matched with a reference to marriage fraud presumably committed by immigrant spouses seeking 'green cards,' directing a study of both marriage fraud and domestic violence" (Jackson 2002, 502).

The resulting 1999 report and a study by Robert Scholes (Appendix A of the report) provided further information on the prevalence of the practice and suggested that there was a higher risk of domestic abuse within these relationships. The regulatory focus continued to shift further toward protecting women from domestic abuse. In 2000, Congress passed the Battered Immigrant Women's Protection Act, intended to improve access to immigrant protections for battered immigrant women. Although the mail order bride industry was not specifically targeted, mail order brides who experienced domestic abuse would be able to access the protections. In 2005, Congress passed the International Marriage Broker Regulation Act (IMBRA) as part of the authorization of Violence against Women Act. The new legislation required that international marriage brokers conduct background checks of male applicants and disclose to prospective brides any restraining orders, arrest, convictions for murder, domestic and/or sexual abuse, prostitution, controlled substances or alcohol offenses, as well as the applicant's marital history (number and date of marriages and divorces, and previous marriage immigration sponsorships) and age of all children under the age of 18 (§ 833 (d)(2)(B)

This legal regulation and its shifting normative visions can be compared to the cultural representations of the practice of mail order brides. The 2000s saw an explosion of filmic representations of mail order brides. In Birthday Girl (2001), John, a British banker, orders Nadia (Nicole Kidman), a mail order bride from Russia. On her birthday, her cousins arrive, to celebrate. But they take Nadia hostage and demand a ransom from John, who is forced to steal from his bank to pay the ransom. John learns that the kidnapping is a hoax, and Nadia is an accomplice. But, in a further twist, Nadia gets into trouble, and it is John who comes to her rescue. The representation of Nadia as an outlaw, not seeking genuine marriage but money, resounds with the early regulatory efforts in which it was the men who needed to be protected from women seeking fraudulent marriages. She is bad. He is naïve. But, in a melodramatic twist, Nadia is redeemed by John's gallantry.

In *A Foreign Affair* (2003), two brothers in need of domestic help travel to Russia to find a wife. Jake is upfront about their needs. They are not looking for love, and there is no sex involved. They just need a woman to do the housework for them, and in exchange she will get citizenship. Along the way, Jake encounters Angela, a British documentary filmmaker, who is making a film on the mail order bride industry. She becomes fascinated with Jake because he is not looking for a bride in a traditional sense. While Jake doggedly pursues the perfect housekeeper, Josh goes his own way and decides that he wants to find love. And Jake is ultimately side-tracked by the filmmaker, where fascination turns to romance. The mail order brides are not the central characters in this film but rather provide a backdrop for protagonists to discover that real love and real marriage are the answer. Jake and Josh are initially represented as a little bit pathetic—they need a wife but are unable or unwilling to attract one in the American marriage market—but not as naïve. They know what they want (housekeeping), and they know what the mail order bride wants (citizenship). They are not bad, just a little lost.

Mail Order Wife (2004) offers a slightly more complex set of representations of the men and women in the mail order bride industry. It is presented in a kind of mockumentary style, with Andrew, a New York filmmaker, making a documentary of his friend Adrian's mail order bride. He is on hand for the arrival of Lichi, a young Asian mail order bride. Adrian is an obese slob living in Queens, who orders a mail order bride to serve as a maid and an s/m porn actress. Upon arrival Lichi seems to be the stereotype of the perfect Asian bride—beautiful, submissive, and servile. But, Adrian's desires are too much, and Lichi takes refuge in the filmmaker's home, where a new romance develops. Andrew and Lichi marry. In a dramatic exchange of racialized stereotypes, Lichi transforms from the submissive Asian bride she pretended to be to the duplicitous, greedy, and vindictive one she actually is. Adrian and Andrew then join forces to seek their revenge against her.

The film engages the contested visions of the practice of mail order brides. Adrian, the man who orders the mail order bride, is marked as thoroughly unbecoming: fat, disorderly, and sexually deviant. He seeks in marriage not an equal partner but a submissive slave. His sexual desire is deployed to mark him as beyond the realm of the reasonable; he is not simply an American man legitimately rejecting feminist equality in favor of a more traditional gendered division of labor. His abject sexual desires mark him as beyond the bounds of normalcy. Lichi, the mail order bride, is represented in the contested duality of mail order brides, with a particularly racialized twist: first as innocent submissive who needs protection from abuse and then as selfish, materialistic, vindictive, citizenship seeker from whom American men need protection.

Then there is Adrian, the self-righteous, liberal-minded filmmaker who condemns the practice but then crosses the boundaries of appropriate documentary film-making by seeking to rescue Lichi and falling for her masquerade. The film exchanges one set of stereotypes for another: Male clients are bad and female brides are innocent is displaced by the plot twist in which the female bride is actually duplicitous and the male clients are her victims.

The legal and cultural representations of the mail order bride industry appear to gesture in different directions. In legal discourse, the men have become suspect citizens, and the women are their potential victims. In the films, the representations are flipped: The women are suspect, and the men are their potential victims. Both the legal and cultural representations leave space for the possibility of redemption, through real marriage or otherwise, although again, they do so in different directions. IMBRA does not prohibit the practice, nor foreclose the possibility of real marriages. Rather, it adopts a regulated marketized approach with disclosure requirements, whereby individual women are to be provided information and allowed to make their own decisions. The women are to manage their own risk. But, the risk is not entirely privatized, since the women are afforded some exit options; if the relationship turns violent, they can access the heightened immigration protections for battered women.

Yet, the mail order bride industry remains a possible avenue to real marriage and real citizenship. The films are harsh on the practice, with happy endings possible primarily through repudiating it in favor of more romantic or "pure relationships" (Giddens 1992). Real marriages are possible, but not through the mail order bride industry. The protagonists in the films must overcome their limitations, represented by their participation in the practice.

By the end of the films, each has learned to make better choices, to choose love according to the terms of sexual citizenship. Intimacy, love, and romance triumph over commercialized exchange.

Despite these differences, the legal and cultural representations share some elements of contemporary sexual citizenship. Both emphasize choice and the importance of individuals making the right choices in marriage. They also share a vision of the practice of mail order brides as inherently suspect; in all of the representations something is potentially a little bit wrong. In the law, the practice is framed as high risk, painting the men as potential abusers, justifying heightened surveillance. In the films, the men may not be abusers, but they are flawed; there is something a little bit wrong with them. They are lost or naïve, looking for love—or at least a wife—in all the wrong places. They are sympathetic, yet also pathetic. They have failed for some reason in the domestic marriage market. The law is prepared to overlook their failure, provided that it is not criminal or abusive, and to let the prospective brides decide for themselves on the marriageability of these men in this international marriage market. The films, on the other hand, frame the flaws as that which the men must overcome.

The legal and cultural representations of the mail order bride industry, despite their marked differences, reflect the idea that sexual practices are central to contemporary citizenship. Marriage is a key sexual practice, and individual citizens are called upon to make responsible choices about who and how to marry, managing their risks through self-discipline. The participants are each framed as border dwellers, whose marriage choices and practices can tip them over the edges, into or out of citizenship. The overt introduction of the global market into the marriage practice produces anxieties that need to be managed. The discourses of marriage and market as private sit in awkward juxtaposition. The law allows the possibility of this highly marketized citizenship, while the films seek to drive a wedge between them. Yet, both seek a privatized resolution, in which individuals—prospective bride and groom alike—make the "right" choice, and in so doing, affirm or refute not only their sexual citizenship, but also the potential formal citizenship of the prospective bride.

This brief foray into the regulation and representation of mail order brides is offered as an example of how the analysis of sexual citizenship developed in the preceding chapters might also be deployed in transnational issues, wherein geographic borders and formal legal citizenship are at stake. It gestures toward the possibility that the legal and cultural analysis of a modality of sexual citizenship that is privatized and self-disciplined might be insightful in this and other transnational contexts. It further suggests that it might be productive to decenter state practices in these transnational border crossing cases. State practice is obviously important in whether an individual is able to cross borders and obtain formal citizenship, which is after all, about formal state recognition. But, the preceding chapters have not argued against the relevance of legal regulation, but rather, argued for a more expansive analysis of modes of regulation. In a similar vein, the current controversy over mail order brides is not only about state practices. It is also about cultural practices, about the cultural norms of marriage, and about the contested cultural representations of those norms and practices.

In the post-9/11 era, these transnational border crossings are acquiring a heightened and more urgent significance. The events of September 11 have produced intensified anxieties and heightened demands for patrolling the borders of both the imagined community and its very real geographic boundaries. Under the sign of homeland security, these borders have been produced as sites of profound national angst and insecurity, requiring dramatic new powers of surveillance and exclusion. A new wave of anti-immigration sentiment has captured the imagination, with contested points of focus ranging from a specific focus on potential terrorists to a broad net of restricting any and all illegal immigration.

While many of these anxieties and contested regulatory responses, from the Patriot Act to the reform of immigration law, may not appear to be directly relevant to sexual practices, future analysis of sexual citizenship will need to explore the possibility that some might be. How are the new spaces of exclusion sexualized? How are the new outlaws produced partially through sexual practice or sexual abjection? One need look no further than the images that emerged from Abu Ghraib in April 2004 to sense that the abjection of the new outlaws—Iraqi prisoners and enemy combatants—took a specifically sexual turn. The pictures of hooded, naked Iraqi men in positions of simulated sex and sexual humiliation revealed a range of torturous practices at the hands of American soldiers. As Susan Sontag observed, "most of the pictures seem part of a larger confluence of torture and pornography: a young woman leading a naked man around on a leash is a classic dominatrix imagery" (Sontag 2004). The sexually saturated public sphere and the "the vast repertory of pornographic imagery available on the Internet" provides the background from which these images came forth and were given meaning.

Some commentators have begun to connect the images from Abu Ghraib with new sexualized nationalist discourses of the post-9/11 moment. Kim Pearson, for example, identifies a new "patriotic homosocial discourse" that is producing heterosexualized, normalized patriots and homosexualized, deviant non-patriots (Pearson 2005). Pearson deploys Eve Sedgwick's idea of homosociality to explore contemporary border anxieties, arguing that there is an "intense fear of penetration and concern about protecting bodily integrity" that bears more than a passing resemblance to homosexual panic (Pearson 2005). "Much of the current political discourse mirrors homosexual panic due to ambiguity about masculine/nationalist identity, concern about porous borders/penetration and fear of non-outed enemies of the state" (Pearson 2005). Pearson sees this patriotic homosocial discourse in images of sexualized violence of Abu Ghraib, where "sexualized torture demonstrates that nothing is inviolable—neither the physical body itself nor the sexual identity of the person are invulnerable" (Pearson 2005).

Abu Ghraib as a violent performance of exclusion is but one admittedly extreme example of how current national anxieties and practices of border patrol may assume a sexualized dimension that future analyses of sexual citizenship will need to further explore, along with other transnational sites of inclusion and exclusion that may implicate sexual practices. The analysis of sexual citizenship in the preceding chapters may be a helpful template for these transnational issues. For example, while the patrolling of geographic borders from those who seek to infiltrate and destroy the real and imagined communities invokes the most coercive of state practices, it will also be important to consider the role of other forms of regulation in this process. From the reitieration of the photographs of Abu Ghraib in the 24/7 news media to the contested cultural representations, ranging from "Courtesy of the Red, White, and Blue (The Angry American)," the chart-topping country music song by Toby Keith that performed an aggressive American nationalism ("And you'll be sorry you messed with the U.S. of A., cause we'll put a boot in your ass. It's the American way"), to Michael Winterbottom's controversial and critical film *The Road to Guantanamo* (2006), the meaning of these new modalities of inclusion and exclusion, becoming and unbecoming, citizen and alien, will not be produced by state practice alone.

These final comments gesture toward important sites of further interrogation of the contemporary modalities of sexual citizenship, several of which point toward transnational border issues. While speculative in nature, they are suggestive of some of the ways in which the norms and practices of sexual citizenship explored in the preceding chapters may be relevant beyond the figurative borders of belonging to the literal ones of more traditional invocations of citizenship. It is also suggestive of why the register of citizenship has a value added to the analysis of the legal and cultural regulation of sexuality, by linking up the norms and practices of the figurative with the literal, of the national with the transnational.

Contemporary norms of belonging and abjection are deeply implicated in sexual practices. These are the norms that we are all up against, the norms that constitute and measure our degrees of belonging or exclusion, whether inside or outside of the literal and/or figurative borders. Sexual freedom has become a terrain to be managed, preferably through a privatized self-disciplined subject. We are all called upon to manage our sex lives, to make "good" sexual choices and engage in the "right" sexual practices, affirming both our sense of sexual autonomy while governing in and through it. To the extent that we conduct ourselves as ethical sexual subjects (Foucault 1985), through appropriate sexual practices, choices, and desires, we may be constituted and reconstituted as eligible for sexual citizenship—with sex and belonging, freedom and governance, intimately and irrevocably linked. And if we fail to do so, we risk unbecoming citizens, through the subtle and not so subtle interplay of legal and cultural interdictions, once again, interlacing sex with belonging and sexual freedom with sexual self-governance.

Notes

Introduction

1. Civil rights include "the rights necessary for individual freedom—liberty of the person, freedom of speech, thought and faith, the right to own property and to conclude valid contracts." Political rights include "the right to participate in the exercise of political power as a member of a body invested with political authority or as an elector of the members of such a body." Social rights include "the right to a modicum of economic welfare and security to the right to share to the full in the social heritage and to live the life of a civilized being according to the standards prevailing in the society" (Marshall 1950, 10–11).

2. By "gay and lesbian subject," a term I deploy throughout the book, I am referring to an identity constituted by legal, cultural, and other discourses.

3. "Making the claim for inclusion may seem assimilationist, but actually making demands on a culture that denies you is extremely radical; it identifies the frontiers of the conventional, it demarcates the lines of struggle. So, you can see transgression and citizenship as simply different faces of the same moment of challenge. One is separating, the other is calling for belonging. But you can only do one with the other" (Weeks 1997, 323, see also Weeks 1999).

4. As Michael Katz has observed in *The Price of Citizenship* at 2, "The word 'welfare' initially meant 'well-being.'" According to Katz, in the early twentieth century, "welfare range with a progressive tone, it signified the increased assumption of public responsibility for dependence, the professional administration of programs, the rejection of charity, and initial steps of the recognition of entitlement" (Katz 2001, 2).

Chapter 1

1. The Texas Court of Appeals never actually describes the act other than as "engaging in homosexual conduct" and then uses the language of the statute, namely, "deviate sexual intercourse," which includes genital/mouth contact or anal penetration.

2. *Glucksberg* established a two-part test for the recognition of a new fundamental right. First, it must begin with a careful description of the asserted right. Second, the court must determine whether the asserted right is one of "those fundamental rights and liberties which are, objectively, deeply rooted in this Nation's history and tradition, and implicit in the concept of ordered liberty, such that neither liberty nor justice would exist if they were sacrificed" (*Glucksberg*, 720–721).

3. Merl Storr, who has studied the Ann Summers Tupperware-style sex parties in the United Kingdom, has argued that the parties are a form of female homosociality—a performance of a certain kind of femininity that allows women to belong, and to exclude those who do not fit in (Storr 2003). While the parties are all women, the tension between homosociality and lesbianism is carefully policed: Lesbians are not generally welcomed within this heterosexual enclave, and although there may be a range of games and banter in which the women may even "flirt" with other women, the male gaze, the woman as sex object for her man, is ever present. Storr suggests that the range of products on sale—sex toys, the massage oils, the sex guides, the lingerie—all invoke the male gaze, even in its absence. Martha McCaughey and Christina French have similarly observed the extent to which women's sex toy parties assume the heterosexuality of its participants (McCaughey & French 2001, 90). For example, while a broad range of dildos and vibrators are displayed, many parties do not mention or sell strap-on vibrating dildos. As McCaughey and French observe, "it's as though the companies and/or their dealers presume all women have male partners—and male partners who do not want to be penetrated—or as though keeping the 'clean' image of sex toys involves pretending women use them only with men or when alone" (McCaughey & French 2001, 90).

4. The facts of the story of Joanne Webb are all taken from Whitley (2004).

5. The bad publicity led the County Attorney Moore to seek a gag order to "protect" Joanne's right to a fair trial. Sisemore objected, but Judge Robert Mayfield was allegedly furious with all the publicity and temporarily imposed the order. Eventually, the judge ordered that the defense and the prosecutors reach their own agreement. The compromise worked out between Sisemore and Moore was that the defendant and her lawyer could talk about anything except the events of October 7, 2003, namely, the police sting operation.

6. KBOO provided its response to the NAL, but the FCC never issued its final order.

7. Cambria defends the list as identifying the subject matters and themes that have attracted prosecution. On the "no black men/white women" themes, he stated "The last five cases I had involved tapes with black men/white women. That's one of the things they pick. Well, the black women/white men they don't pick" (Calvert & Richards 2004, 164).

8. It is a sentiment echoed by Chairman Kevin Martin in his first public remarks after taking charge of the FCC in 2005. Martin urged cable operators to rein in their shows before Congress cracks down (Hofmeister 2005).

Chapter 2

1. I am indebted to Robert Leckey for this insight and turn of phrase.

2. As Nicholas Rose argues, freedom becomes the terrain on which liberal governance is exercised. Freedom is not the negation of power but one of "its vital elements." Liberal democratic governance is "autonomizing: [it] seeks to govern through constructing a kind of regulated autonomy for social actors. The modern liberal self is 'obliged to be free,' to construe all aspects of its life as the outcome of choices made about a number of options" (Rose 1999, 100). Experts in the "technologies of psychology" acquire their power "because they share this ethic of competent autonomous selfhood, and because they promise to sustain, respect, and restore selfhood to citizens of such polities. They constitute technologies of individuality for the production and regulation of the individual who is "free to choose" (Rose 1999).

3. This Dr. Philification of marriage exemplifies the extent to which the self-governance literature seems to be indebted to both the early and later Foucault, operating in unresolved tension. While there is an emphasis on the role of the self and discourses of freedom, there is simultaneously a borrowing of the early Foucault, with its emphasis on expert intervention, confessionals, and other disciplinary practices (Leckey, personal communication, 2005).

4. However, the New Jersey statute only allowed an annulment where the marriage had not subsequently been ratified. The court held that the husband's actions of continuing to live with the wife for three years and attempting to have sexual intercourse with her had in fact ratified the marriage.

5. According to Giddens, sexual exclusiveness is something to be negotiated between the parties: "Sexual exclusiveness here has a role in the relationship to the degree to which the partners mutually deem it desirable or essential" (Giddens 1992, 62).

6. Adultery remains criminalized—most often as a misdemeanor—in the following states: Alabama: Code of Ala. § 13A-13-2 (2004); Arizona: A.R.S. § 13-1408 (2004); Colorado: C.R.S. 18-6-501 (2004); Florida: Fla. Stat. § 798.01 (2004); Georgia: O.C.G.A. § 16-6-19 (2004); Idaho: Idaho Code § 18-6601 (2004); Illinois: 720 ILCS 5/11-7 (2004); Kansas: K.S.A. § 21-3507 (2003); Maryland: Md. CRIMINAL LAW Code Ann. § 10-501 (2004); Massachusetts: ALM GL ch. 272, § 14 (2005); Michigan: MCLS § 750.30 (2004); Minnesota: Minn. Stat. § 609.36 (2004); Mississippi: Miss. Code Ann. § 97-29-1 (2004); New Hampshire: RSA 645:3 (2004); New York: NY CLS Penal § 255.17 (2004); North Carolina: N.C. Gen. Stat. § 14-184 (2004); North Dakota: N.D. Cent. Code, § 12.1-20-09 (2003); Oklahoma: 21 Okl. St. § 871 (2004); Rhode Island: R.I. Gen. Laws § 11-6-2 (2004); South Carolina: S.C. Code Ann. § 16-15-60 (2004); Utah: Utah Code Ann. § 76-7-103 (2004); Virginia: Va. Code Ann. § 18.2-365 (2004); West Virginia: W. Va. Code § 61-8-3 (2004); Wisconsin: Wis. Stat. § 944.16 (2004).

7. In Alabama, for example, in 2002, of 24,002 divorces, only 101 were granted on the basis of adultery, in contrast to 22,601 granted on the basis of incompatibility. Similarly, in New York State in 2000, of a total of 59,864 divorces, only 273 were granted on the basis of adultery, in contrast to 36,808 on the basis of abandonment (the closest New York State gets to a no-fault ground).

8. These cases blur some of the typical liberal/conservative fault lines. Is it liberal or conservative to recognize same-sex sex as adultery? On the one hand, it seems liberal insofar as it is consistent with the recognition of same-sex relationships more generally. On the other hand, it can be seen as conservative, insofar as it is cast as a repudiation of the monogamous marital heterosexual relationship and a broadening of the fault-based grounds for divorce.

Chapter 3

1. It is important to emphasize that the story of the welfare queen and the deadbeat—of the production of these political and cultural subjects—is not the story of actual single mothers on welfare or noncustodial fathers. Many have sought to dispel the myth of the welfare queen—to illustrate the enormous discrepancy between the discourse and the material reality of these women's lives (see, e.g., Zucchino 1997). This chapter focuses on the production and deployment of these mythic cultural icons—on their production as bad citizens, on the ways in which their identities are deployed to support welfare reform, and on the remedial strategies for transforming these bad citizens into good ones. It is a discursive analysis of the political representations deployed in support of public policy initiatives. It does not reflect the material realities and daily struggles of the single mothers receiving AFDC or the noncustodial fathers who are not providing financial support for their children. Throughout the chapter, I use the pejorative terms "welfare queen" and "deadbeat dads" to keep attention on these discursive productions and their political uses. It is intended to highlight the artificiality of the constructs that are in turn punitively deployed against poor women, poor men, and their children.

2. The Supreme Court had struck down a number of the eligibility restrictions. In *Shapiro v. Thompson*, 394 U.S. 618, the Court struck down AFDC residency requirements, and in *King v. Smith*, 390 U.S. 903 (1968), the Court struck down a state substitute father provision that denied AFDC benefits to families on the ground that the mother had a sexual relationship with a man. See generally Gwendolyn Mink, *Welfare's End* (1998).

3. Many liberals supported this emphasis on workfare on the basis that social norms for women had changed, and that most non-poor women with children are now expected to work. Therefore, it would be reasonable to expect the same from poor women. See David Ellwood, *Poor Support: Poverty in the American Family* (1988); Irwin Garfinkel and Sarah McLanahan, *Single Mothers and Their Children: A New American Dilemma* (1986).

4. Social conservatives do not oppose the workfare approach. Rather, they agree with the underlying emphasis on personal responsibility and have supported welfare reforms that have encouraged and/or mandated work. However, work appears to be secondary to their emphasis on the traditional family as the solution to welfare dependency and poverty. For social conservatives, transforming single women into workers is an inadequate solution, insofar as it addresses the problem after the fact. While it would reduce state expenditures on welfare, it would fail to reverse the problem of illegitimacy and all its attendant social costs. See for example Butler and Kundratas (1987) who argue that although promoting work and responsibility is important, "work requirements within the welfare system do not improve work incentives or opportunities for absent fathers; their effect is to transform mothers into primary earners. . . . Thus, long-term welfare reform has to focus on strengthening the two-parent family" (Butler & Kundratas 1987, 146).

5. Unlike those social conservatives that place a primary emphasis on promoting traditional families, Mead would use this paternalist approach to promote work. Workfare is an important part of Mead's vision for reforming welfare. See Mead 1997, "Welfare Employment" in *The New Paternalism*. This is yet another example of individual positions not mapping perfectly onto these two conservative positions and of the "labels fitting arguments better than people."

6. Historians of social welfare have illustrated that single mothers being able to stay at home to care for their children was never realized for the vast majority of poor women (see Handler 1987/1988, 476). Under both the Aid to Dependent Children program enacted in 1911, and its successor, the Aid to Families with Dependent Children enacted in 1935, highly restrictive conditions disqualified many single mothers, and work remained their only option. For example, the requirement that recipients provide "a suitable home" was used to regulate the sexual behavior of single women—the presence of a man in the house or the birth of an illegitimate child was sufficient to make the home "unsuitable." The maternalist programs were primarily designed to benefit a subset of single mothers, namely, widows—who were single due to no fault of their own. (See Handler 1990, 919; see also Abramovitz 1988; Gordon 1994; Kessler Harris 1982). As Joel Handler and other social welfare historians have illustrated, these programs were highly racialized: The overwhelming majority of recipients were white, as mothers' pensions programs and then AFDC implicitly and explicitly excluded women of color (Mink 1990).

7. The objectives of PRWORA included (ii) ending dependence of needy parents on government benefits by promoting job preparation, work and marriage; (iii) preventing and reducing out of wedlock pregnancies; and (iv) encouraging the formation of two-parent families. While a number of substantive provisions were designed with the objective of reducing illegitimacy, there were few substantive provisions specifically directed toward the objective of promoting marriage. The increased flexibility given to states in relation to eligibility was used by thirty-five states to make it easier for two-parent families to qualify for assistance. Some spend TANF funds

on activities intended to strengthen marriages (Parke 2003). But, these changes were largely the result of the increased flexibility given to states to spend their TANF block grants in accordance with the purposes of the legislation, rather than as a result of any substantive provision of the legislation. This lacuna in the legislation has subsequently become a focus of neo-conservative critique and debate.

8. According to PRWORA, the TANF program required congressional reauthorization by September 2002. Congress has approved several temporary extensions of TANF, while they debate the substance of the reauthorization. There have been several TANF reauthorization proposals before Congress, including the H.R. 4737 passed by the House on May 16, 2002; a Democratic substitute for H.R. 4737 offered by Rep. Cardin on the House floor; a list of provisions agreed to by a bipartisan group of Senate Finance Committee members; a bill introduced by Sen. Rockefeller (S. 2052); a bill introduced by Senators Bayh and Carper (S. 2524); and H.R. 4, passed by the House in 2003. For a comparison of these bills, see "Summary Comparison of TANF Reauthorization Provisions: Bills Passed by Senate Finance Committee and the House of Representatives and Related Proposals," Center on Budget and Policy Priorities, August 2002. See also "Revised Side-by-Side Comparison of Family Formation Provisions in TANF Reauthorization Legislation," Center on Budget and Policy Priorities, June 2002.

9. See Representative Wally Herger, chairman of the House Ways and Means Committee's Human Resources Subcommittee, who stated "During the first phase of welfare reform, we made sure we were putting people to work. I believe that now is the time to stress the importance of marriage" (as quoted in Fremstad & Primus 2002).

10. Regina Austin recounts the story of Liz Walker, a black news anchorwoman in the Boston area, who became the subject of a major controversy when she decided to have a child outside of marriage. Austin quotes from a *New York Times* article "many of the critics . . . said that as a black woman, Ms. Walker had a special responsibility as a role model for black teenagers who are responsible for a disproportionately large share of out of wedlock births." Austin notes the way in which the motherhood of an unmarried black adult is treated as linked to, if not the cause of, black teenage pregnancies, concluding that: "Single black mothers get blamed for so much that there is little reason not to blame them for teenage pregnancies as well" (Austin 1989, 564–565). The controversy is remarkably similar to the Lauryn Hill controversy a decade later, where even then a partnered adult black woman is linked to unmarried teenage pregnancies.

11. Cheryl Dunye had previously directed *The Watermelon Woman* (1996), a critically acclaimed, ground-breaking film about African American lesbians.

Chapter 4

1. This is not to suggest that the battles over same-sex marriage have been won. Clearly, they have not, as legal defeats in constitutional challenges to the opposite-sex definition of marriage and state constitutional amendments protecting traditional

marriage continue to pile up. In July 2006 the New York Court of Appeals and the Washington State Supreme Court reversed lower court rulings and upheld the opposite-sex definition of marriage; the Georgia Supreme Court reinstated a constitutional amendment banning gay marriage; a federal appeals court reinstated a Nebraska voter-approved ban on same-sex marriage; and the Tennessee Supreme Court dismissed an effort to keep a proposed ban on same-sex marriage off the November ballot. Forty-five states have banned same-sex marriage through statute or constitutional amendment. But, despite the ongoing struggles and setbacks, gay men and lesbians are getting married and entering civil unions in the United States and beyond. Same-sex marriage may be contested, but it has also become part of the present.

2. The superior court ruling was affirmed by the appellate division in *Lewis v. Harris* 2005.

3. This opinion was overruled by the New York Court of Appeals in a 4-2 decision in July 2006 (*Hernandez v. Robles*, 2006 WL 1835429). The majority held that the law excluding same-sex couples from marriage was supported by a rational basis. The legislature could rationally decide that for the welfare of the children it was more important to promote the stability of opposite-sex couples. In an opinion echoing the holding in *Morrison*, the court held: "'Heterosexual intercourse has a natural tendency to lead to the birth of children; homosexual intercourse does not. . . . The Legislature could find . . . that an important function of marriage is to create more stability and permanence in the relationships that cause children to be born. . . . The Legislature could find that the rationale for marriage does not apply with comparable force to same sex couples. These couples can become parents by adoption or artificial insemination or other technological marvels, but they do not become parents as a result of accident or impulse.' Because opposite sex relationships may be more unstable and present a greater risk to children, it is rational for the Legislature to promote stability in these relationships through marriage" (*Hernandez*, para. 2).

4. According to Massachusetts General Laws Annotated; Chapter 208, §§ 4, 5, and 6, if the grounds for divorce occurred in Massachusetts, one spouse must be a resident. If the grounds occurred outside of the state, the spouse filing must have been a resident for one year.

5. West Virginia and Massachusetts courts have dissolved Vermont civil unions. In *Re The Marriage of Misty Gorman and Sherry Gump*, a West Virginia court issued a dissolution (Unreported, January 2003; see Paul Olsen, "Texas Judge Grants, Rescinds CU Divorce," *Out in the Mountains* (5 May 2003): http://www.mountainpridemedia.org/oitm/issues/2003/05may2003/news02_texas.htm). Similarly, in *Salucco v. Alldredge* (2004), a Massachusetts court dissolved a civil union. In contrast, a Connecticut court has refused to dissolve a civil union on the ground that there is no valid marriage and therefore nothing to dissolve. In *Rosengarten v. Downes*, July 30, 2002, a Connecticut court refused to dissolve the civil union on the ground that the court had no jurisdiction. It should be noted that this case was decided prior to the passage of An Act Concerning Civil Unions in Connecticut in 2005, which recognizes civil union, and its validity is now in question. In both Texas and Iowa, divorce decrees

initially ordered by the courts have been vacated and appealed, respectively. In Texas, Russell Smith and John Anthony were initially given a divorce decree, but that decree was subsequently vacated and a new trial ordered after the intervention of the Texas attorney general. Similarly, in Iowa, Brown and Perez were granted a divorce under the court's equitable jurisdiction. A group of plaintiffs, including six state legislators, brought an application for certiorari to challenge the court's dissolution of the couple's civil union (*Alons v. Iowa*). The application in *Alons* was ultimately dismissed, on the grounds that the plaintiffs had no standing to challenge the court's decree.

6. Dr. Phil in "Extreme Marriages," for example, tells a married couple who have tried to remain married despite the husband's attraction to and affairs with men: "However you define a marriage, for sure it's about commitment, it's about fidelity, it's about being there for another and in a way that is based on trust. . . . Now just take out that it's men he's involved with. If marriage is what I just said—it's commitment, it's fidelity . . . that's not happening here, right?" Dr. Phil concludes that this marriage is "not going to work."

These stories of gay or transsexual husbands (and occasionally lesbian wives) often tell a rather sympathetic, even heroic story. After the wife overcomes her emotional devastation at the loss of her marriage and seemingly goes through the multiple stages of grief, she sometimes articulates not only an acceptance of her husband but respect for the difficult choice that he made. In a television show on Lifetime entitled "My Husband Is Gay," one of the four women interviewed stated "I've not only forgiven him—I'm actually proud of him. By coming out, he did the right thing, which is a lesson we both want to teach our children." A similar sympathetic affirmation is sometimes found in the shows chronicling the struggle of couples where the husband undergoes a sex change. In several *Oprah* shows ("The Husband Who Became a Woman," "More Husbands Who Became Women"), the narrative is one of self-realization: The husband must self-realize by becoming a woman. And sometimes, their wives choose to stay with them after the operation, affirming their difficult journey toward self-realization. While raising its own unique challenges, the transsexual husbands—as highlighted in these shows—do not raise the same infidelity issues, and therefore they are not seen to have engaged in the same kind of violation of the marital relationship. Self-realization can be affirmed without running into the problems of infidelity.

7. Inclusion into marriage—or marriagelike relationships—need not incorporate the norms of fidelity quite so completely. For example, the U.K. Civil Partnerships Act 2004 does not specifically recognize adultery as a ground for dissolution. Rather, dissolution of a civil partnership is available on the basis that the partnership has irretrievably broken down. This ground may be proven by the existence of one of four facts that are the same as those set out for divorce in the matrimonial cases— with the exception of adultery. However, sexual infidelity might still be taken into account as constituting unreasonable behavior, which is one of the facts establishing breakdown.

Notes to Conclusion   215

Conclusion

1. It is not that the sex has been uncontested; rather the preceding chapters have focused on the contested discourses around many sexual practices and norms. Instead, it is that the consensual nature of the sex has mostly not been contested. With the exception of the slasher pornography of Extreme Associates, wherein the consent of the parties may be contested by social conservatives and/or feminists, most of the examples of sex and sexuality have been drawn from the consensual side of the consent/coercion dichotomy. And while this dichotomy has itself been the subject of considerable controversy and deconstruction, the examples of the legal and cultural regulation of sex and sexuality—from sodomy and sexual representations in hip-hop music in Chapter 1, consummation and adultery in Chapter 2, premarital or nonmarital sex in Chapter 3, to same-sex marriage and sexuality in Chapter 4—the consent of the participants has not been at issue. Future analyses of sexual citizenship could explore this consent/coercion dichotomy more explicitly, by considering examples where consent is contested and/or where coercion produces non-citizenship.

The very instability of the distinction between consent and non-consent may itself be an important site of further interrogation of the norms and practices of sexual belonging. From s/m practices of consensual non-consensuality to debates over the relative consent/coercion of sex workers, consent is itself contested, as is its role in constituting legitimate sexual citizens.

2. Companies provide listings of photographs and self-descriptions of prospective brides, selling contact information to male clients. Some also organize guided tours where male clients can meet prospective brides.

Bibliography

Abbot, Pamela, & Clare Wallace. *The Family and the New Right*. London: Pluto Press, 1992.

Abramovitz, Mimi. *Regulating the Lives of Women: Social Welfare Policy from Colonial Times to the Present*. Boston: South End Press, 1988.

Alexander, Brian. "Sex Toys and Porn on her Terms." *MSNBC* (18 March 2004). http://www.msnbc.msn.com/id/4314184.

Ali, Lorraine, & Lisa Miller. "The Secret Lives of Wives." *Newsweek* (12 July 2004). www.msnbc.msn.com/id/5359395/site/newsweek.

Altman, Dennis. "Rupture or Continuity? The Internationalization of Gay Identities." *Social Text* 48 (1996): 77–94.

American Decency Association. "Desperate Housewives" Advertisers (3 October 2004). http://americandecency.org/email_updates/email11.01c.04.htm.

Anderson, Kathy. "My Vermont Civil Union Divorce." *The Advocate* (28 September 2004).

Arendt, Hannah. *The Human Condition*. Chicago: University of Chicago Press, 1958.

Asimov, Michael. "Introduction: UCLA's Law and Popular Culture Seminar." *UCLA Enter. L. Rev.* 9 (Fall 2001): 87–88.

Austin, J. L. *How to Do Things with Words*. Cambridge, MA: Harvard University Press, 1962.

Austin, Regina. "Sapphire Unbound." *Wisc. L. Rev.* (1989): 539–78.

Austin, Regina. "'A Nation of Thieves' Securing Black People's Right to Shop and to Sell in White America." *Utah L. Rev.* 149 (1994): 147–78.

Beato, G. "Xtreme Measures: Washington's New Crackdown on Pornography." *Reasononline*. http://reason.com/0405/fe.gb.xtreme.shtml.

Beck-Gernsheim, Elisabeth. "On the Way to a Post-Familial Family: From a Community of Need to Elective Affinity." In Mike Featherstone (ed.), *Love and Eroticism* (pp. 53–70). London: Sage, 1999.

Bell, David. "Pleasure and Danger: The Paradoxical Spaces of Sexual Citizenship." *Political Geography 14* (1995): 139–53.

Bell, David, and Jon Binnie. *The Sexual Citizen: Queer Politics and Beyond.* Cambridge, MA: Polity Press, 2000.

Bell, Vikki. "Governing Childhood: Neo-Liberalism and the Law." *Economy and Society 22* (3) (1993): 390–405.

Berlant, Lauren. *The Queen of America Goes to Washington City: Essays on Sex and Citizenship.* Durham, NC: Duke University Press, 1997.

Blankenhorn, David. *Fatherless America: Confronting Our Most Urgent Social Problem.* New York: Basic Books, HarperCollins, 1995.

Bordieu, Pierre. *Distinctions: A Social Critique of the Judgement of Taste.* Cambridge, MA: Harvard University Press, 1984.

Borten, Laurence Drew. "Sex, Procreation, and the State Interest in Marriage." *Col. L. Rev. 102* (2002): 1089–1128.

Bosniak, Linda. "Citizenship Denationalized." *Indiana Journal of Global Legal Studies 7* (1999–2000): 447–509.

Brito, Tonya. "From Madonna to Proletariat: Constructing a New Ideology of Motherhood in Welfare Discourse." *Vill. L. Rev. 44* (1999): 415–43.

Brodie, Janine. "Meso-Discourses, State Forms and the Gendering of Liberal Democratic Citizenship." *Citizenship Studies 1* (1997): 223–42.

Brodie, Janine. "Restructuring and the New Citizenship." In Isabelle Bakker (ed.), *Rethinking Restructuring: Gender and Change in Canada* (pp. 126–40). Toronto: University of Toronto Press, 1997.

Brook, Heather. "How to Do Things with Sex." In C. Stychin & D. Herman (eds.), *Sexuality in the Legal Arena* (pp. 132–50). London: Athlone Press, 2000.

Brown, Janelle. "Porn Provocateur." *Salon Magazine 20* (June 2002). http://www.salon.com/mwt/feature/2002/06/20/lizzy_borden/index.html.

Brown, Trent. "Flynt and Black Each Make One Last Response in Debate on Obscenity." *Adult Video News* (15 April 2004). http://www.avn.com/index.php?Primary_Navigation=Articles&Action=View_Article&Content_ID=80701.

Burchell, Graham. "Liberal Government and Techniques of the Self." In Andrew Barry, Thomas Osborne, and Nikolas Rose (eds.), *Foucault and Political Reason* (pp. 19–36). London: University College London Press, 1996.

Butler, Judith. "Against Proper Objects." In Elizabeth Weed and Naomi Schor (eds.), *Feminism Meets Queer Theory* (pp. 1–30). Bloomington: Indiana University Press, 1997.

Butler, Judith. *Excitable Speech: A Politics of the Performative.* New York: Routledge, 1997.

Butler, Judith. *Undoing Gender.* New York: Routledge, 2004.

Butler, Stuart, & Anna Kundratas. *Out of the Poverty Trap: A Conservative Strategy.* New York: Free Press, 1987.

Califia, Pat. *Public Sex: The Culture of Radical Sex.* Pittsburgh: Cleis Press, 1994.

Calvert, Clay, & Robert Richards. "Adult Entertainment and the First Amendment: A Dialogue and Analysis with the Industry's Leading Litigator and Appellate Advocate." *Vand. J. Ent. L & Pract. 6* (2004): 147–70.

Carbone, June. "Morality, Public Policy and the Family: The Role of Marriage and the Public/Private Divide." *Santa Cl. L. Rev. 36* (1996): 267–86.

Carey, George (ed.). *Freedom and Virtue: The Conservative/Libertarian Divide.* Lanham, MD: University Press of America, 1984.

Chambers, David. "Fathers, the Welfare System, and the Virtues and Perils of Child Support Enforcement." *Va. L. Rev. 81* (1995): 2575–2605.

Chandra-Skekeran, Sangeetha. "Theorising the Limits of the 'Sadomasochistic Homosexual' Identity in R. v. Brown." *Melb. U. L. Rev. 21* (1997): 584–600.

Clark, H. *The Law of Domestic Relations in the United States.* St. Paul: West, 1968.

Cooper, Davina. "The Citizens Charter and Radical Democracy: Empowerment and Exclusion Within Citizenship Discourse." *Social and Legal Studies 2* (1993): 149–71.

Cornyn, John. *Statement of the Honorable Senator Cornyn on the Proposed Constitutional Amendment to Preserve Traditional Definition of Marriage*: Hearing Before the Senate Committee on the Judiciary 108th Congress, March 23, 2004.

Cossman, Brenda. "Family Feuds: Neo-Liberal and Neo-Conservative Visions of the Reprivatization Project." In B. Cossman & J. Fudge (eds.), *Privatization, Law and the Challenge of Feminism.* Toronto: University of Toronto Press, 2002.

Cossman, Brenda. "Gender Performance, Sexual Subjects and International Law." *Can. J. of L. & Juris. 15* (2002): 281–96.

Cossman, Brenda. "Contesting Conservatisms, Family Feuds and the Privatization of Dependency." Amer. U. J. of Gender, Social Policy & the Law 13 (2005): 415–509.

Cossman, Brenda, & Judy Fudge (eds.). *Privatization, Law and the Challenge of Feminism.* Toronto: University of Toronto Press, 2002.

Cossman, Brenda, & Bruce Ryder. "What Is Marriage-Like Like? The Irrelevance of Conjugality." *Can. J. of Fam. L. 18* (2001): 269–326.

Cott, Nancy. *Public Vows: A History of Marriage and the Nation.* Cambridge, MA: Harvard University Press, 2000.

Crenshaw, Kimberle. "Demarginalizing the Intersections of Race and Sex: A Black Feminist Critique of Anti-Discrimination Doctrine, Feminist Theory and Anti-racist Politics." *U. Chi. Legal F.* (1982): 139.

Crooms, Lisa. "Don't Believe the Hype: Black Women, Patriarchy and the New Welfarism." *How. L. J. 38* (3) (1995): 611–28.

Crooms, Lisa. "The Mythical, Magical 'Underclass': Constructing Poverty in Race and Gender, Making the Public Private and the Private Public." *Journal of Gender, Race and Justice 5* (2001–2002): 87–129.

- Cruikshank, Barbara. *The Will to Empower: Democratic Citizens and Other Subjects.* Ithaca, NY: Cornell University Press, 1999.

Dargis, Manohla. "In Buoyant Secretary, Romance for Consenting Adults." *L.A. Times* (20 Sept. 2002).

Dean, Mitchell M. *Governmentality: Power and Rule in Modern Society.* London: Sage, 1999.

DeJean, Joan. *The Reinvention of Obscenity: Sex, Lies, and Tabloids in Early Modern France.* Chicago: University of Chicago Press, 2002.

Dickerson, Debra. 1999. "Lauryn Hill: Hoochie or Hero?" *Salon Magazine* (22 June 1999). http://www.salon.com/news/feature/1999/06/22/hill/index.html.

Diller, Matthew. "Working Without a Job: The Social Messages of the New Workfare." *Stan. L. & Pol'y Rev. 9* (1998): 19–32.

Dunn, Charles, & David Woodards. *American Conservatism from Burke to Bush: An Introduction.* Lanham, MD: Madison Books, 1991.

EGALE. *In the Supreme Court of Canada Between Little Sisters Book and Art Emporium and Canada (Minister of Justice). Factum of the Intervenor,* 1999.

Ellwood, David, *Poor Support: Poverty in the American Family.* New York: Basic Books, 1988.

Evans, David. *Sexual Citizenship: The Material Construction of Sexuality.* London: Routledge, 1993.

Farber, Daniel A. "Whither Socialism?" *Denv. U. L. Rev. 73* (1996): 1011–16.

Farrar, Charles. "Black Questions Fight of My Business." *Adult Video News* (7 April 2004). http://www.avn.com/index.php?Primary_Navigation=Articles& Action=View_Article&*Content_ID=79688.*

Federal Communications Commission. "Industry Guidance on the Commission's Case Law Interpreting" 18 U.S.C. § 1464 and "Enforcement Policies Regarding Broadcast Indecency, Policy Statement" 16 F.C.C.R. 7999, para 1, 23 Comm. Reg. (P & F) 857 (2001).

Fevre, Ralph. *The Demoralisation of Western Culture.* London: Continuum, 2000.

Fineman, Martha. "Masking Dependency: The Political Role of Family Rhetoric." *Va. L. Rev. 91* (1995): 2181–2215.

Flynt, Larry. 2004. "Life, Liberty and the Pursuit of Porn." Interview with Larry Flynt. *Wired News* (14 Feb. 2004).http://www.wired.com/news/privacy/ 0,1848,62343,00.html.

Foucault, Michel. *The History of Sexuality: Volume I: An Introduction.* New York: Vintage House, 1980.

Foucault, Michel. *The Use of Pleasure. The History of Sexuality: Volume II.* New York: Vintage House, 1985.

Foucault, Michel. "On the Genealogy of Ethics: An Overview of Work in Progress." In P. Rabinow (ed.), *The Foucault Reader.* Harmondsworth: Penguin, 1986.

Foucault, Michel. "Technologies of the Self." In L. H. Martin, H. Gutman, & P. H. Hutton (eds.), *Technologies of the Self.* London: Tavistock, 1988.

Foucault, Michel. "Governmentality." In G. Burchell, C. Gordon, & P. Miller (eds.), *The Foucault Effect: Studies in Governmental Rationality* (pp. 87–104). Hemel Hempstead: Harvester Wheatsheaf, 1991.

France, David. "The Invention of Patient Zero." *New York Magazine* (22 April 2005). http://newyorkmetro.com/nymetro/health/features/11840.

Franke, Katherine. "The Domesticated Liberty of Lawrence v. Texas." *Col. L. Rev. 104* (2004): 1399–1426.

Franke, Katherine. "The Politics of Same Sex Marriage Politics" *Col. J. of Gender & L. 15* (2005): 236–48.

Fraser, Nancy. *Justice Interruptus: Critical Reflections on the "Postsocialist" Condition.* New York: Routledge, 1997.

Fraser, Nancy, & Linda Gordon. "A Genealogy of Dependency: Tracing a Keyword in the U.S. Welfare State." *Signs 19* (1994): 309–36.

Freeman, Jody. "Extending Public Law Norms Through Privatization." *Harv. L. Rev. 116* (2003): 1285, 1287.

Freitas, Anthony. "Belongings: Citizenship, Sexuality, and the Market." In Jodi O'Brien & Judith Howard (eds.), *Everyday Inequalities: Critical Inquiries.* Oxford: Blackwell Publishers, 1998.

Fremstad, Shawn, & Wendell Primus. "Strengthening Families: Ideas for TANF Reauthorization." *Center on Budget and Policy Priorities* (22 Jan. 2002). http://www .cbpp.org/pubs/recent_2002.htm.

Friedman, Milton. *Capitalism and Freedom.* Chicago: University of Chicago Press, 1982 (orig. pub. 1962).

Garfinkel, Irwin, & Sara McLanahan. *Single Mothers and Their Children: A New American Dilemma.* Washington, DC: Urban Institute Press, 1986.

Gavanas, Anna. *Fatherhood Politics in the United States.* Urbana: University of Illinois Press, 2004.

George, Lianne. "Toyland in the Torrid Zone" Maclean's Magazine (17 May 2004). http://www.macleans.ca/topstories/life/article.jsp?content=20040517_80625_ 80625.

Gertler, Stephanie, & Adrienne Lopez. *To Love, Honor, and Betray: The Secret Life of Suburban Wives.* New York: Hyperion, 2005.

Giddens, Anthony. *Modernity and Self Identity.* Cambridge: Polity Press, 1991.

Giddens, Anthony. *The Transformation of Intimacy: Sexuality, Love and Eroticism* Cambridge: Polity Press, 1992.

Giddens, Anthony. *The Third Way: The Renewal of Social Democracy.* Cambridge: Polity Press, 1998.

Gillens, Martin. *Why Americans Hate Welfare: Race, Media and the Politics of Antipoverty Policy.* Chicago: University of Chicago Press, 1999.

Gillies, Val. "Family and Intimate Relationships: A Review of the Sociological Literature." (2003). *www.lsbu.ca.uk/families/workingpapers/familieswp2pdf.*

Glass, Shirley. "Shattered Vows: Getting Beyond Betrayal." *Psychology Today* (July/ August 1998). www.shirleyglass.com/pyschologytoday.htm.

Glass, Shirley. *Not "Just Friends": Rebuilding Trust and Recovering Your Sanity After Infidelity.* New York: Free Press, 2003.

Goldstein, Richard. "Red Slut, Blue Slut." *The Nation 280* (1) (3 Jan. 2005): 20.

Goodwin, Andrew. "The New Infidelity." *Salon Magazine* (28 Feb. 2003). www.salon .com.

Gordon, Linda. *Pitied, but Not Entitled: Single Mothers and the History of Welfare.* Cambridge, MA: Harvard University Press, 1994.

Graff, E. J. *What Is Marriage For? The Strange Social History of Our Most Intimate Institution.* Boston: Beacon Hill Press, 1999.

Halley, Janet. "Reasoning About Sodomy: Act and Identity in and After Bowers v. Hardwick." *Va. L. Rev. 79* (1993):1721–72.

Handler, Joel. "Transformation of the Aid to Families with Dependent Children: The Family Support Act in Historical Context." *N.Y.U. Rev. L. & Soc. Change 16* (1987/88): 457–533.

Handler, Joel. "Constructing the Political Spectacle: The Interpretation of Entitlements, Legalization and Obligations in Social Welfare History." *Brook. L. Rev. 56* (3) (1990): 899–974.

Handler, Joel. "'Ending Welfare as We Know It': The Win/Win Split or the Stench of Victory." *J. Gender Race & Just. 5* (2001): 131–74.

Haney, Lynne, & Miranda March. "Married Fathers and Caring Daddies: Welfare Reform and the Discursive Politics of Paternity." *Social Problems 5* (2003): 461–81.

Hanna, Fadi. "Punishing Masculinity in Gay Asylum Cases." *Yale L. J. 114* (2005): 913–20.

Hare, David. *The Judas Kiss.* New York: Samuel French, 1999.

Hatch, Orrin. 108th Congress § 8089. Federal Marriage Amendment—Motion to Proceed (14 July 2004). Statement by Senator Orrin Hatch.

Hayek, F. A. *The Constitution of Liberty.* Chicago: University of Chicago Press, 1978 (orig. pub. 1960).

Held, D. "Between State and Civil Society: Citizenship." In G. Andrews (ed.), *Citizenship* (pp. 19–25). London: Lawrence and Wishart, 1991.

Herman, Didi. *The Anti-Gay Agenda: Orthodox Vision and the Christian Right.* Chicago: University of Chicago Press, 1997.

Hill Collins, Patricia. *Black Sexual Politics: African Americans, Gender and the New Racism.* New York: Routledge, 2004.

Hindness, Barry. "The Liberal Government of Unfreedom." *Alternatives: Global, Local, Political 26* (2)(April–June 2001).

Hofmeister, Sallie. "Indecency Proposal Getting Static from Cable." *Los Angeles Times* (5 April 2005): C1.

Horn, Wade. "Wedding Bell Blues: Marriage and Welfare Reform." *Brookings Review* (Summer 2001): 39–42.

Horn, Wade, David Blankenhorn, & Mitchell Pearlstein (eds.). *The Fatherhood Movement: A Call to Action.* Lanham, MD: Lexington Books, 1999.

Huda, Perida. "Singled Out." *W. & M. J. of Wom. & L. 7* (2001):341–80.

Hunt, Alan. *Governing Morals: A Social History of Moral Regulation.* Cambridge: Cambridge University Press, 1999.

Huntington, Keston. "How to Survive Infidelity." n.d. *http://www.lezbeout.com/howtosurviveinfidelity.htm.*

Ignatieff, Michael. "The Myth of Citizenship." *Queen's Quarterly 94* (1987): 966–85.

Jackson, Suzanne. "To Honor and Obey: Trafficking in Mail Order Brides." *G. W. L. Rev. 10* (2002):475–568.

Kaplan, Morris. *Sexual Justice: Democratic Citizenship and the Politics of Desire.* New York: Routledge, 1997.

Katz, Michael. *The Price of Citizenship: Redefining the American Welfare State.* New York: Metropolitan Books, 2001.

Kaufman, Moises. *Gross Indecency: The Three Trials of Oscar Wilde.* New York: Vintage Books, 1998.

Kerber, Linda. *No Constitutional Right to Be Ladies: Women and the Obligations of Citizenship.* New York: Hill and Wang, 1998.

Kernes, Mark. "Extreme Associates Defendants Arraigned, Released on Bail." *Adult Video News* (28 Aug. 2003). http://www.avn.com/index.php?Primary_Navigation=Articles&Action=View_Article&Content_ID=36904.

Kessler Harris, Alice. *Out to Work: A History of Wage-Earning Women in the United States.* New York: Oxford University Press, 1982.

King, Desmond. *The New Right: Politics, Markets, and Citizenship.* Basingstoke: Macmillan Education, 1987.

King, Steve. "King Reacts to Lesbian Divorce in Sioux City." (12 Dec. 2003). http://www.house.gov/apps/list/press/ia05_king/pr_031212.html.

Kipnis, Laura. *Against Love: A Polemic.* New York: Vintage, 2003.

Klatch, Rebecca. "Coalition and Conflict Among Women of the New Right." *Signs: Journal of Women in Culture and Society 13*(4) (1988): 671–94.

Klesse, Christian. "Bisexual Women, Non-Monogamy, and Differentialist Anti-Promiscuity Discourse." *Sexualities 8*(4) (2005): 445.

Knight, Tim. "Review: 'We Don't Live Here Anymore.'"(2004). www.reel.com.

Kramer, Larry. *The Tragedy of Today's Gays.* New York: Tarcher/Penguin, 2005.

Krasnow, Iris. *Surrendering to Marriage: Husbands, Wives, and Other Imperfections.* New York: Miramax Books, 2001.

Krause, Harry. "Child Support Reassessed: Limits of Private Responsibility and the Public Interest." *Family Law Quarterly 1* (24) (1990): 1–34.

Kushner, Tony. *Angels in America.* New York: Theatre Communications Group, 1993.

Kymlicka, Will, & Wayne Norman. "Return of the Citizen: A Survey of Recent Work on Citizenship Theory." *Ethics 104* (1994): 352–81.

Lasch, Christopher. *Haven in a Heartless World.* New York: Basic Books, 1977.

Levin-Epstein, et al. "Spending Too Much, Accomplishing Too Little: An Analysis of the Family Formation Provisions of H.R. 4737 and Recommendations for Change." *Center for Law and Social Policy* (2002). http://www.clasp.org/publications.php?id=2&year=2002#0.

Lindsay, Matthew. "Reproducing a Fit Citizenry: Dependency, Eugenics, and the Law of Marriage in the United States 1860–1920." *Law and Social Inquiry 23* (1998): 541–85.

Lipset, Seymour Martin, & Earl Raab. *The Politics of Unreason: Right Wing Extremism in America, 1790–1970.* New York: Harper & Row, 1970.

Lister, Ruth. *Citizenship: Feminist Perspectives.* London: MacMillan, 1997.

Little Sisters Book and Art Emporium. *In the Supreme Court of Canada between Little Sisters Book and Art Emporium and Canada (Minister of Justice), Factum of the Appellant.* 1999.

Lloyd, Carol. "Veritable Wilde Explosion." *Salon Magazine* (30 April 1998). www .salon.com.

Lode, Eric. "Slippery Slope Arguments and Legal Reasoning." *Calif. L. Rev. 87* (1999): 1469–1543.

Macklin, Audrey. "Dancing Across Borders: Exotic Dancers, Trafficking, and Immigration Policy." *International Migration Review 37* (2003): 464–500.

Marshall, T. H. *Citizenship and Social Class.* Cambridge: Cambridge University Press, 1950.

Marber, Patrick. *Closer.* New York: Atlantic Monthly Press, 1999.

McCaughey, Martha, & Christina French. "Women's Sex-Toy Parties: Technology, Orgasm, and Commodification." *Sexuality & Culture 5* (3) (2001): 77–96.

McCluskey, Martha. "Efficiency and Social Citizenship: Challenging the Neoliberal Attack on the Welfare State." *Ind. L. J. 78* (2003): 783–876.

McElroy, Wendy. 2006. "Law Brands All American Men Abusers." *Fox News* (10 Jan. 2006).

McGraw, Phillip. *Relationship Rescue: A Seven Step Strategy for Reconnecting with Your Partner.* New York: Hyperion, 2000.

McNair, Brian. *Striptease Culture: Sex, Media and the Democratisation of Desire.* London: Routledge, 2003.

Mead, Lawrence. *The New Paternalism: Supervisory Approaches to Poverty.* Washington, DC: Brookings Institution Press, 1997.

Mincy, Ronald. "What About Black Fathers?" *American Prospect* (8 April 2002). http://www.prospect.org/print/V13/7/mincy-r.html.

Mincy, Ronald, & Elaine Sorenson. "Deadbeats and Turnips in Child Support Reform." *Journal of Policy Analysis & Management 17* (1) (1998): 44–51.

Mink, Gwendolyn. "The Lady and the Tramp: Gender, Race, and the Origins of the American Welfare State." In Linda Gordon (ed.), *Women, the State and Welfare.* Madison: Wisconsin University Press, 1990.

Mink, Gwendolyn. "Welfare Reform in Historical Perspective." *Conn. L. Rev. 26* (1994): 879–99.

Mink, Gwendolyn. *Welfare's End.* Ithaca, NY: Cornell University Press, 1998.

Minow, Martha. *Partners, Not Rivals: Privatization and the Public Good.* Boston: Beacon Press, 2002.

Mnookin, Robert H., & Lewis Kornhauser. "Bargaining in the Shadow of the Law." *Yale L. Rev. 88* (1979): 950–977.

Moll, Rob. "Workplace Romance: The New Infidelity." (2005). http://www.family .org/married/romance/a0026483.cfm.

Moon, Richard. "R. v. Butler: The Limits of the Supreme Court's Feminist Re-interpretation of s. 163." *Ottawa L. Rev. 25* (1993): 361–84.

Morgan, Deborah. "Not Gay Enough for the Government: Racial and Sexual Stereotypes in Sexual Orientation Asylum Cases." *Law and Sexuality 15* (2006): 135–61.

Morgan, Joan. *When Chicken-Heads Come Home to Roost: A Hip-Hop Feminist Breaks It Down.* New York: Touchstone Press, 1999.

Morgan, Laura. "Family Law at 2000: Private and Public Support of the Family: From Welfare State Poor Law." *Fam. L. Q. 33* (1999): 705–18.

Moynihan, Daniel Patrick. *Report on the Black Family.* (1965).

Murray, Charles. *Losing Ground: American Social Policy 1950–1980.* New York: Basic Books, 1984.

Myers, Jack. "Gays Are America's New Role Model." (2003). *www.jackmyers.com/ JMER_Archive/08–06–03ER.pdf.*

Naughton, Keith. "The Soft Sell: Pitching a New Male-Impotence Drug with Romantic Images of Tender Moments." *Newsweek* (26 Jan. 2004). http://msnbc.msn.com/id/ 4051447.

Nisbet, Robert. "Uneasy Cousins." In George Carey (ed.), *Freedom and Virtue: The Conservative/Libertarian Divide.* Lanham, MD: Intercollegiate Studies Institute, 1984.

O'Neal, Parker. "Battle Station in a Rap Revolution." *Washington Post* (2 Feb. 2002).

Orloff, Ann, & Renee Monson. "Citizens, Workers, or Fathers? Men in U.S. Social Policy." In Barbara Hobson (ed.), *Making Men into Fathers: Men, Masculinities, and the Social Politics of Fatherhood.* Cambridge: Cambridge University Press, 2002.

Pa, Monica. "Beyond the Pleasure Principle: The Criminalization of Consensual Sadomasochistic Sex." *Texas Journal of Women and the Law 11* (2001): 51–92.

Pakulski, Jan. "Cultural Citizenship." *Citizenship Studies 1* (1) (1997): 73–86.

Parke, Mary. "Marriage-Related Provisions in Recent Welfare Reauthorization Proposals: A Summary." *Center for Law and Social Policy* (June 2003, updated March 2004). http://www.clasp.org/publications/marr_prov_upd.pdf.

Parke, Mary, et al. "One Step Forward or Two Steps Back? Why the Bipartisan Senate Bill Reflects a Better Approach to TANF." *Center for Law and Social Policy* (2002). www.clasp.org/publications.

Pearson, Kim. "Patriotic Homosocial Discourse" *W. & M. J. of Wom. & L. 12* (2005): 627–70.

Perlmutter, David. "Incapacity for Sexual Intercourse as Ground for Annulment." *American Law Reports 52* (3) (1974): 589.

Peter, Jennifer. "First Gay Divorces Filed in Massachusetts." Associated Press (10 Dec. 2004).

Peterson, Karen. "Infidelity Reaches Beyond Having Sex." *USA Today* (1 Aug. 2003): 8D. http://www.usatoday.com/news/nation/2003-01-08-workplace-usat_x.htm.

Phelan, Shane. *Sexual Strangers: Gays, Lesbians, and the Dilemmas of Citizenship.* Philadelphia: Temple University Press, 2001.

Plotz, David. "Oscar Wilde: Why the 1890s Insurgent Has Made a 1990s Comeback." *Slate.com* (10 May 1998). www.slate.msn.com/id/1864.

Plummer, Ken. "The Square of Intimate Citizenship: Some Preliminary Proposals." *Citizenship Studies 5* (3) (2001): 237–53.

Popenoe, David. *Life Without Father.* New York: The Free Press, 1996.

Rector, Robert. "Using Welfare Reform to Strengthen Marriage." *American Experiment Quarterly* (Summer 2001):63–7.

Richardson, Diane. "Sexuality and Citizenship." *Sociology 32*(1) (1998): 83–1000.

Richardson, Diane. *Rethinking Sexuality.* London: Sage Press, 2000.

Roberts, Dorothy. "Deviance, Resistance, and Love." *Utah L. Rev. 1* (1994): 179–91.

Roberts, Dorothy. "Welfare and the Problem of Black Citizenship." *Yale L. J. 105* (1996): 1563–1602.

Roberts, Dorothy. *Killing the Black Body: Race, Reproduction, and the Meaning of Liberty.* New York: Vintage Books, 1999.

Rose, Nicholas. *Inventing Our Selves: Psychology, Power, and Personhood.* Cambridge: Cambridge University Press, 1996.

Rose, Nicholas. *Powers of Freedom: Reframing Political Thought.* Cambridge: Cambridge University Press, 1999.

Rose, Nicholas. "Community, Citizenship, and the Third Way." *American Behavioral Scientist 43* (9) (June/July 2000): 1395–1411.

Rubin, Gayle. "Thinking Sex: Notes for a Radical Theory of the Politics of Sexuality." In Carole Vance (ed.), *Pleasure and Danger: Exploring Female Sexuality* (pp. 267–319). London: Routledge, 1984.

Sarat, Austin, & Jonathan Simon. "Beyond Legal Realism: Cultural Analysis, Cultural Studies, and the Situation of Legal Scholarship." *Yale J. of L. & the Humanities 13* (3) (2001): 3–34.

Sawyer, Terry. "Blind Leading the Bland." *Popmatters* (2003). http://www.popmatters.com/tv/reviews/q/queer-eye-for-the-straight-guy.shtml.

Schauer, Frederick. "Slippery Slopes." *Harv. L. Rev. 99* (1985): 361–83.

Scholes, Robert. "The Mail-Order Bride Industry and Its Impact on US Immigration." In *International Matchmaking Organizations: A Report to Congress* (Appendix A). Washington, DC: Immigration and Naturalization Services and Violence Against Women Office at the Department of Justice, 1998.

Schudson, Michael. *The Good Citizen: A History of American Civic Life.* New York: Free Press, 1998.

Scobey, David. "The Specter of Citizenship." *Citizenship Studies 5* (1) (2001): 11–26.

Scott, A. O. "Sexual Politics in a Noir Mood." *New York Times* (13 Aug. 2004): E1.

Seidman, Steven. "From Identity to Queer Politics: Shifts in Normative Heterosexuality and the Meaning of Citizenship." *Citizenship Studies 5* (3) (2001): 321–28.

Senior, Jennifer. "Sex Tips for Red State Girls." *New York Times Magazine* (4 July 2004): 32.

Shader Smith, Diane. *Undressing Infidelity: Why More Wives Are Unfaithful*. Avon, MA: Adams Media, 2005.

Shallenbarger, Sue. "Co-Workers Can Wreck a Marriage: At the Office, Divorce Is Contagious." *Wall Street Journal* (12 Nov. 2003). http://www.careerjournal.com/columnists/workfamily/20031114–workfamily.html.

Shaw Spaht, Katherine. "Louisiana's Covenant Marriage: Social Analysis and Legal Implications." *Louisiana L. Rev. 59* (1998): 63.

Shimes, Stephen. "Building Bridges, One Manicure at a Time." (2003). http://www.filmsnobs.com/www/shimes/queereye.htm.

Shklar, Judith. *American Citizenship: The Quest for Inclusion*. Cambridge: Harvard University Press, 1991.

Sigle-Rushton, Wendy, & Sara McLanahan. "Father Absence and Child Wellbeing: A Critical Review." Working Paper 2002–20, Fragile Families Project, Center for Research on Child Wellbeing. (November 2002).

Silbergleid, Robin. "Oh Baby! Representations of Single Mothers in American Popular Culture." *Americana: The Journal of American Popular Culture 1* (2) (Fall 2002). http://www.americanpopularculture.com/journal/articles/fall_2002/silbergleid.htm.

Singer, Linda. *Erotic Welfare: Sexual Theory and Politics in the Age of Epidemic*. New York: Routledge, 1993.

Smith, Anna Marie. "The Politicization of Marriage in Contemporary American Public Policy: The Defense of Marriage Act and the Personal Responsibility Act." *Citizenship Studies 5* (2001): 303–20.

Smith, Rogers. *Civic Ideals: Conflicting Visions of Citizenship in U.S. History*. New Haven: Yale University Press, 1997.

Sontag, Susan. *AIDS and Its Metaphors*. New York: Farrar, Straus and Giroux, 1989.

Sontag, Susan. "Regarding the Torture of Others." *New York Times* (23 May 2004).

Specter, Michael. "Higher Risk." *New Yorker 23* (April 2005). http://www.newyorker.com/fact/content/?050523fa_fact.

Storr, Merl. *Latex and Lingerie: Shopping for Pleasure at Ann Summers Parties*. New York & Oxford: Berg, 2003.

Stychin, Carl. *A Nation by Rights: National Cultures, Sexual Identity Politics, and the Discourse of Rights*. Philadelphia: Temple University Press, 1998.

Stychin, Carl. "Sexual Citizenship in the European Union." *Citizenship Studies 5* (2001): 285–320.

Stychin, Carl. *Governing Sexuality: The Changing Politics of Citizenship and Law Reform*. Oxford: Hart Publishing, 2003.

Tapper, Jake. "Court Deals Blow to U.S. Anti-Porn Campaign." *ABC News* (4 March 2005). http://abcnews.go.com/nightline.

Themba, Makani. 1998. "Real Women Have Men: The New Cultural Offensive Against Black Career Women." *Colorlines* (Summer 1998). http://www.arc.org/C_Lines/CLArchive/story1_1_05.html.

Thomas, Kendall. "Beyond the Privacy Principle." *Col. L. Rev.* 92 (1992): 1431–1516.

Turner, Bryan. "Postmodern Culture/Modern Citizen." In B. V. Steenbergen (ed.), *The Condition of Citizenship* (pp. 153–68). London: Sage, 1994.

Turner, Bryan. "Outline of a General Theory of Cultural Citizenship." In Nick Stevenson (ed.), *Culture and Citizenship* (pp. 48–62). London: Sage, 2000.

U.S. Census. "The Black Population in the United States." (April 2003). www.census.gov/prod/2003pubs/p20–54.pdf.

U.S. Department of Justice. "Ceos Renews Obscenity Prosecutions." Obscenity Prosecution News *1* (1)(Spring 2005): 2–3.

U.S. Department of Justice. "Justice Department to Appeal District Court Ruling Dismissing Obscenity Charges in the Extreme Associates Case." Press Release (15 Feb. 2005).

Vaughan, Peggy. *The Monogamy Myth: A Personal Handbook for Dealing with Affairs.* New York: Newmarket Press, 2003.

Ventura, S. J., & C. A. Bachrach. "Non-Marital Child Bearing in the United States, 1940–99." *National Vital Statistics Reports 48*(16). Hyattsville, MD: National Center for Health Statistics, 2000.

Voet, R. *Feminism and Citizenship.* London: Sage, 1998.

Volokh, Eugene. "The Mechanism of the Slippery Slope." *Harv. L. Rev.* 116 (2003): 1026–1137.

Walby, Sylvia. "Is Citizenship Gendered?" *Sociology 28*(2) (1994): 379–95.

Warner, Michael. *The Trouble with Normal: Sex, Politics, and the Ethics of Queer Life.* New York: Free Press, 1999.

Weed, Elizabeth, & Naomi Schor. *Feminism Meets Queer Theory.* Bloomington: Indiana University Press, 1997.

Weeks, Jeffrey. "The Delicate Web of Subversion, Community, Friendship, and Love: In Conversation with Sue Golding." In Sue Golding (ed.), *The Eight Technologies of Otherness* (pp. 320–32). London: Routledge, 1997.

Weeks, Jeffrey. "The Sexual Citizen." *Theory, Culture and Society 15* (3–4) (1999): 35–52.

Weitzman, Lenore. *The Divorce Revolution: The Unexpected Social and Economic Consequences for Women and Children in America.* New York: Free Press, 1985.

White, Melanie, & Alan Hunt. "Citizenship: Care of the Self, Character, and Personality." *Citizenship Studies 4* (2) (2000): 93–116.

Whitehead, Barbara Dafoe. "Dan Quayle Was Right." *Atlantic Monthly* (April 1993): 47.

Whitley, Glenna. "Sex Toy Story." *Dallas Observer* (8 April 2004). http://www.dallasobserver.com/issues/2004–04–08/news/feature.html.

Williams, Linda. "Second Thoughts on Hard Core: American Obscenity Law and the Scapegoating of Deviance." In Pamela Church Gibson & Roma Gibson (eds.), *Dirty Looks: Women, Pornography, Power* (pp. 46–61). London: British Film Institute, 1993.

Williams, Lucy. "The Right's Attack on Aid to Families with Dependent Children." *The Public Eye 10* (1996): 1.

Wilson, Erin Cressida. *Secretary: A Screenplay.* New York: Soft Skull Press, 2003.

Wilson, Julius. *The Truly Disadvantaged: The Inner City, the Underclass, and Public Policy.* Chicago: University of Chicago Press, 1987.

Wintemute, Robert, & M. Andaneas (eds.). *Legal Recognition of Same-Sex Relationships: A study of National, European, and International Law.* Oxford: Hart Publishing, 2001.

Women's Legal Education and Action Fund. *In the Supreme Court of Canada Between Little Sisters Book and Art Emporium and Canada (Minister of Justice), Factum of the Intervenor.* (1999).

World Entertainment News Network. "Eva Longoria to Produce Documentary on Latino Labor Workers." (12 April 2006). http://www.starpulse.com/news/index .php/2006/04/12/eva_longoria_to_produce_documentary_on_l.

Zicari, Robert. "Rob Black's Open Letter to Larry Flynt." *Adult Video News* (12 April 2004). http://www.avn.com/index.php?Primary_Navigation=Articles& Action=View_Article&Content_ID=80365.

Zucchino, David. *The Myth of the Welfare Queen.* New York: Touchstone, 1997.

Films

Baby Boy. Dir. John Singleton. Sony Pictures, 2001.

Claudine. Dir. John Berry. 20th Century Fox, 1974.

Closer. Dir. Mike Nichols. Sony Pictures Entertainment, 2004.

Double Indemnity. Dir. Billy Wilder. Paramount, 1944.

Fatal Attraction. Dir. Adrian Lyne. Paramount, 1987.

The Graduate. Dir. Mike Nichols. Embassy Pictures, 1967.

My Baby's Daddy. Dir. Cheryl Dunye. Miramax, 2004.

The People vs. Larry Flynt. Dir. Milos Forman. Columbia Pictures, 1996.

Philadelphia. Dir. Jonathan Demme. Written by Ron Nyswaner. Columbia Tristar, 1993.

The Postman Always Rings Twice. Dir. Tay Garnett. Metro-Goldwyn-Mayer, 1946.

Secretary. Dir. Steven Shainberg. Screenplay by Erin Cressida Wilson. Lions Gate Films, 2002.

Soul Food. Dir. George Tillman Jr. 20th Century Fox, 1997.

Unfaithful. Dir. Adrian Lyne. Epsilon Motion Pictures, 2002.

The Watermelon Woman. Dir. Cheryl Dunye. Dancing Girl Productions, 1996.

We Don't Live Here Anymore. Dir. John Curran. Front Street Films Productions, 2004.

Wilde. Dir. Brian Gilbert. British Broadcasting Corporation, 1997.

Music

Hill, Lauryn. *The Miseducation of Lauryn Hill.* Sony Music, 1998. Compact disc.

Jones, Sarah. "Your Revolution." http://www.sarahjonesonline.com/press/ VillageVoice.html.

U.S. Cases

Alons v. Iowa, 698 N.W. 2d 858 (Iowa 2005).

Anderson v. King County, WL 1738447 (Wash. Sup. Ct. 2004).

Baker v. State, 170 Vt.194, 744 A 2d 864 (1999).

Re: Blanchflower, 150 N.H. 226 (2003).

Bonura v. Bonura, 505 So. 2d 143 (1987).

Bounds v. Caudle, 560 S.W. 2d 925 (Sup. Ct. Tex. 1977).

Bowers v. Hardwick, 478 U.S. 186 (1986).

Castle v. State, WL 1985215 (Wash. Sup. Ct., 2004).

Dean v. District of Columbia, 120 Daily Wash. L. Rep. 769 (1991).

Dolan v. Dolan, 259 A.2d 32 Me. (Sup. Jud. Ct. Maine, 1969).

Donati v. Church, 13 N.J. Super. 454, 80 A.2d 633 (N.J. Super. A.D., 1951).

Eisenstadt v. Baird, 92 S. Ct.1029 (1972).

Franzetti v. Franzetti, 120 S.W.2d 123 (Tex. Civ. App., 1938).

Goodridge v. Department of Public Health, 798 N.E. 2d. 941 (Mass. 2003).

Griswold v. Connecticut, 85 S. Ct. 1678 (1965).

H. v. H., 59 N.J. Super. 227, 236 [157 A.2d 721] (App. Div., 1959).

Heller v. Heller, 116 N.J. Eq. 543. (1934).

Hernandez v. Robles, 794 N.Y.S. 2d 579 (N.Y. Sup., 2005).

Sarah Jones v. FCC, U.S. Dist. Ct. So. NY, 02 Civ 693 (Sept. 4, 2002).

KBOO Found., Notice of Apparent Liability for Forfeiture, 16 F.C.C.R. 10731 (2001).

KBOO Found., Memorandum Opinion, 18 F.C.C.R. 2472 (2003)

King v. Smith, 390 U.S. 903 (1968).

Kshaiboon v. Kshaiboon, 652 S.W.2d 219 (Mo. App. E.D., 1983).

Lawrence v. Texas, 123 S. Ct. 2472, 2484 (2003).

Lewis v. Harris, 2003 WL 23191114.

Lewis v. Harris, 875 A. 2d. 259 (2005).

In Re Marriage Cases, WL 583129 (Cal. Superior) 2005.

Menge v. Menge, 491 So. 2d 700 (La. App. 5 Cir., 1986).

Miller v. California, 413 U.S. 15 (1973).

Morrison v. Sandler, 821 N.E. 2d 15 (2005).

Poe v. Ullman, 147 Conn. 48, 156 A. 2d 508 (Conn., 1959).

Roe v. Wade, 410 U.S. 959 (1973).

Rosengarten v. Downes, 71 802 A. 2d 170 (Conn., 2002).

S.B. v. S.J.B., 609 A.2d. 124, 126 (N.J. Super. Ct. Ch. Div., 1992).

Salucco v. Alldredge, 17 Mass. L. Rptr. 498 (2004).

Santos v. Santos., 80 R.I. 5 (1952).

Shapiro v. Thompson, 394 U.S. 618 (1969).

Standhardt v. Superior Court ex rel. County of Maricopa, 77 P. 3d 451 (2003).

Stanley v. Georgia, 394 U.S. 557 (1969).

State v. Lash, 16 N.J.L. 380, 384 (N.J. Sup. Ct., 1838).

State v. Wallace, 9 N.H. 515, 517 (1838).

Steinberger v. Steinberger, 33 N.Y.S.2d. 596 (1940).

Stepanek v. Stepanek, 193 Cal.App.2d 760 (1961).

T. v. M., 100 N.J.Super.530, 242 A. 2d 670 (1968).

Turney v. Avery, 92 N.J. Eq. 473, 113 A. 710 N.J.Ch. (1921).

U.S. v. Extreme Associates, 352 F. Supp. 2d. 578, W.D. Pa. (Jan. 20, 2005).

U.S. v. Extreme Associates, 2005 WL 3312634. U.S.C.A., 3d Cir. (2005).

Washington v. Glucksberg, 521 U.S. 702 (1997).

Williams v. Pryor, 41 F.Supp.2d 1257 (N.D. Ala., 1999).

Williams v. Pryor, 240 F. 3d. 944 (11 Cir., 2001).

Williams v. Pryor, 220 F. Supp. 2d.1257 (N.D. Ala., 2002).

Williams v. State of Alabama, 378 F. 3d 1232 (2004).

Television

"American Porn." *Frontline* (7 Feb. 2002). http://www.pbs.org/wgbh/pages/frontline/shows/porn.

"Cheating Husbands Confess." *Oprah* (1 Nov. 2004). http://www.oprah.com/tows/pastshows/200411/tows_past_20041101.jhtml.

Desperate Housewives. ABC. http://abc.go.com/primetime/desperate.

"Dr. Phil on Adultery." *Oprah* (26 Feb. 2002). http://www.oprah.com/tows/pastshows/tows_2002/tows_past_20020226.jhtml.

"How I Found Out My Husband Was Cheating." *Oprah* (23 Sept. 2003). http://www.oprah.com/tows/pastshows/200309/tows_past_20030923.jhtml.

The L Word. Showtime. http://www.thelwordonline.com.

Nightline (27 Aug. 2003). http://abcnews.go.com/Nightline.

"Oprah's 2000 Time Capsule, Dr. Phil on Coping with the Aftermath of an Affair." *Oprah* (19 Oct. 1999). http://www.oprah.com/relationships/relationships_content.jhtml?contentId=con_20020916_trustadultery.xml&section=Couplehood&subsection=Infidelity.

"Passion Parties Expand Female Freedom." *ABC News Primetime* (7 Feb. 2004). http://abcnews.go.com/Primetime/story?id=132402&page=1

"Porn in the USA." *60 Minutes* (21 Nov. 2003). http://www.cbsnews.com/stories/2003/11/21/60minutes/main585049.shtml.

Queer as Folk. Showtime. http://www.sho.com/queer.

Queer Eye for the Straight Guy. Bravo. http://www.bravotv.com/Queer_Eye_for_the_Straight_Guy.

"Secret Sex in the Suburbs." *Oprah* (19 Nov. 2004). http://www.oprah.com/tows/pastshows/200411/tows_past_20041119.jhtml.

Sex and the City. HBO. http://www.hbo.com/city.

Six Feet Under. HBO. http://www.hbo.com/sixfeetunder.

"When Women Cheat." *The Early Show* (18 Jan. 2005); see also "Summary of the 'When Women Cheat' Report," *CBS News* (18 Jan. 2005). http://www.cbsnews.com/stories/2005/01/17/earlyshow/living/main667380.shtml.

Legislation

Anti-Obscenity Enforcement Act, 2003. Ala. Code § 13A-12–200.2 (Supp. 2003).
The Child Support Act, 1974. U.S.C. §§ 651–660 (1975).
Child Support Enforcement Amendments of 1984, Publ. L. No. 98–378, 98 Stat. 1305.
Child Support Recovery Act of 1992, 18 U.S.C. § 228 (1992).
Family Support Act, Pub. L. No. 100–485, 102 Stat. 2343 (1988).
Fathers Count Act, 1999–(bill).
Omnibus Budget Reconciliation Act, 1981.
Personal Responsibility and Work Opportunity Reconciliation Act, 1996.
Personal Responsibility, Work and Family Promotion Act, 2002 (bill).
Personal Responsibility, Work and Family Promotion Act, 2003 (bill).
Social Security Amendments of 1967, Pub. L. 90–248, Title II, 81 (Stat. 821).

Government Reports

Report of the Senate Finance Committee on the Personal Responsibility and Individual Development for Everyone Act (PRIDE), October 3, 2003, Report 108–162, 108th Congress.
The Family Connection of St. Joseph County. Responsible Fatherhood.http://community.michiana.org/famconn/respfath.html

Websites

Dr. Phil Website:
"Affair Proof Your Marriage." www.drphil.com/articles/article/335.
"Is Internet Porn Cheating." www.drphil.com/articles/article/64.
"Putting Passion Back into Your Relationship." www.drphil.com/articles/article/158.
"Put Your Relationship on Project Status." www.drphil.com/articles/article/367.
"Relationship Rescue." www.drphil.com/articles/article/368.
"Sexless Marriages." www.drphil.com/articles/article/60.
"Top Ten Relationship Myths." www.drphil.com/articles/article/26.

Oprah Website:
"Dr. Phil on Adultery." www.oprah.com/tows/pastshows/tows_2002/tows_past_20020226.jhtml

Peggy Vaughan Website:
"Questions About Monogamy." www.dearpeggy.com/monogamy.html.

Responsible Fatherhood Website:
http://community.michiana.org/famconn/respfath.html.

Index

Abbot, Pamela, 11

ABC, 65; *Nightline,* 66

abortion, 24, 146

Abramovitz, Mimi, 211n6

Abu Ghraib, 204–5

ACLU, 33–34, 36

adultery, 83–114, 214n7, 215n1; among celebrities, 112; *Closer,* 19, 95–97, 101, 102, 104; confession of, 97–98, 101, 111, 184; *Desperate Housewives,* 19, 102–6; epidemic of, 94–95; as failure of citizenship, 3, 10, 27, 83, 84, 96, 109, 110, 111–12, 113–14, 124, 180, 184, 197; as failure of self-discipline, 83, 84, 85, 96, 109, 110, 113–14, 124, 180, 184; *Fatal Attraction,* 91; fear of, 81; as grounds for divorce, 84, 108, 210n7; and law, 23–24, 30, 70, 79, 83–84, 85–89, 107–9, 114, 184–85, 209n6, 210n7; and the new infidelity, 83, 84–93; responsibility for, 97, 98, 106–7; and same-sex marriage, 177–85, 214n6; same-sex sex as, 86–88, 180–81, 210n8; *Scarlet Letter,* 92, 97; treatment and recommitment after, 83, 84, 95–102, 111, 180, 182, 184; *Unfaithful,* 90–93; *We Don't Live Here Anymore,* 94, 99–102. *See also* infidelity; marriage

AFDC. *See* Aid to Families with Dependent Children

affirmative action, 4

African American men: as deadbeat dads, 19, 116, 132, 137–42, 144, 158; exclusion of,

54–55, 137–38; out-of-wedlock children fathered by, 122, 137, 142–43, 145–48, 151–57; responsible fatherhood programs for, 124, 128, 133, 139–41, 143, 156, 157; stereotypes of, 19, 115–19, 132, 142–44, 151–58

African American women, 55, 67–68; *Claudine,* 115–18, 158; feminists among, 143, 146; lesbians among, 212n11; out-of-wedlock children born to, 122, 137, 142–43, 145–48, 151–57; stereotypes of, 19, 115–18, 120, 142–51, 158, 212n10; as welfare queens, 19, 116, 118–19, 120, 121, 122–23, 128, 137, 142–51, 158

AIDS, 94, 95, 197

Aid to Dependent Children (ADC), 119, 211n6

Aid to Families with Dependent Children (AFDC), 11, 119–20, 124–25, 126, 133–35, 137, 210nn1,2, 211n6

Airs, Kim, 38–39

Alabama: Anti-Obscenity Enforcement Act, 33–39; divorce in, 210n7

Alexander, Brian, 39

Alger, Horatio, 99

Ali, Lorraine, 84–85, 91, 92, 93

Alons v. Iowa, 214n6

American Decency Association, 103

American Dream, 99, 152

anal sex, 28, 31, 57. *See also* sodomy

Anderson v. King County, 172, 176–77, 179

Aniston, Jennifer, 112